Roger Welsch

Forty Acres and a Fool

HOW TO LIVE IN THE COUNTRY AND STILL KEEP YOUR SANITY

Voyageur Press

First published in 2006 by Voyageur Press, an imprint of
MBI Publishing Company, Galtier Plaza, Suite 200,
380 Jackson Street, St. Paul, MN 55101-3885 USA

The information in this book is true and complete to the best of our
knowledge. All recommendations are made without any guarantee on the
part of the author or Publisher, who also disclaim any liability incurred in
connection with the use of this data or specific details.

We recognize, further, that some words, model names, and designations
mentioned herein are the property of the trademark holder. We use them
for identification purposes only. This is not an official publication.

MBI Publishing Company titles are also available at discounts in bulk
quantity for industrial or sales-promotional use. For details write to
Special Sales Manager at MBI Publishing Company, Galtier Plaza,
Suite 200, 380 Jackson Street, St. Paul, MN 55101-3885 USA

ISBN-13: 978-0-7603-2256-7
ISBN-10: 0-7603-2256-2

Library of Congress Cataloging-in-Publication Data

Welsch, Roger L.
  Forty acres and a fool : how to live in the country and still keep
your sanity / by Roger Welsch.
    p. cm.
  ISBN-13: 978-0-7603-2256-7 (hardbound)
  ISBN-10: 0-7603-2256-2 (hardbound)
  1. Welsch, Roger L. 2. Authors, American--20th century--Biography. 3.
Farmers--Nebraska--Dannebrog--Biography. 4. Farm life--Nebraska--
Dannebrog. 5. Country life--Humor. I. Title.
  PS3573.E4944Z46 2006
  630.9782--dc22
                                        2006018891

Editor: Darwin Holmstrom
Cover Designer: Tom Heffron
Page Designer: Liz Tufte

Cover image is from the Roger Welsch collection.

Printed in the United States of America

CONTENTS

for Dee

AN EXPLANATION OF THE DEDICATION
AND INTRODUCTION TO THE WORK

I know it's not customary for an author to explain his dedication. You just write something like "For Mom," or "For Dick and Deb," and that's it. It's a personal and private matter between you and the dedicatee. But in this case I dedicate this book to my old friend Dee Steffenhagen not simply because she is an old and dear friend but because she is in a substantial way central to the idea of this book. I acquired this sandpile of a farmstead on the banks of the Middle Loup River in central Nebraska, not far outside the little town of Dannebrog (population 352) in the winter of 1975. I bought the land without so much as placing a bid even though it was covered in no less than four feet of snow at the time—the single dumbest condition in which you can possibly buy farm ground. I was in love with it the moment I saw it. I first slept on *my* land that next February, still under four feet of snow. After having buried our car in a drift a couple hundred yards above the river bottoms, I set up a plastic tarp for a lean-to and built a small, utterly ineffectual fire. That spring, as the snow melted and I finally saw what I had purchased, I was amazed and delighted at how lucky I had been. Every new revelation emerging from under the melting snow proved that this was indeed a wonderful piece of land, and precisely what I would have had in mind if I had had the presence to actually consider what I should have had in mind.

I had had a five-acre mountain lot on the back side of Pike's Peak and in a way that was handy because it was near in-laws in Colorado Springs. There were wonderful trees (that are there no longer because the area has since burned over), a trout pond and stream (now ruined), and it seemed a great place to put a vacation home near our family (now dissolved). I bought a kit to build an aluminum and steel shell of a house, only to find once I shipped it out to the site that newly enacted zoning laws forbade such construction. Then gas prices soared and speed limits dropped, making the trip from our home in Lincoln, Nebraska, to Colorado Springs no longer an easy, inexpensive weekend jaunt. And the idea of vacationing the rest of my life next to former in-laws . . . well, let's just say that this land no longer seemed like a good plan for my future.

Well, swell, now I had land that was no longer easily accessible, where I couldn't build the house that I had bought. So I sold off that ground and began casting about for something else, maybe something in the Nebraska Sandhills, which I love, and perhaps on Nebraska's Platte River, which I also admire. A friend pointed me toward this ground, which met neither requirement, being on the *Loup* River and only *near* the eastern edge of the Sandhills. Both of those lapses wound up being decided advantages later on but at the time I couldn't anticipate that.

Nonetheless, the first time I saw this place under four feet of snow on that cold, wintry day, I was sold. I bought the plot without so much as considering what lay under all that snow, that day only walking down into the bottoms along the river and returning to the realtor's car, wet, cold, and exhausted . . . and exhilarated.

In fact, the land is so gorgeous, I began to have real doubts about putting up the crummy shelter I had originally bought for the Colorado property and had since moved to this new Nebraska property. So I sold off the tin house kit I had purchased for the Colorado site, trading it for a battered old Ford F-150 pickup that came to be known as "Blue Thunder." Then by pure, crazy serendipity I came into the possession of a fine old oak-and-walnut log house built not far outside of Lincoln in 1872 by a Civil War veteran. With the help of friends I dismantled the house, hauled it 125 miles west, and rebuilt it. Now my new land on the

Loup was doubly wonderful in my eyes because it was not only a beautiful retreat of wildlife, trees, and water but also had the perfect house on it—a place just about as romantic as you can imagine. Almost immediately I began spending more time out here than I did at my home in Lincoln. I came to know the little town nearby and made more and more friends. I cherished my hours here and hated every time I had to close and lock the gate and return to "civilization," as those who didn't know any better put it.

After one weekend here on "the farm"—it isn't really a farm, even though it is now officially designated as a "tree farm" because of the immense number of trees I have planted and maintained—I was in town, about to head back to Lincoln when I happened to encounter my friend Dee Steffenhagen on Main Street. Quite matter-of-factly she asked me as we parted, "When will you get home again?"

I said, "Well, if I make good time I should be back in a little over two hours."

There was a puzzled moment of confusion. Dee said, "No, I mean, uh, when will you get *home* again?"

I thought I had answered her question the first time, but I patiently tried again. "I'll be home tonight, if I get started right away."

"No," she said. "When will you be *home* again?" and she made her point clear by waving her hand in a half circle across the Main Street beside us. Wow. Her gesture and choice of words almost knocked me out. Dee was right. I hadn't realized it but in just a few years Dannebrog had become "home" for me. Yes, I was living in Lincoln—but I was at home in Dannebrog.

My mind churned as I drove home that evening. Why should I be living where I was not at home? How stupid is that? You only get one life—shouldn't it be lived where you are at home? Was there any way I could somehow translate my life as a professor in a university city where I had lived most of my life to this little burg in the middle of absolutely nowhere—central Nebraska, for God's sake!—into something other than a total abandonment of making a living?

Then things got even more complicated for me. I remarried. And we had a child. Now I had—eek!—responsibilities. But just as I had been lucky in finding the perfect piece of land, I was also fortunate enough to find the perfect mate: friend, partner, lover, sympathetic soul. Eventually I found the courage to tell Linda that I couldn't live in Lincoln anymore, as it became increasingly a city, that my fire for teaching was fading, as students were increasingly thinking of education as job training. As my University increasingly dedicated itself to entertaining football-crazy boneheads, becoming little more than a mechanism for providing football-nuts with Saturday entertainment rather than educating its young, my heart was more and more in Dannebrog, something she already knew of course. Our painful mutual conclusion was that as our daughter Antonia approached school age, we were going to have to make a huge decision: have her start school in Lincoln and maybe move out to the countryside in thirteen or fourteen years, or throw away a superb job, sell a nice house, leave behind friends and family, and move out to the Unknown.

Others asked us the question and uneasily we had to ask it too: how were we going to make a living if I left my lifelong occupation of teaching in higher education? I joked that we would simply live on my good looks. Or maybe on Linda's art. Yeah, there are a couple of great career choices! But I have been a hustler all my life, never satisfied with only one job, showing an uncanny capability for turning my hobbies and sidelines into income-producing jobs that provided both income and entertainment. And during our analyses we figured out that whenever we had plenty of money, we still never seemed to have enough, and conversely when we had no money at all we still seemed to get by. And at the bottom, there was no choice. We had to follow our hearts into the rural countryside. We'd figure out some way to put food on the table.

All that was here on this land was that log cabin, a smoke-house, an outhouse, and a couple sheds for firewood and tools. Moving from our Lincoln home into this new context was a nutty notion. And everyone we shared the idea with agreed: this was nuts. People fight and scramble all their lives to get a full profes-sorship with tenure at a major university. No one throws away a plum like that. No one. We agonized long and hard over the deci-sion, but the date for Antonia to begin school drew nearer, and I grew more and more discontented. Our neighborhood grew increasingly noisy and unpleasant, and the farm and village became ever more attractive. Could we do it? Could we make this crazy, life-shattering change? Would we starve? The point came where the question was moot: we no longer had a choice. We had to do it, loony or not. Our souls required it, and maybe we were just trying to convince ourselves but we also suspected that Antonia's soul was in play too. Would she grow up in a city screaming with sirens, rude and inconsiderate neighbors, neigh-bors whose first names we never learned, crime, dirt, and traffic, or would we all survive somehow on the banks of a beautiful clean river, in a friendly little town, with the sounds of migrating cranes, coyotes, and the noon whistle from up in town? Okay, I'll admit that life here on the farm turned out not to be all that idyllic, and we discovered advantages as well as disadvantages we hadn't con-sidered before we made our decision, but we did make the decision. I turned in my resignation at the University, we bought and moved an ancient, abandoned farmhouse to our land, and we left Lincoln to come home, or at least to where Dee Steffenhagen and I had decided I was indeed at home.

So this book is dedicated to Dee. She may not have been the first even to recognize the inevitability or reality of our living here (where at this very moment I lie in a hammock in the shade of some now-huge cottonwood trees we planted the year we came) but she was the first to *say* it. Now I can't imagine being anywhere else.

And apparently neither can a lot of other people. More and more people are moving from the cities of America to the rural country-side and facing the same kinds of new situations Linda and I had to deal with cold. Every day in our new home brought new considera-tions we had never thought of, and while it was a rewarding learning process, it was also one fraught with difficulties. The purpose of this book is not so much to give you answers because you are going to have totally different questions. But my intention in these pages is to give you a start at thinking about the sorts of things you should con-sider in making a similar decision for yourself.

I suppose the bottom line is, *do it!* I can't imagine living any-where else now. I wouldn't trade this rural life for anything else. I will never move from right where I am at this very moment. I do wish some moments had been easier. I wish I had thought of some things earlier. But that's okay. Even with all the problems we've had, it has been worth the trouble. For us.

When I tell you about my experiences and conclusions about moving to the rural countryside, you may change your mind and decide this is definitely not what you had in mind. That too is a posi-tive result: a move like this is way too big to wind up a mistake. If I can save you just a few complications, so much the better. But even if I don't help you decide one way or the other what you are going to do about who or what your neighbors are going to be, and how far away they will be, and if there will be thousands or only a handful, do con-sider that bottom line: you only have one life and you shouldn't spend it wondering if you made the right choice in staying where you are or even worse, regretting that you are living where you have to live rather than where you are at home. No matter where you live now, Dee and I will tell you, it may be time for you to consider coming home.

Chapter 1

CONSIDERING THE RIDICULOUS:

Is a Move to the Country Even Something You Want to Consider?

ONCE AN OUTSIDER

It's not a coincidence that my training and academic experience is in anthropology. Transplanting oneself from an urban setting to the rural countryside or small town is not just a matter of moving from one place to another, an apartment to a house, a tenth of an acre plot to fifty acres, a street to a gravel road, a zip code shared by thousands to one that is exclusive to your driveway. Believe me, when you go rural you are entering another world. The more prepared you are for the jarring transition, the better you'll cope with it. If you are moving from one state to another, or one region to another, you can multiply those differences by a factor of five or ten.

You are going to have to adjust to another world; if you think that world is going to adjust to you, you have another think coming. You may not want to go native—to pick up the accent, dress style, politics, and drinking habits—of your new environment but neither can you expect everyone around you to change to fit your understanding of what is normal, decent, or neighborly. You are going to be the outsider and you are going to have to decide how far you will go to fit in. If you decide not to fit in at all, you are going to have to figure that as an outsider you are going to encounter some major problems along the line. On the other hand, maybe you will find the changes to be welcome improvements on your life. The least you can do in the new situation is to observe and listen, to consider new ideas and learn, and maybe even evaluate what you have always thought was the best way to do things.

I came to a very small town in a remote area well removed from my previous urban home, to a life well removed from my previous life as a professor, a writer, an intellectual, a liberal. I arrived in this new world substantially different from everyone native to the place. But I liked my new neighbors and respected them. I found that I didn't have to endorse or adopt all of their styles of living to be dealt with civilly, and while now it is clear to me that I will always be an outsider—after thirty years of being here—I also know that this is indeed my home. I had already been an occasional denizen of the community for fifteen years, coming regularly and for long periods to my cabin by the river. I knew everyone in town and everyone in town knew me. Nonetheless one day as I walked into the Chew 'n' Chat Café on Main Street, I was greeted by one of my closest and dearest friends, Bumps Nielsen, with the wonderfully ironic words, "Whoops! Well, look here. The *tourists* are in town!"

The tourists . . . I realized then and there that the inscription on my tombstone, even if I lived in Dannebrog another fifty years, would almost surely read "Roger Welsch: Tourist."

And my daughter's tombstone when she died would read similarly: "Antonia Welsch: Tourist." You can live in a new rural area for decades, even generations, but unless one of your ancestors is listed on the monument in front of city hall as one of the founders of the community, you will forever be an outsider. There's nothing to be done about that, and there's nothing wrong with that. Sometimes there are advantages to being an outsider. America, after all, is made up of outsiders.

THE VIEW FROM THE OUTSIDE

Don't let all this "outsider" talk discourage you! It's not as if you're going to be lynched, or shunned, or have to wear a sign around your neck saying "Warning: City Slicker." There is something to be said for being an outsider—that is, a relatively objective observer. After I'd been coming out here maybe ten years or so, while sitting around the coffee table in the café I made some comments about how great life is in rural America, and how wonderful a small town is, and how great it was to be out here. I think I even may have published some articles to that effect somewhere. I was writing at the time for *Natural History* and the *Nebraska Farmer* magazines so I probably said something romantic about the noble life of the Jeffersonian yeoman or some such nonsense. At any rate, a friend of mine gave me a look of thorough disgust and tore into me: "Jeez, Rog, life here in this little town may seem charming and quaint to you, but you just come out here for weekends and holidays and maybe a break from work so you really don't know what it's like to *live* here on a day-to-day basis. It can get to be a real pain, if you know what I mean. The things that you consider so terrific are exactly the kinds of things that get to grinding on your nerves when you have to put up with them every day. I grew up here. I've spent every day of my life living here. Life here is not nearly as great as you think it is."

Well, that hit me pretty hard. This woman is no dummy. She was almost certainly right, at least to some degree. I gave her complaint some considerable thought over the next couple weeks. I tried to see things as she saw them, and to figure out if she was right, and if maybe I was wrong. That would be the American way: one problem, one answer. One *right* answer. No ambiguity, no doubt, no overlap, no gray area.

That kind of thinking is what gets presidents elected perhaps but that's not the way the world works. I decided that we were both right; my friend was right about what it was like to live here and I was right about what it was like to come here as an outsider. And I decided that I should keep both things in mind. I couldn't simply see this place from the eyes of an outsider; if I was going to live here, I also needed to give some thought to what it must be like to live here.

On the other hand, as I explained the next time I talked with her, I have something to say about this too. Maybe a town like Dannebrog needs an outsider like me to come along every so often to remind the old-timers in town what truly wonderful benefits come with living here, the things they may have forgotten or not see because they *are* here every day. I made her promise to keep me honest about the reality of the problems of living in the middle of nowhere, and I would do what I could to keep on reminding her of how lucky she was to live in the middle of a nowhere that was at the same time something of a paradise.

ON THE OTHER HAND

It was about that time that I came up with a really great example of how that double-thinking could work. One morning I drove to town in Blue Thunder to get some hardware at the lumberyard and drove into the yard and up to the big door. I went in and looked around the hardware display to find what I needed. I kept expecting one of the lumber people to come around to ask if they could help me, but nope, no one showed up. So I looked around a little more. I even went into the office. The radio was on—right beside the cash register—but no one was there. I walked around in the lumber stacks . . . no one. There was Loosey, the lumberyard cat, a famous mouser and the mother eventually of our cat of eighteen-year tenure, Love Heart Love Angel Love Kitty, as christened by our four-year-old daughter; "Hairball" as retagged by me. But no human beings.

So I drove a couple blocks to Main Street and there were the lumberyard trucks, all parked in front of the Chew 'n' Chat Café. I went in and found all the workers, sitting around a table drinking coffee and eating donuts. They greeted me and I said to Swede Peterson, proprietor of the lumberyard, "Swede, I was just over to the yard and no one is there. You know, I could have backed up my pickup and loaded up with half your inventory." Obviously undisturbed by my report of his lax security, he responded, "And before you got out of town, I'd know how many board feet you had in the back of that truck." Some people might call that an example of small-town nosiness. Others would call it a case of small-town people looking out for each other. It just depends on your point of view.

Outsider or not, it is possible for the newcomer to become a part of the rural community. The small town and rural community still have room for the unconventional—as long as it isn't a matter of making trouble. Ten years ago the name of the main street through my little town was changed from "Pioneer Boulevard" to "Roger Welsch Avenue." The governor of our state even came out to make the change official since it is a state highway. (Although the governor, being from a small town herself, probably hit the nail on the head when she commented that about all that probably meant was that I would be expected to shovel the snow off of it during the winter.) I have my supporters here in my little town, and my detractors. That's the way it is anywhere. The really great part is that it has worked out that the people who have become my friends are precisely the ones I would have wanted to be my friends; and I guess in all honesty there is even something to be said about being considered an undesirable by precisely those I would feel queasy about having embrace me. It's kind of a situation where you get double points for the very same thing.

I'LL SHOW YOU MINE IF YOU SHOW ME YOURS

This range of tastes is not simply a matter of native versus immigrant. We all have our own taste when it comes to preferences and dislikes. As you read these pages you can be sure that you and I are no more the same than city people and rural residents. What I love about life out here may be precisely the kind of thing that will drive you screaming from the gravel roads back to the city streets.

The following pages describe what I find attractive in rural living but these things may not suit your taste at all. I wake up at night often and hear a pack of coyotes—wild dogs—screaming through our river bottoms, not a hundred yards from the house. We have even looked out our back-door window and seen coyotes walking past our back gate, not twenty feet from the house. We have heard the scream of a mountain lion down along the river late at night, again only a couple hundred yards from our home. I find that absolutely thrilling. I wake up and grin like an idiot. I consider those sounds one of the most important reasons I am here and would never leave. A friend in Vermont is currently hesitant about walking far from her front porch because of a bear that has been visiting her house at unexpected times. Another friend in Wyoming deals with rattlesnakes in his backyard. But do understand that I can imagine you simply reading these words, closing the book, and saying, "Honey, you know what I said to you about how we should consider moving out of here and into the country someplace where we can enjoy nature? I just changed my mind. . . ."

CELEBRATE THE ORDINARY

My area of research, writing, and interest is folklore, the study of what various groups of people consider usual. When Charles Kuralt invited me to be an essayist on his wonderful invention, *CBS News Sunday Morning,* he said, "Rog, what I want you to do with your pieces for Sunday Morning is *celebrate the ordinary.*" And that was fine with me because that's what I do best and love most. That has some real bearing on what I tell you in these pages. First, one of the reasons I am qualified to shoot off my mouth is because I am something of a specialist in the typical. Kuralt urged me to wear overalls for my pieces because, as he so poetically put it, "With that potato-face of yours, no one is going to remember you other-wise." I am not only enchanted by the ordinary, I *am* the ordinary. Therefore, I think I represent a lot of ordinary people who would move from a city to a rural landscape.

On the other hand, maybe you are not ordinary, don't want to be ordinary, even go to some ends to have nothing to do with the ordinary. Or maybe you're a different kind of ordinary. In that case, you may not come to the same conclusions I have. I think that's fine. My experience may not be your experience, but then again it will help you avoid some pitfalls I walked right into. As I have insisted all along with my books about tractor restoration for this same publisher, this is not a manual on how to do things; it's an exemplar of how things have been done. And that's pretty much what all history is, after all. The lessons of George Bush's presidency are not simply "Let's not do this again," but "We tried this and it didn't work."

THE SIMPLE LIFE

In large part the question is "What are you looking for?" I can tell you one thing for damn sure, if you are looking for the simple life with this move to the country, you can go back to your drawing board. I knew that was pure nonsense before I even came out here. I am not only a folklorist, I am also a historian and an anthropologist, so one thing I know for dead certain is that while other living systems may seem simple on the surface, they are anything but that. Pioneer life, Indian life, subsistence living is not a life without technology, or even simply a life with an alternate technology. In fact, almost any social and economic system other than mainstream American middle-class life is remarkably more complex. And therefore also substantially more satisfying.

During the hippie years—oh man, did I <u>love</u> the hippie years—I had dozens of students at the colleges and universities where I taught coming to my office and announcing that they had decided to leave the ugly pollution of modern, urban, technology-dependant life and to move to an eight-acre plot they had plans to buy in Nevada and establish a subsistence, organic farm—you know—live the simple life. They came to me because I was a hippie too, not exactly the image of your stereotypical professor. But they didn't find in me the enthusiasm for their schemes that they expected when they approached me. In fact, I would get almost violent in my response. I simply did not want to see them dying in the desert as a result of their stupidity.

The thing is, in devoting my life and energy to studying pioneer and native life I had learned that it is anything *but* a simple life. In fact, it is the exact opposite of a simple life. In the modern city, things are indeed complicated. But our relationship with those complicated, highly technological things is ridiculously simple. Yes, they are complicated but we actually have very little to do with their complications. I write these words on a computer and send them to the publisher through cyberspace. I don't have the foggiest notion what the hell that means. I am a mechanic—in fact, I have something of a reputation for being an expert mechanic. On tractors manufactured before 1960. I can totally dismantle and rebuild an Allis-Chalmers WC tractor. In fact, if you show me any part from that model of tractor, a part as small as your fingernail or one way too big to lift without a hoist, I can tell you what it is, and how it works.

On the other hand, I open the hood on the Taurus or Ford F-150 pickup sitting in our garage and I haven't any idea what I am looking at. I can rebuild the carburetor of that old tractor; I can't even tell you where the carburetor *is* on the modern car or truck. Oh . . . cars and trucks these days don't have carburetors? They have fuel injectors? Oh . . . well . . . never mind. You see, we throw switches in incredibly complex electrical devices, but haven't any notion how they work. The technology is complex; our relationship with it is not.

That's not the way the simple life works. Homesteaders, the Pawnee, Inuits, any people living within a basic living format lead incredibly complex lives. They provide their own food, water, clothing, and shelter, after all. They provide their own entertainment, deliver their own children, and provide all other health-related processes they need. They forecast their own weather and defend themselves against threats from all manner of neighbors. They are their own veterinarians and priests. They provide their own fuel, light, and justice. Folks, take it from me—that is *not* a simple life!

Why then, in the name of all that makes sense, would anyone actually want to abandon a system where there are all manner of conveniences: grocery stores, automatic heating and cooling systems, sewage disposal systems, public roads, a wide variety of entertainment and cultural offerings, fuel-injected engines, and on and on? Or more precisely, the layered human mechanisms for developing, installing, maintaining, and repairing those systems—you know— wholesalers and retailers, plumbers, electricians, techies, mechanics, professionals, that kind of thing? Why would anyone want to live an independent subsistence life? I know what you're thinking: "Hey, Welsch! We're not thinking of going out into the wilderness and establishing an organic foods co-op in the Nevada desert! We just want a home in the country! You know, one with flush toilets and electricity!" But the thing is, there is something in an awful lot of us that draws many of us to the simple/complicated life. Given a chance for a vacation away from the tensions and torsions of everyday modern life, some carry their lives of dependence on others to an even *further* extreme by going to a resort somewhere where someone else does absolutely *everything*. Still there are a substantial proportion of us who opt instead to go camping. Or fishing, or hunting, or hiking, or canoeing, or rafting, leaving behind all the comforts and retreating to primitivism.

Some of us are not all that content with having systems on which we depend swirling around us—systems controlled by others without any input from us. While we enjoy the benefits of technology and modern civilization, there is still a yearning for some closer, deeper relationship with the mechanisms of our lives. There is something truly gratifying about living in a log house where there is light only if we tend to our lamps and candles, heat only if we cut the wood and tend the fire, food only if we prepare it (or even grow it!), entertainment only if we are inventive and active enough to devise some. The most satisfying moments in my family's life were those dark, deep, cold nights at my old log cabin down in the river woods, carrying in firewood and carrying out ashes, cooking up a squirrel or rabbit ragout, heating bathwater on a wood stove, playing word games until the kerosene ran down in the lamps and we could crawl into our beds, our psyches undisturbed by the most recent disasters reported on the television evening news.

LEAN ON ME

One does not have to go quite that primitive to enjoy some of the benefits of self-reliance. Now we have a modern house on our farm. The old log house is still in the bottoms and we still retreat there on occasion but our home is as modern as any, but in the country. That means it is still up to me and my tractor to clear the snow from our lane in the winter or grade out the ruts in the spring. We have a modern heat pump to warm the house in the winter, but we are at the very end of our power line and a good wind or snow storm can bring down that line, leaving us once again dependent on a kerosene lamp for light and our fireplace for heat. Even if we ratchet up the technology, it is still up to me to make sure our portable generator is fueled and running before winter sets in, still up to me to make sure there is plenty of firewood stacked under the roof of the back porch, still kerosene for the lamps, and that the emergency power packages scattered around the house are charged and ready to go.

And having even control over that little bit of our well-being in my own hands is a good feeling.

Even when we don't or can't take care of the technology we depend on, there is the comfort in the rural countryside of knowing personally the people who do. I wouldn't try to do any major work on our household plumbing, for example, but in our adopted rural setting our plumber is one of my best friends. The guy who does all our computer work is another. We are not just acquainted or even just on a first-name basis—we are friends. We aren't gardeners, and the "soil" (actually *sand*) of our farmstead wouldn't grow much if we were, but we have friends who keep us in zucchini and sweet corn, and there are produce stands just down the road where we can buy wonderful, fresh, beautiful, nutritious food from other friends, the very people who do grow it. I have a good friend who keeps bees and supplies us with our honey, and another who is a mechanic and fixes our tractors and cars. Even our mail is something personal and direct because in a town as small as ours, the postmaster and rural carrier are friends and neighbors. Few letters sent to me are returned to the sender stamped "addressee unknown," even if my name is misspelled. Or absent. I wrote in my book *It's Not the End of the Earth But You Can See It From Here* (University of Nebraska Press, 1987) that you could send a letter to "Roger 68831" and I'll get it. As a result, I do get a lot of mail addressed exactly like that. There is only one other Roger in this zip code area and he doesn't have friends goofy enough to send him mail addressed like that, so anything that says "Roger 68831" must be for me, the postmaster figures. (I have since found that the situation is even wackier than that: the zip code for our driveway is 68831-4007. So that number will get mail to us!)

The point is that in the idea of sacrificing the conveniences of city living in order to live the simple life resides something of a triple error: city life isn't all that convenient. So it isn't a sacrifice to leave it behind. And while rural living may be anything but simple, it is also more satisfying. At least for some of us. Definitely for me. It is actually a question of what you are looking for. Or more precisely, of finding out what you are looking for. And only you can know that. And you can only get there by thinking seriously about it and doing some footwork. Like reading this book.

THE FARMER IS THE MAN

One presumption I am going to be making throughout is that you are probably not moving to the country to be a full-time farmer. For one thing, there aren't very many of those any more. Way too many farmers have to have a real job, often in a city, at a factory, to support their real love, which is farming. That has to be the stupidest arrangement any nation has ever tolerated (with the possible exception of our own medical delivery system, our transportation debacle, and our chaos of an electoral process). Nothing is more crucial to a people than its food; nothing is harder and riskier than growing food. To put that occupation so far down, well, down the food chain, is sheer madness. But that's the way we do it.

It costs millions of dollars to get into a real farming operation: land, equipment, home, livestock, supplies, and tools. You can make a small fortune in farming, but only if you start with a large fortune. No occupation is so demanding technologically as farming; you have to be an economist, CPA, botanist, veterinarian, mechanic, chemist, meteorologist, and philosopher, all rolled into one. And I am not kidding about that last listed item. There is a mentality about farming that you can't get from classes, books, or inherent talent. Frankly, I don't believe you can become a farmer if you haven't grown up a farmer. Okay, maybe you can grow some soybeans, maybe prairie hay, plant an orchard or vineyard, set up some trees. (This place of mine is officially a tree farm, certified by the state, but actually it is a word farm. I've planted tens of thousands of trees, did some watering—never any real irrigation—pruned, even harvested a few downed or dead trees for firewood. But me a farmer? I don't think so!) You might set up a few beehives, breed dogs, goats, or horses, tap a few maples for sugar or syrup, plant some pumpkins or gourds and set up a roadside stand in October just in time for Halloween, but that's not farming. About the only advice I have for you if you are thinking of moving to the country to farm is, forget it. If you want to gamble that badly, go to a casino. That'll even save you some time in losing your grubstake. I want to talk with you about moving to the country in order to better enjoy life, not commit slow suicide.

On the other hand, with the new freedom of having some ground that is actually useful, you might find yourself in the wonderful position of being able to indulge some mad agricultural fantasy, maybe plant a vineyard or an orchard. Perhaps you might build a fishpond based on the Japanese model of layers of carp at various depths, or maybe work at breeding the perfect daylily. Ducks . . . how about raising ducks? Horses for the kids? Goats? How about keeping bees for that comb honey you love so much? None of this is simple, but this is your chance to learn about it and do what you want. Read, study, do some research, talk with some people, and go ahead and do it. You may very well find what seemed utterly trivial or even foolish in the beginning will wind up being the most profitable thing you've done in your life. I didn't so much as own a socket wrench before I was fifty years old. I never even changed the oil in a car. Then I got this wild notion about fixing a broken brake on an ancient tractor a friend had given me, and the next thing I knew I had a full-blown shop, had become something of a tractor guru, and was writing and publishing books about repairing and restoring old tractors. Maybe there's a book in you about bees, daylilies, or goats?

You don't even have to decide right up front just how far you want to go into agriculture—a full half-gainer into the deep end or just a dip of the toe to test the water. But once you have your rural homestead, the door is open. You might as well at least peek in to see what's on the other side.

Chapter 2

THE BIG DECISION:

Now That the Thinking Is Behind You, What Do You Need to Consider As You Look Ahead?

IF THERE IS ONE

For us there wasn't much of a decision to make. I had owned this land for twelve years and loved it and the associated town. My daughter was approaching school age and I wanted her to grow up in the rural countryside (and as I always like to add, I wanted to grow up in the rural countryside too!), I was sick of my job in the city, and increasingly sick of the city. It was almost a matter of survival. I believe to this day that if we hadn't taken the enormous risk of giving up everything we'd been working towards for a lifetime and moved out here, I would have been dead many years ago.

Hopefully you are saved a lot of your own agony by being in that same situation. If it is easy for you to give up urban living, you are spared the first half of a hard decision. If you don't have to give up much to move to the country, that's just another way of saying the same thing. "Freedom's just another word for nothin' left to lose," as that excellent philosopher Kris Kristofferson once put it. If you have no choice, well, what the heck, enjoy the ride.

But if you are conflicted in making the decision to move to the rural countryside, if you have even the slightest suspicion that you might not know enough or more importantly don't feel that you don't have a real grasp on what you don't know, then you should take more time and think things over. It's a bigger move than you think it is, believe me, and you want to be as sure about this huge change in your life as you can be.

One thing's for sure: take plenty of time to talk about your inclinations with everyone involved, and I don't mean just your wife, partner, or banker. Be sure to talk with your friends and larger family. Is your mother eighty-nine years old and in poor health? This might not be the best time to move to a place where you are a six-hours' drive away from her.

Are your kids already in school? How much trauma is this move going to cause them? If you have only one child, have you considered the isolation you are going to inflict on him or her?

DO UNTO OTHERS

I feel pretty strongly about that last consideration because Linda and I brought Antonia out here without considering that problem. I had older children from another marriage but the youngest had graduated from college and was off making her own life in Seattle by the time we settled in out here. Antonia was essentially alone here on our farm for a lot of years. She survived, but it was not easy for her. And she was the city kid thrown into a pit with a bunch of snotty provincial farm kids. That didn't help. Yes, one of the things I had brought her out here to avoid was the horrendous life I remembered in a huge city high school with its cliques, jocks, nerds, and socialites. What I didn't realize until too late was that exactly the same groups of adolescent poops populate rural schools too. But in the country school Antonia had fewer options for escape and companionship because there were only thirty-five other kids in her graduation class. Even if we had known those things, we probably would have made the same decision to move here, but with more thought and perhaps more preparation. Antonia paid for our lack of fore-thought. She now says that the discomfort she went through in our consolidated school system might have popped up in any city school too, and her experiences have helped her appreciate her collegiate life and the more abundant intel-lectual and social choices in higher education, but still, the years in the school here were hard on her. And hard on us.

My dreams of Antonia growing up to be a "nature's child," walking the woods with me to teach her about edible wild plants, moon phases, and animal tracks never quite came to pass. She really didn't care much about anything other than what most teenage girls care about, no matter where they grow up.

That could have been simply a matter of the nature of children, or it might have resulted from one little incident when we were building our house. We were all gathered in what would become the basement/main room of our house, talking about details. The cement floor hadn't been poured yet so we were standing in construction rubble on the loose, sandy earth. Our dog Slump was nosing around in some of the wood scraps when out ran a field mouse. Slump pounced and pounded the unfortunate mouse into the sand. I man-aged to stop Slump before he ate the mouse, but not before it was badly maimed. Linda and Antonia were horrified, but I thought aha! here is my first chance to teach four-year-old Antonia a lesson about life in the wild. I picked up the pathetic little beastie and said, "I'll take care of it," whereupon Antonia announced that she was going to go with me. Great. This kid is on her way.

What I failed to consider however is that the phrase "take care of" has two meanings. As I dispatched the unfortunate mouse, Antonia was thinking of my offer in terms of little bandages, splints, and maybe mini-crutches, and as I delivered the coup de grace, she sputtered, "That's not what I call taking care of it!" Her zest for Dad's nature lessons pretty much ended right then and there. The moral is, lots of things can mean a lot of different things to different people, including notions like country living!

As with so much in my life, I didn't so much decide that I was going to move into the country, or where in the country I was about to move, as things just sort of happened. Often I didn't even know what it was I wanted. And then I saw it and thought, "Yeah, that's what I want! In fact, that's exactly what I want!" If you're lucky, maybe that's the way it will go for you too.

If not, then I would recommend that you approach going rural like you would work at planting a spring flower garden: Spend as much time as you can poring over the seed catalog dreaming about how beautiful that garden is going to be, because believe me, that is the best part of gardening. Start looking at sale bills for a site, talk with real estate agents, go driving and shopping, look long and hard at the kind of landscape you think you'll want—mountains, pastures, un-farmable waste land, prime ground—for livestock? Crops? Tobacco? Corn? Radishes? Soybeans? Grapes? Tulips? Ramps?

SOMETIMES A HOUSE *IS* A HOME

Think about houses and outbuildings. Are you going to look for a place with a farmstead already in place or are you thinking—and saving—with an eye toward building everything from scratch? I like old buildings. New lumber doesn't come with ghosts. Or maybe it's just that I'm cheap. The first two buildings I moved onto our land were throwaways. I heard some folks had a couple outbuildings near Lincoln that they wanted to be rid of and I had just bought a trailer and needed some practice moving big stuff, so. . . . If you want some real entertainment, get yourself a CB radio in your vehicle and tow a trailer with an outhouse on it down the Interstate highway system. You'll be amazed and amused at what other drivers have to say about what they presume is your camper setup. Yep, the first building I moved into my new digs was an outhouse. I have my priorities.

Moving the outhouse turned out to be an excellent beginning lesson for me. Over the period of the next few years I would be moving lots of buildings—a total of seven on my own, not counting a military-surplus water tower, not counting some minor and amateur participation in the moving of two entire houses. In my opinion, that's recycling in spades. Think of the trees you save when you buy an old house or even just an outhouse and move it to a new home.

And don't for a moment discount the, uh, economy of the matter. I paid $2,500 for one house we have here, Linda's art studio. For our huge two-story seven-room house (twelve-room after we moved it and spiffied it up) I paid a grand total of $350. It had a stained-glass window and etched window that were easily worth the price of the whole thing. Nice old yellow-pine floors, a bay window, lots of room, $350.

When the farmer-friend told me that's what he wanted for the building, I essayed, "Uh, Arnie, would you be willing to take $250?"

"No," he said, "But I'll throw in the basement." The joke came free, making the house even more of a bargain.

It's a matter of fortune, I suppose, if you buy a piece of country land with a house already on it. On one hand, a lot of your problems are solved without you having to make decisions: you need a house? There's a house. But I can also imagine that starting with someone else's notion of a perfect home isn't going to be everyone's cup of tea. If you plan to build a brand-new house, there are plenty of plans on the market, plenty of lumberyards ready to supply the lumber, and plenty of contractors willing to build to your specifications. Increasingly in this part of the country—the central Plains—a new house means "manufactured housing," not exactly a mobile home but a house that is put together in a house factory and then trucked, sometimes in segments, to the site where it is put together on a permanent foundation. Some of these houses are really quite nice and of course some are pretty cheesy, but I wince at the notion of using up new lumber while empty houses that are perfectly good are sitting around waiting for someone to adopt them and move them to a new home.

MOVING ON UP

I know what you're thinking: "Okay, yeah, you paid $350 for your house, but then how much did it take you to move this huge house six miles to a new foundation?" Well, not that much actually—a couple thousand dollars, and it would have cost even less if there hadn't been a couple unexpected snags. For example, our house mover was the legendary Butch Williams from Hastings, Nebraska, about thirty miles south of here. I knew I had a good man when he gave me an estimate on moving the building the next spring and, when I asked him if he wanted me to sign a contract for our agreed terms, he said, "If your word ain't no good now, it wouldn't make much difference if you signed a paper, would it?" That was yet another lesson in country logic and business ethnics. He trusted me and I trusted him.

And it was a good thing we had that arrangement. The next spring my buddy Mick built a foundation for the old house (the land we bought had not a single building on it when I bought it) and we organized for the move. Butch, his son Allen, and a couple helpers came drifting in with massive dollies, trucks, winches, and jacks and set to the task of moving the huge old house. By that time I had moved a lot of buildings myself; I was asked in an interview with the Omaha *World-Herald* what sports I participated in and I said, "Moving buildings," so I considered myself something of a veteran by the time we got to the job of moving the huge house. But nothing like Butch and his gang. It was fun just to drive around the mid-Nebraska countryside with him and hear his tales that went something along the lines of: "Moved that house over there, from Chapman . . . thirty miles . . . ten bridges . . . Moved that barn. And that airplane hangar. Those three houses over there came from North Platte. . . ." As it turned out, Butch had pretty much rearranged the landscape furniture all across Nebraska in his long life of moving buildings.

At any rate, I watched with awe and admiration as Butch set about what seemed like an impossible task, making it seem easy. It was amazing how fast the process went. Within a couple hours he was at the controls for the hydraulic jacks, slowly lifting the huge building from the foundation where it had sat for almost a century. It was a tense moment for everyone, lifting this huge house up on the fingers of what seemed to be a hopelessly fragile rig of hydraulic hoses and jacks, but I already knew about what a legend Butch Williams was and what utterly impossible buildings he had moved—barns, airplane hangers, brick houses—and from my own experience I knew that it was a matter of some simple mechanics and equipment, a little muscle and a lot of patience, and virtually any building can be lifted, loaded, and moved. But I sensed a moment of concern as Butch sat at the hydraulic controls.

"Something wrong?" I asked.

"There must still be cables or pipes connected underneath," he said. "We might have missed disconnecting some plumbing or wiring." He dismounted from the cab of his huge truck and we approached the house. Gulp. We went down into the basement, now lit with sunlight for the first time in a century as a two-foot gap had opened up between the stones it sat on and the wooden sill of the house itself. I wondered about the wisdom of this as the house above us creaked and groaned and little popping sounds came from the wooden blocks shoring under the jacks and beams lifting the house. Hmmm. We found no connected pipes or wires. Nothing was between the house and the earth but air and Butch's lifting mechanisms.

"Something is definitely wrong here," he said. From his gauges he had read that the house weighed almost twice as much as he had estimated, and his long experience gave him the skill to estimate almost to the pound what a house weighed. He wouldn't miss an estimate by one hundred percent. No way. We climbed out of the basement and entered the house now up on the jacks, still making those ominous creaking sounds. Butch looked around the house a moment and then picked up a large maul that we had used to knock off some small additions . . . a shambling kitchen addition for example, that we wound up pushing into the old basement and burning. He swung it at one of the inside surfaces of an exterior wall . . . something of a surprise since we were hoping we could save all the interior plastering, perhaps blowing in new insulation through surgical holes bored in the plaster and lath and then resurfacing it.

But I would have never questioned Butch Williams' authority when it came to moving houses. He was like the captain of a ship. A very <u>large</u> ship. As he broke away the plaster, we were all astonished to find . . . a brick wall— inside the wooden frame studs of the wall. Well, okay, I was astonished. Butch wasn't surprised. "I saw this once before," he said. "Not too far from here, in fact." The old Danes were used to building houses in Denmark with wooden framework, stuffing the empty spaces in between with bricks, mud, adobe, whatever they had to fill the space. Cut down on the wind, was a kind of insulation, and I suppose it was a kind of protection in case of attack. "There were still some Indian troubles out this way back then, you know."

All the outside walls of that house were filled with soft bricks, making it both a frame house and a brick house, and a good deal heavier than both. "What do we do now?" I said in dismay.

"Get out of the way while I move this house," Butch said, and that's what he did. He moved it as it was, and not down the road as planned, which would have required the moving of some power lines. No, that wasn't Butch's style. He dragged that brick-filled house across three hundred yards of bog with his huge truck until the dollies under the double-weight house sank into the muck. Then he hooked up his huge winch truck, using another truck parked sideways in a ditch as a dead man, and with engines howling he pulled that house out and across the swamp, with the huge steel cables sparking fire in the dark. All I saw at every new scream of gears, pop of cables, and whine of engines was disaster. Butch just smoked his cigar and shouted commands.

And then, there it was, high on a hill, on road, on its way to our farm—our big old house. But not for long. Once Butch started moving a house, it was a matter of everyone else getting the hell out of the way. The power company trucks frantically dashed ahead of Butch and our house barreling on down the gravel road, lifting or dropping power lines, the cable television people were moving their lines, Butch's crew was lopping off overhanging branches, and literally within two hours that enormous, two-story, brick-lined house had traveled five miles cross-country, over fragile county bridges, across a railroad track, and down a highway, down our drive, and into what was about to become our farmstead.

I still break out in sweat as I recall the moment—the one when I looked at the house on the dollies, imagined Butch backing his monstrous truck up to the new basement, and setting the building onto its new foundation . . . backwards. I cannot for the life of me imagine now how I could have missed this fairly important point, but the way we loaded up that house, the way we hauled it, the final orientation as Butch backed it up to the blocks and rails to slide it onto the foundation . . . would have put it backwards on the foundation. I waited for what was sure to be untold fury when I ran up to Butch and broke the news: "Uh, Butch, it's backwards. We, er, need to, uh, like, well, uh, turn the house around."

His response was pretty much the same as it had been when we found the house walls full of bricks. Okay. It's full of bricks. Get out of the way. Big deal. It's now backwards. Stand back and we'll just spin her around. And just like that, with some kind of magic, Butch had that house turned around on the dollies and, still on schedule, we began the dramatic slide of the house off the truck dollies and onto its new foundation.

And then Butch stopped. He turned off his truck engine and took off his gloves. "Tank time!" he announced. I had spent enough time with Butch to translate that command: time to call it a day and head up to the tavern for a few cold pitchers.

"Butch," I stammered in dismay, "We are only a few feet from getting this house onto the foundation! It's Friday! If we stop now, it'll sit here perched on the back dollies, the beams, the cribbing, the blocks, for over two more days, just sitting here! Shouldn't we finish these last few feet before calling it a day? And a week?!"

Butch leaned against his truck and from the look on his face I could see he was mustering up all the patience he could to explain this to me. "Rog, if we finished this whole job in one day, next week you'd look at my bill and think, 'Man, that's a lot of money he's charging me for one measly day's work.' But if we stop now and come back Monday, you're going to look at my bill and think, 'You know, that's really not all that bad for four days work.'" And so we quit right then and there, and finished the job on Monday. And I did feel better about his bill.

Which, incidentally, wasn't all that bad. It was in fact precisely what he said it would be. Despite the brick-lined walls, having to turn the house around, and a dozen other minor glitches along the way, Butch said that he had told me what it would cost and that's what it would cost. In part it was a matter of his sense of honor: he agreed to a price and whether he made money or not was not nearly as important as maintaining his reputation as the greatest house mover on the Great Plains. But in later conversations he explained seriously that it's also a matter of practical reality: You lift the house up, you move it, you set it down. Whether you move it two miles or ten, really doesn't make much difference. Or fifty for that matter. At least not to Butch. It would have cost me a lot more to move more power or cable lines, to block off a highway for any distance, to cross railroad tracks, but lifting it, trucking it, and setting it down was really pretty much a matter of, well, lifting it, trucking it, and setting it down. Same equipment, same crew, same tools, same trucks.

Moving a building is, to my mind, an important option. Whatever it costs, it is nowhere near the cost of building a new home. In our case, we wound up pouring a lot more into reconstruction because we now had to gut the building to get the bricks out—in order to re-insulate it—and then drywall it, but we still came out ahead of buying and building with new lumber. And there is something to be said about people driving into your yard and asking, "Is that the Johnson House like they tell me? Would you mind if I went in and looked at that room on this end of the second floor? I am told that my great-grandmother was born in that room."

HOUSE HUNTING

Okay, say you want to find yourself an old farmhouse, move it to your land, and refurbish it. How do you go about finding an old farmhouse? It's not as if there is a used farmhouse lot like a used car lot. Well, there should be! As I drive around America's countryside and see house after house after house falling in on itself, just begging to be rescued, I wonder why someone hasn't started buying them up, moving them to a hunk of open ground somewhere so people could look them over and buy them just as they might a trailer house. Abandoned, fine old farmhouses are not unique to the Great Plains. As farming becomes ever more a matter of big business, you can't make a living on forty acres and a mule any more. Not even 360 acres and a tractor in a lot of places. In large areas of the West, when you talk about a "spread," you measure the land area in "sections," or square miles. It is not unusual to find ranches here of twenty or even a hundred sections—*one hundred square miles!* Since they aren't making any more land, the ground that goes into these ever-larger holdings comes from smaller holdings. Which means there are fewer and fewer farmers and more and more empty houses.

The countryside is littered with very nice houses and other buildings: empty, falling apart, costing somebody taxes while providing the owner with no revenue. Landowners are often eager to be rid of these structures. And people like you and me want them. So how do we get together, this old house and us? There are local, small-town newspapers, where ads cost little and where the opportunities are best for finding good houses or buildings close to where you want them. But as I will note later, newspapers are not the way news is broadcast in the rural countryside. At least not most effectively. I have never advertised for a building and yet, as I have mentioned, I have acquired almost a dozen, most for nothing more than the hauling, and most of the time I have done this pretty much by myself.

The secret is *tell* someone. It's that easy. When we were ready to move out here and decided to look for an old farmhouse to move onto our ground, we told our friend who owned the tavern here in town. Within a week he had a list of a dozen houses we could look at, with a range of prices from $250 to $5,000, in a variety of conditions and sizes, at varying distances from our location. When Linda needed a studio for her artwork, all I had to do was mention it in a conversation at the local mechanic's shop. That same day I heard from someone at the Lutheran Church that they were thinking of selling off the little house behind the church because they needed the space for parking—$2,500 for a very nice little four-room house with fine woodwork and an etched glass door. Butch Williams moved it for us for another couple thousand dollars.

BUILDINGS NOT BUILT

I spotted the old farmhouse that turned out to be a century-old, oak and walnut log house while shooting a television program. I asked the owner if he would be at all interested in selling it to me, and he said "If you can move it out of there within four weeks and rebuild it the way my grandfather did, you can have it. And the Eleanor out back too." (Outhouses built by the WPA government program designed to rebuild employment destroyed by the Great Depression were called Eleanors in honor of their presumed designer, Eleanor Roosevelt. They are particularly splendid structures, truly the Taj Mahals of privies.) I accepted and moved both and they are some of the best buildings I have on this place. Cost? Nothing but my labor and the materials I put into restoration and improvement. And in many cases the price for a building may be nothing more than you getting it out of the owner's way or a nominal figure. A deal is often sealed with nothing more than a cold twelve-pack of the owner's favorite brand of beer.

The outhouse up here by our "new" home (as opposed to the log house) and a splendid 8x8-foot smokehouse I still use were gifts from someone who wanted them moved out of the way. I got them for hauling them, which was half the fun. Cost? Nothing. I have a third outhouse just sitting on blocks down by the cabin. A friend remarked one day that he hated to burn it down but didn't want it sitting in the backyard any longer. And me just not able to let something like that be thrown away . . . add another very nice outhouse to the Welsch Great Plains Outhouse Holdings. Another friend in a town about thirty miles from here told me once in a casual conversation that he had an old storage building back of his city home. Would I want it? I looked at it—perfect for storing wood—and I moved it by myself.

What does it take by way of equipment to move a building? Well, some experience, some mechanical skills, a couple hand-operated cable winches ("come-alongs"), pieces of large (4- to 6-inch) steel pipes for rollers, some steel bars for prying, some short jacks, maybe a "handyman" or "high-boy" jack, some planks, a stout trailer, and that's about it. A tractor or front-end loader would help but I didn't have one in my building-moving days and I did fine. Most people will want to hire someone to move buildings but believe me, while it may seem like a super-human task to move a building, no matter what the size or difficulty, it can be done. And even if it's not something you'd enjoy doing yourself, you will really get a kick out of watching someone who knows what they are doing handle the task of shuffling buildings around the landscape.

LOCATION, LOCATION, LOCATION

On the other hand, land pretty much has to stay where it is. You either have to shop around until you find something that suits your wants and needs or adapt to whatever it is that you wind up with. I presume you are bright enough to give some serious consideration to the part of the world where you want to build your rural home. If you don't like heat and humidity, the Yucatan peninsula may not be your cup of tea even if the land runs ten dollars an acre; on the other hand, if anything below fifty degrees sends you to the sauna, northern Minnesota won't be a good idea either, no matter how much you love fishing. You'd be nuts to move to an area of the world you are not well acquainted with, even if it's only fifty miles from where you live now. Sometimes surprises are nice but not when they are factors that might make the rest of your life miserable.

I love the Plains. I love Nebraska (as hard as that might be for some people to understand). I knew quite well that I wanted to be in Nebraska. I wanted something on a river but didn't get quite the river I wanted; I wanted Sandhills and got a bit of Sandhills enclave at the edge of that larger geography; I would have preferred a town with a Czech heritage like my wife's people but wound up with Danes. Not one of those conditions required much change or sacrifice on my part, however, just a little re-jiggering in my priorities.

I had some vague criteria—running water in the form of a creek or river, low population, not too far from my family and friends in Lincoln, preferably short-grass Plains—which gave me a lot of latitude in exactly where I would settle in. But I have had friends and acquaintances who have made much greater changes in their geography to find their rural paradise. How about the folks who moved from Lincoln, Nebraska, to rural Wisconsin? From Lincoln to Oregon? Urban Baltimore to backwoods Nebraska? Germany to East Texas? Nebraska to Hawaii? Even while you are considering details for relocation, it seems, you need to be thinking big.

What I did know was that I did not intend to farm for a living and so could be satisfied with land that wasn't much more than waste ground, which means I paid a lot less for it than I would have paid for prime agricultural ground. In fact, I paid about a half or third of what the same acreage of arable land would have set me back. I felt better about salvaging and renovating abused land to nicely grassed and treed ground and to watch wildlife return to it, so again this wasn't exactly a sacrifice on my part. We are a little closer to town than we might have chosen but town is out of sight over the hill and far enough away that we don't hear much by way of the sounds of town. And yet it is close enough that in a pinch we can walk the mile for groceries, even through snow.

There are some things to consider when you are looking for a site, some you might think of on your own, but some might come as a surprise.

LAY OF THE LAND

For the gentleman farmer—that is to say, *non*-farmer—well-defined land—that is hilly ground—has its advantages. It is likely to be cheaper than more easily farmed flat ground, it drains better, it makes for better vistas from a bedroom window or patio, and even a small plot with hills provides a better chance for the insulation from neighbors that those who are fleeing to the rural countryside for peace usually prefer. While there is always a temptation to build high on a hilltop for the view and implications of the Lord's manor overlooking the lowly serfs laboring in the fields below, you may want to give this idea some serious thought, especially if you haven't lived on a hilltop before. One of my first homes apart from my parents', was high on a hill from which I could look twenty miles across the Missouri River and over farmlands and villages far and wide. I remember the first day I looked out the huge living room window and wondered, "Why would anyone who has a choice not live like this, high on a hill with a view that inspires Zen-like thinking?"

After a couple years of being battered by the wind until I couldn't hear myself think, insulation blowing out under the wall moldings and onto the floor from the pressure of fifty- and sixty-mile-per-hour sustained winds, after three winters of struggling to get up to the house on the icy roads from the town far below, after trying to mow a lawn holding the mower in one hand while clinging to a porch railing with the other, I bought a house down in the valley.

On the other hand, there are problems to be considered when the water starts rising and you stand directly between the water falling from above and the water inching up from below. If you are considering a landscape with definition, think about the middle ground—above the danger of flooding, below the howling winds of open skies. Our house is big and high, but the main living area is subterranean, making heating and cooling much easier but also protecting us from the wind that drove prairie pioneers nuts. We are constantly astonished at people who build homes in this area on the north slope of hills, thus facing directly into the ferocity of winter winds and losing the advantage of what little winter sun there might be. You might be thinking, well, sure, but facing north they avoid the hot *summer* wind and heat. Well, okay, but the thing is, you can manufacture some of your own summer protection by planting trees, which then do not cut off the winter sun. But once you're facing north, it's pretty hard to turn that hill around 180 degrees to catch some winter sun.

Our house faces south, not only to take advantage of a view of the river, the woods, and the wildlife that constantly passes by our backyard fence but also to avoid the bitter north winds of winter and hopefully shelter us from the ferocious storm winds from the west in spring and summer—if not necessarily from the almost inescapable ferocity of tornados. I suppose that is something we might have checked on before buying ground in, hmmm, tornado alley. The region's nickname might have provided a clue for us. Around here we wonder if folks who complain about flooding note at all that they have chosen to live in Grand *Island*, Nebraska, or Wood *River*.

Increasingly, zoning codes even in rural areas won't let you build in flood plains no matter how dumb you are because that causes problems for everyone around you and downstream even if you are willing to take the chance. But even where there is no code preventing risky construction in flood plains you can find maps at county offices, soil conservation, natural resources district, and insurance offices defining what sort of jeopardy you are likely to have in any particular area. You might want to take a look at that unless you enjoy waking up some morning with the river running through the bedroom door and on under your bed. In fact, even when there is no river, on land that is best described as desert, there is danger of flash flooding, even more dangerous than rising river levels. This would not be a good mistake to make.

SETTING THE TABLE

Just as important but perhaps not quite as obvious is the orientation to a road of your house and stead. On one hand, easy access is a good thing. You want to be able to get in and out of the place just for ordinary things like getting the mail and groceries, but, more importantly, also in the event of emergencies. You'd be amazed at how often and badly you can hurt yourself on a farm. At least in my case. Linda won't even trust me any more with anything sharper than a butter knife or hotter than toast. So getting me to an emergency ward or arranging for EMTs to come in with splints and bandages is always a concern for us. On the other hand, you may not want your place to be quite so convenient for casual visitors or in-laws to drop in. It's a delicate balance.

When I was younger, I didn't mind being totally stranded down by the river in my log house, snowed in so bad I couldn't even get in or out with a tractor and had to walk into town for groceries with snowshoes. But now that I'm nearly seventy years old and have had some health problems, well, I'm interested at least in getting out more easily. On the other hand, as a writer, I need undisturbed time and the Sunday that twelve separate carloads of very nice, friendly, well-meaning folks dropped by just to chat, have a cup of coffee, or invite me up to town for a beer pretty much was the clincher. We put up ugly signs telling people to stay out, go away, beware of dogs, and don't feed the monkeys. (It was the monkey sign that wound up doing the trick. People who figure *Keep Out* signs don't pertain to them and who like dogs, seem to have real doubts about the wisdom of messing around with dangerous monkeys.) Our house sits about fifty yards off of a two-lane state highway and now I wish we were either on a gravel road or had placed our house another hundred yards back into the trees. My intent at the time was that our farmstead would stand near the road as a sentinel to protect our land; we should have given more consideration to using more of the land to protect our privacy and us.

The highway that goes by our gate is not heavily traveled. We hear an occasional truck roar by applying Jake brakes (and just who was this "Jake," the stupid ass who invented those obnoxious devices, anyway? I'm sure there's a special place in hell for that jerk Jake), and now and then someone honks at deer or wild turkeys crossing their path but generally speaking, highway noise is not much of a problem for us.

I still wish we were further back from the road but that was a lesson we learned too late.

On the other hand, when the temperature is fifteen below zero, the wind is blowing thirty miles an hour, and snow is piling up at the rate of a foot an hour—as it was yesterday evening—and I am out there on a tractor trying to clear a path out to the highway so we can get out in the morning, well, that fifty yards from the house to the highway seems quite enough, thank you.

There are ways to make even a short distance between you and civilization more comfortable. Good fences help but the most they will stop is people, not the sights and sounds. Early on in our occupancy—immediately upon acquiring this place in fact—I sensed I wanted more insulation and privacy so we planted trees like crazy, including huge, thick, wide windbreaks of evergreen junipers. They were laughably puny to begin with, barely appearing above the furrows in which we planted them, struggling to rise above the prairie grasses around them. But now they are forty feet tall, four rows wide, fifty feet thick total, on both sides of our ground, from town to the river on both sides, nearly a full mile in all. We also put smaller breaks, groves, rows, and patches of deciduous (ash, hackberry, silver maple, locust) and coniferous (Douglas, ponderosa) trees in between the major windbreaks and now even in winter we can see only faint bits of the highway even though it is just a hundred feet away. And huge, heavy trees like junipers are like soundproof walls, muffling all but the loudest and most obnoxious noises. Our neighboring farmers, especially ranchers, think we're crazy because they consider junipers to be weeds. Not us. We love those big, dense walls of green all around us.

I wish we had some decisions to make over in regard to the layout of our place. I'd set the house further back off the road, as I've already said, but I would also move it one terrace further up the hill, not so much to enhance the view since it would also expose the house to more wind and weather but to make it easier to get in and out of the house. The house sits back into a hill—a kind of split level—so when we drive into the yard and into our garage building, we then have to go down a flight of stairs to get to the main door of the house. That was okay when I was twenty years younger, and isn't all that bad when I am only carrying in the mail, but man, when Linda comes back with a pickup load of groceries and we have to carry them all down those stairs, climb back up for another load, go back down, I cuss my idiocy in locating the house.

My intent was to avoid having the main windows of the house open up on a parking lot with everyone driving in having a full view of whatever we were up to. But now I think I could have come up with other ways of doing that.

And because we have never had a lot of resources to work with, we have placed our other outbuildings—machine sheds, my shop, Linda's studio—piecemeal in our compound. Now I wish they were not in a closed circle, so we could more easily add a new building. I wish we had saved up our money and built one large, more efficient structure instead of tacking things together bit by bit over the years.

If you buy a farmstead already in operation, you may not have many choices and can only hope that builders before you had the sense I didn't.

If you do have a choice, take your time and give plenty of thought to where you erect buildings in terms of your traffic patterns. Consider potentially changing needs you might have as you grow older or your family grows. Take the wind and weather into account, and consider future plans for additional buildings or additions to buildings. Don't box yourself in. Don't set yourself up for a lot of problems you don't need. Consider where electrical and plumbing lines will need to go, or even cable television and fences, light poles and wells, gates and gardens. We made a mistake in just letting things happen as time went along; a little more serious, thoughtful planning at each stage would have saved us a lot of grief later on.

CAVEATING THE EMPTOR

When you buy a used car, hopefully you have the good sense to take it to a mechanic you trust and have him or her check it out for problems you might have missed. That precaution is even more important when you buy land. Have a friend in real estate look at what you are considering and give you some opinions. Ask someone who is experienced in the kind of things you'll be doing—gardening, bird watching, pigeon breeding—and help you think about all the things you need to think about. You might even ask someone in the neighborhood about what sort of neighbors you'll have. For that question you may want to get several opinions! There is a reason that smalltowngossip is one word.

And have a lawyer—a local lawyer—look over the title for liens, easements, mineral rights, pending boundary disputes. One of the things that is going to amaze you is that the law is not the law is not the law. I had a property dispute with a neighbor once and knew I had him dead to rights because his cattle were constantly on my ground and

Nebraska is a "fence in" rather than "fence out" state. That is, if you have livestock, it is your obligation to keep them fenced and on your property; it is not my duty as a non-livestock grower to fence your animals out. The situation grew pretty tense and finally wound up in a flurry of lawsuits. Great. I knew I had the law on my side. There it is, in black and white, right in front of me.

Well, the judge, the county attorney, and the sheriff gently but firmly informed me that that may be the *law*, but it's not the way things are done in this county. The custom and understanding is that as a landowner I stand on my side of the fence and face the fence in the middle of the property line's length. I am responsible for the fence to my right. My neighbor was to do the same, and the other half of the long fence, to his right, is his obligation. And since my neighbor's lawyer was the father of the county attorney, and my lawyer was a city boy who was wise enough to know when we were about to have the poop pounded out of us in the courtroom, we simply walked away, conceding the decision not to the written law, but to the common law of the countryside. Believe me, if you come into a local legal tangle as a city puke about to raise some legal hell with the locals, forget it. You're going to lose.

Again, a lesson I could have learned the hard way, walk the land you are thinking about buying, every foot of its edges, crisscross in every direction, into every gully and swamp, behind every tree and rock, every building from top to bottom. I suppose that telling you not to buy land under four feet of snow is about as unnecessary as telling you not to buy it at night, except that I did exactly that. I didn't buy it at night but I might as well have because it was indeed under four feet of snow. I was incredibly lucky because at the time I came out here, no one was buying land except for agricultural use so all the defects made this plot less desirable for farming. Rough ground, bad soil, marshy bottomlands, eroding riverbanks, heavily treed in places with lots of old-growth timber that might endanger livestock, etc., spoke precisely to what I wanted: wildlife habitat, low-value land for tax purposes, garbage ground just aching to be rescued by an over-aged hippie romantic like me.

I didn't realize it at the time except in a vague sort of way but even the shape of the plot of land I was buying was to my advantage precisely because it is *not* to any agricultural advantage. It is a long triangle with one leg a state highway, a second leg frontage on a river, and the longest and third leg a fence on a pastureland not suitable for much else, as is my plot. That means that anyone planning to put livestock on it—the only thing it was useful for or used as—would have to maintain a lot of fence for a small amount of marginal ground. Add the difficulty of keeping a fence up through heavily wooded marsh ground on a very fragile sand riverbank into the mix, and it wasn't exactly ideal pasture land. Since I had no intentions of keeping livestock, that was not a problem for me, and the fact that it is not good ground meant that it was cheaper, which suited my plans for establishing a word farm.

Not long after I purchased the ground I got a call from my neighbor with whom I later had a boundary dispute but who is now a friend of mine. (That's the way rural living tends to go, I guess—there are too few people to maintain enemies for very long. It's like the town drunk in a small town—everyone has to take his turn.) Anyway, my new neighbor called and asked if I would be interested in renting my ground to him to graze cows.

Well, I was strictly a city boy so I didn't know at all how such things worked. The grass looked pretty thin for much grazing but then what did I know about grass? And would I be responsible for the fences, which were clearly in total disrepair, especially along the river? How many cattle would these sixty acres support? And how much would I charge for such an arrangement?

At that point I did one of the few really smart things I had done through the whole process of going rural: I went to the county courthouse and talked to our agricultural extension agent. He told me that he had some idea of what my ground was like but would like to come by and take another look, which he did. We walked the ground a bit and then went up to the café in town for a cup of coffee and a conversation.

"Do you need to make a living off of this ground?" he asked. "Do you need to make money on it?"

I said no, that I intended to build a cabin retreat down by the river but didn't have any real plans for the uplands. "Well," he said, "to be perfectly honest, that sandpile won't support much to begin with but after years of overgrazing, it is really a mess. I wouldn't put a single cow-calf combination on it if you don't have to."

Okay, that was fine with me. "In fact," he continued, "let me make you a proposition. How about you work with me on restoring and rehabilitating that ground to keep it from getting any worse." Great. What do we do? "I'll contact the Natural Resource District, and the Soil Conservation folks, and put together a package for you to look at. I think we can have some fun while doing ourselves a good deed here, Roger, and maybe even make you some money."

And that's what he did. The plan he showed me in about a month was stunning: huge, long, dense windbreaks made up of thousands of evergreen and deciduous trees, along the two long boundaries, a total of almost a mile and a half of woodland. And the ground in between would be planted to a combination of native wild grasses. The Game Commission would even provide seed for wildlife plantings. And what would this cost me? Pennies: trees planted by various agencies under a wide range of conservation and agriculture programs. He would also see about seed for wildlife plantings if I would plant it, and he would have the entire uplands seeded to wild grasses for a token amount. In fact, if I would sign a contract not to use the ground for agricultural purposes for ten years, they would pay me a sum per annum that would more than cover my taxes.

Wow! They were essentially going to pay me for doing what I would have done anyway for nothing. What was in all this for them? Wildlife habitat and food, for one thing. And a chance to rescue some ground that was about to blow up into sandstorms that in some other areas of our state would soon block highways and bankrupt farmers, even those who practiced good and careful farming but had the bad luck to be downwind from those who didn't. Some marginal land out of agricultural production. And beautification along a state highway. The funds involved weren't much money but at the time they sure were welcome to me, and now we enjoy wonderful grasslands and woods and all the rich wildlife that has flourished because of them. As it turns out, sometimes land that is worthless because of its condition, shape, or poor natural qualities winds up being the very best option of all for the country gentleman. There are fixer-upper homes of course, but it turns out there are also fixer-upper lands.

BUT I'VE *ALWAYS* HUNTED DOWN HERE!

On the other hand, land that is not all that desirable for agriculture may be all the more attractive for other reasons, like recreation, for example. And now things really get touchy because folks often figure that land they've been using for years has somehow become theirs. And for that matter, it may have. There is a thing called "adverse possession" for "open and notorious occupation or use." That is, if someone has used a piece of land, even if it belongs to someone else, openly and obviously for a length of time, they may have acquired rights to that land. If some guy has set up a cabin and garden back on a far corner of the ground you are looking at and has been living there for ten years or so, you may have trouble evicting him when you take over. Or if a neighbor has kind of edged his fence over onto yours a few yards, maybe putting your pond or creek on his side of the fence, and it's been that way for quite a while, it may have in fact become his.

Even where there is no question of legal ownership, you may be walking into a problem if your neighbors or people in town have the distinct feeling that they have a right to use your pond for fishing, or your driveway as access to the river, your pasture for target shooting, or your woods for hunting mushrooms. The very reasons this parcel of ground may be attractive to you may have drawn its share of attention before, after all. Our ground here is not far out of town and has well-wooded land along a beautiful river. While that is lovely for us, it hasn't been easy convincing people that they aren't welcome to help themselves to it for fishing, hunting, swimming, or even cutting firewood. The law (at least in Nebraska where we are) is clear: not only is the riparian area—the woods along the river—ours but so too is the ground *under* the river. Canoers are fine as long as they are afloat, but the moment they step out of that canoe onto the bed of the river, they are trespassing.

That's not easy for people to understand or accept. And having done some canoeing myself, I understand the problem. So we have had to exercise some common sense and diplomacy regarding our ownership of these grounds that have been used by the community now and again for everything from skinny-dipping to baptisms. A highway runs along one boundary of our land and crosses the river on a large bridge, which was a traditional place for partying, drinking, courting, and, inevitably, vandalism. Our lawyer took one look at this situation and said we were headed for real trouble because this is what is commonly called an "attractive nuisance." It wasn't any fun for us hearing breaking bottles, screaming, roaring engines, and fireworks on a corner of our own land well into the early hours of the morning almost every summer weekend but it was also a formula for disaster because increasingly the sandy riverbed became attractive to halfwits on recreational (read: destruction) vehicles from a nearby city. Apparently, people who have money to buy "all-terrain" vehicles rarely have enough to buy the *terrain* or consider working at getting some, and therefore presume that all-terrain means *all* terrain, including yours. We therefore were making payments and covering insurance for land other people were using recklessly and destructively. And as our lawyer correctly warned, if some stupid parents put their twelve-year-old on a four-wheel ATV and the kid wound up killing himself on our land, we would almost certainly be sued for what they would call *our* negligence in making it possible for them to be impossibly irresponsible.

So we closed a road that illegally left the highway at our land and went—on our property—to the area under the river bridge. Well, the hue and howl from people in town was even more than we expected. People who own land along a nearby creek but do not give the public open access across *their* land were indignant about no longer having access to the river across *our* land. It was that nuts. The Baptist Church complained that now they would have to cross the river to some state-owned ground for baptisms and youth parties. I suggested that if they would all get together and pay the premiums on our liability insurance, close down riotous parties under the bridge when we called them at 3 a.m., and would get together along our road to pick up broken bottles and used condoms every Monday, we would reconsider closing the road. They opted out of that arrangement, but some people in town are still indignant about us thinking we should control the land just because we paid for it, insure it, and cover the taxes on it.

On the other hand, we don't protest people swimming, even on our "land," or fishing, or picnicking on our sandbars. The problem remains with recreational vehicles. The noise, litter, and habitat destruction caused by them is unconscionable—and illegal—but sooner or later the sheriff's office gets tired of telling people to load up their infernal machines and consider buying some ground of their own to tear up—and they just keep coming. The only cure I can see for this is a habitat tax (hopefully substantial if not prohibitive) on all three- and four-wheel ATVs and other off-road vehicles not used in agriculture to cover the cost of the damage they cause and maybe pay for educational programs to make it clear to ATV owners that if their tires are on the ground, they are on someone's property—hopefully their own and not mine.

WELCOME TRESPASSERS

Remarkably, one way to avoid some such problems is to make arrangements for specific visitors to use your land for precisely the same purposes trespassers come for, especially if you are not a permanent and full-time resident. I owned our place for twelve years before we moved here and became residents. I was here weekends and vacations but rarely during the week. One way I could prevent theft, vandalism, and trespassing was to give a few trusted people a key to our gate and permission to use the place for hunting, fishing, bird watching, mushrooming, or camping. That way I could also tell people who were not as desirable that the land was already in use.

Even then I found a surprising problem arose when we eventually moved in a house and settled onto this ground ourselves. For ten years I had allowed two men to hunt deer on this ground, but once we had moved in, I had to tell them that now we didn't care to have high-powered rifles being fired within a hundred yards of our bedroom window, or for that matter, even arrows. To my astonishment, even though they had enjoyed ten years of free access to the ground I had paid for and covered all expenses for, they were outright indignant that now I had the gall to end the generous arrangement. They had come to think of the gift of privilege as their undeniable right. As they say, no good deed goes unpunished.

GUARDING YOUR PERIMETER

Less moot is the neighbor who simply makes an effort to pre-empt your ground, by grazing livestock on it (perhaps under the pretext of failing fences) or simply hoping you won't notice. We were surprised one autumn to get a call from a help-ful neighbor who had spotted another neighbor building a hunting blind on our ground. We quickly checked—we couldn't see the intrusion from our house—and sure enough, this fellow with plenty of river frontage of his own had extended his ter-ritory another few hundred yards onto our property, cutting down trees to make an access road and building a blind. Over the years, this guy's horses had shown up on our ground now and then, but you expect that kind of thing in the country: live-stock strays. But you don't get hunting-blind construction growing by natural growth like a mushroom.

We tried to contact the trespasser but with no response. The sheriff said he didn't want to get involved in property line disputes, leaving us to wonder what sort of problems he would be interested in taking care of. I suspect he mostly didn't want to fight his way through the undergrowth down by the river. To even get to my land, my invasion-prone neighbor had to cross another neighbor's ground, too, so I contacted him and asked if he had perhaps given this guy permission to help himself to our ground. He said he cer-tainly hadn't and hotfooted it down to the river to see the damage for himself.

Well, the bottom line was that we eventually had to take the problem to lawyers to sort out and it wound up being like something from a bad Three Stooges movie. First, the trespasser said he didn't know anything about the hunting blind or road cutting, which was way too obvious a lie to be taken seriously. Then he said he thought river land belongs to everyone, again an absurdity. Finally he opined that river bottom ground is wasteland, so he didn't think anyone would mind him just helping himself to mine. I told him that sounded fine with me because in that case I would be helping myself to ten or fifteen acres of his "wasteland" along the river the very next summer. Somehow he didn't like that idea at all.

There were more lawsuits and surveying costs and lots of huffing and puffing, all nonsense, but sometimes that is exactly what you have to do to protect land rights, especially where the land is not easily watched, or clearly valuable, like river bottoms or woodland. Take it from me, before you buy such land, walk it carefully to check what sort of intrusions are already there and then watch your property lines and fences carefully and walk them regularly to guard against boundary bounders and claim jumpers.

You will definitely want to have a lawyer or deeds expert look at any land documents to check for legal liens or easements in place on the ground you are looking at. If such things are in place, they may or may not be a problem. A fiber-optic company put a cable across our ground here and has access to their cable if they need to work on it but that hasn't happened in ten years and wouldn't be a problem if they did. They were swift and careful when they put the cable in and I imagine they would be the same if they had to return. There is a power line to our place and a highway along one boundary, so there are easements in place for the controlling agencies to maintain their installations, but hey, that's good for us. We need that power and the highway! You will also find that surveyors may occasionally be crossing your ground to plot such things as highways, rights-of-way, bridges, and other people's property lines. That's just part of owning property.

Of course all roads have a right-of-way. That is, only rarely is the total of the ground involved in a road or highway simply what you see with gravel or macadam stuck on it. The shoulders, ditches, maybe even a wider path is reserved by whatever governmental agency is responsible for that road for maintenance, shoulder, signage, repair work, that kind of thing. Just this past month I was headed to town to pick up the mail one morning and was stunned to find all the trees cut down on one corner of my land. Since State Roads Department workers had been knocking down dead and overhanging trees along the highway the day before, and since two big yellow Highway Department trucks were still blithely sitting right there on my ground in what remained of my trees—stumps, ground-up branches, and huge trunks—it didn't take a detective to figure out who the vandals had been who wreaked the havoc. I'll have to admit that I was damned mad about the damage, not to mention the insult and loss, but some phone calls, a couple registered letters, and a meeting with some district supervisors settled the matter in a mutually congenial way. But the moral of the story is, there is constant pressure on the boundaries of even the smallest kingdom with the most clearly defined ownership lines. So stay alert and don't be shy about insisting that others respect the integrity of your ownership.

It's possible, in fact, that you may even want to encourage certain kinds of outsiders using your ground. I think of Old Jules Sandoz of Plains pioneer literature fame. He loved nothing more than a good conversation—okay, what I mean is that the old goat loved a good argument—so he gave a good-size parcel of his homestead claim to the Catholic Church, knowing that then he would have a priest—that is, an educated man he was certain to disagree with—living just down the road and available for a good yelling match any time Jules felt so inclined. Another friend of mine put in a second house on his place and moved in his in-laws. Last I heard he was coming up for parole in a couple more years.

DON'T SPIT INTO THE WIND

You wouldn't think it'd be necessary to tell someone not to build a home downwind from a hog lot if they are at all fussy about nasal insults but it seems to be a regular occurrence out here that someone from the city buys a plot of ground in precisely such a situation and then complains once the spring thaw makes the disadvantage of such an arrangement obvious. I will say it again: you can't move into a new environment, rural, urban, or suburban, and expect to change it into something else. That smell you feel creeping under the door? That's part of country living too.

A couple weeks ago there was a report on television about people having trouble with bears getting into their garbage and lounging around their pools and patios. Well, uh, yes, they had built their homes in an area well known to be occupied by bears. That's why they moved there—to enjoy nature. But not *bears*! So now, of course, they want someone (paid by you and me) to solve the problem for them . . . *by moving out the bears*! Linda finally had to throw cold water on me to stop me from screaming at the ignorant dolts, "You half-wits! If you didn't want bears, why did you move into the bears' backyard? If you don't want bears, get your sorry, stupid asses out of bear country!" Please, don't make me yell at you.

A couple we know recently moved from their suburban home in Lincoln to some acreage about ten miles east of the city, not far from a tiny town on one of the main highways leading out of the city. I don't know what this says to you, or what it says to them, but I know what it says to me: Folks, enjoy country living while you can because like it or not, the city is on its way out to you. A growing city doesn't creep out one house lot at a time; these days cities gobble up a mile at a time and what was a cornfield or orchard one week, the next week becomes a mushroom garden of stick houses growing so fast you can't keep up with the "progress." And voilà, my friends are all at once not in the country any more but are surrounded by exactly the kind of activity they thought they were escaping . . . but which, after all, they are in part responsible for bringing to the country. If you build within a half-hour drive of a city in a direction in which that city is expanding, you have only a couple years before you are back in that city. If you intend to stay in the country, you better keep that consideration in mind.

WATER RUNS DOWNHILL AND OTHER SCIENCE

Some geographic features that would seem to be about as permanent as a mountain or river aren't. Certainly not rivers. We have some assured stability on our place because of that highway along one side and the bridge crossing the river. It's not likely that the state of Nebraska is going to move that bridge very soon (although it is always possible they might!) nor are they likely to let the river go crazy and erode away an approach.

They are fairly determined to keep the water under the bridge.

Irrigation ditches, drainage canals, pits, channels, basins, even canyons and small washes are important clues to where water wants to go on any particular piece of land, and the prospective owner would do well to study and interpret the signs. They may be good, they may be bad, but either way, they are worth knowing and considering.

Which is not to say that the river doesn't still have a mind of its own. God, I was so green when I bought this place! As the snow melted (you'll recall that like the cosmic idiot I was, I bought the ground under four feet of snow), I watched to see what kind of river frontage I had. I found a huge old cottonwood in a string of huge old cottonwoods, leaning out over the channel of the river—the perfect place for a rope swing and swimming hole! I crawled out on the tree and tied a stout rope in place and anticipated a lifetime of pleasure in my own private swimming spot. Better than a movie star's Oscar-shaped pool, I thought.

I came out a few weeks later to find my rope dangling over a sandbar sticking well above the river's waters. It didn't take long for me to learn that while this particular river pretty much stays within its main banks from year to year, decade to decade, it is not quite so particular about where it puts its channel between the banks. In fact, the Platte River not far south of here was called The Old Harlot because she changed beds so often! But I wasn't even done there. You know that row of big old cottonwoods? Each maybe fifty years old? A month or so later the entire row was gone—washed on downstream somewhere. And then an island developed and for ten years I was fifty yards farther from the river than I had been when I first looked over my land. And at this moment the channel is swinging back over to my side and eating away that island that now has ten-year-old cedar and cottonwood trees on it.

Nonetheless, I feel I'm pretty lucky. For one thing, when I lose a couple acres to the river, I can be pretty sure that in a couple years I'll be getting a couple acres back. Maybe not in the same place, but . . . I remember a time long before I got this land I was camped with some buddies along this same river. The landowner—a farmer—came by our camp to join us for some beans and beer and we talked for a while. We commented on the fact that even as casual canoers over the years we had seen some pretty dramatic changes in the channel of the river, and even the banks. He pointed a quarter mile across the broad, shallow river and said, "See that line of trees over there? That used to be on this side of the river, and it was therefore mine. A couple years ago the river shifted almost a half mile in this direction, and now it belongs to the guy on that side of the river."

For many years in an effort to gain some understanding of the river and its workings I kept a daily journal, complete with a map of what the river seemed to be doing. The main thing I learned from that record is how dynamic that river of mine is. There has been at least one occasion when the river about five miles upstream from our place ate through the neck of a huge oxbow curve and cut off a lake, while shortening its own length a good quarter mile. While the constant change of the river is one of the things I now cherish about it, that particular development made the river all the more wonderful because the ancient ground it cut through had been in place for centuries, perhaps millenniums, and as a result old bison skulls and bones washed out and down the river making my every skinny-dipping jaunt down to the river an adventure in paleontology.

When we bought our place, one of the things I was most excited about was an old slough, an old, abandoned riverbed. (Since then I have found that there are actually three or four old beds that can be detected; old-timers here have told me they recall sitting on the riverbank and fishing where our backyard fence is now, a good three hundred yards from the current banks.) I love wetlands because that is where the most dynamic wildlife can be found. And this marshy ground was going to be perfect. Until the river moved out another hundred yards and the slough dried up. And a new slough developed further out. . . . And is now just about to disappear as the river returns.

The moral of this is that you can't depend on permanence when it comes to Mother Nature, as people can tell you who build on cliff sides in California, barrier reefs in North Carolina, or beaches in Florida. If you elect to take the chance, you better be ready to deal with the consequences. There ain't no whining in risky real estate.

OTHER THINGS RUN DOWNHILL TOO

Which is not to say you can't use your head. If you have the time and good sense, read everything you can about the area in which your land lies and about features near it like rivers, wetlands, mountains, and oceans. Look at topographical maps for flood plains, intermittent watercourses, and potentially recurring riverbeds. Talk to old-timers in the area about what you can expect on that piece of ground. Look back into the archives of the local newspaper. Hang around the tavern, café, or co-op and ask questions. Maybe the locals won't be all that helpful. On the other hand, maybe they will. If you think the locals in the immediate area may not be giving you straight information, perhaps to protect someone or something, ask folks in the next town over. They'll be more than happy to give you the bad news.

This is especially important when it comes to building or moving in a house or other buildings. You want to know exactly what you can expect from that nearby river or mountainside. Drive around and look at industry, agriculture, and settlement patterns in the area of the land you are looking at. Is the town moving in your direction? How soon is it going to reach you? Is that going to be a problem? Check with the country courthouse and city hall. Do they know of any plans to develop a garlic packing factory just across the fence upwind from the ground you are about to buy? A feedlot perhaps? A ten-thousand-acre landfill for big-city garbage?

Is there a chance you could rent the land you are thinking about buying for a year or two before buying? Or perhaps something in the area you can sit around on for a while, watching for what you want to buy as a permanent location? I used my land for thirteen years before deciding to move out here and locate a house, and even then I made a lot of mistakes. We've been damn lucky with this ground of ours, but we could have done better.

If a farmstead—that is, a house and buildings—is not already in place, sooner or later—preferably sooner—you're going to have to think about bringing in utilities. As we will note later, water and sewage can be relatively self-contained—that is, you can sink a well and get water and get rid of your wastes in most rural areas without bringing in water and sewer lines from a central source. For heating you can set up a propane, fuel oil, firewood, or other heating system (for example, burning corn, or wood pellets, or as in our case, using a water-based heat pump) without linking to outside sources. Not so generally with electricity and telephone. Oh yes, I know, you can run a generator, or wind power system, or put together something solar, but I'm talking about more conventional (and one might add reliable) methods. You can pretty much figure on getting power to almost anywhere these days, but the farther the lines have to be run and the more difficult the terrain, the more it is going to cost you. I don't want to throw cold water on your ardor, but this is something to think seriously about. One of the advantages we have of living along a highway and not all that far out of a town is that we didn't have a lot of trouble or expense running power and telephone lines to the house. I did without such conveniences when all I had on the land was my log house but once I got married and had a child and decided to live out here, well, discretion was indeed the better part of valor. Besides, it's getting tougher and tougher to find kerosene-powered word processors.

We found it a real convenience to build one major outbuilding before we moved in the house so we could live in it while the house was being put together, and that also meant that we had to run power in here before the house was brought in—not a bad idea since the contractor putting together everything for the house needed power too.

In most places in this country, you need to give some thought to heating and/or cooling, not to mention cooking, lights, and your electric toothbrush. How much of a problem is it going to be to get heat into your new location? Is a power line close? In the city we don't usually have to worry about such things—gas and power lines seem to be a given. But not so in the rural countryside. If you are planning to heat with propane or fuel oil, how close is a supplier? How hard is it going to be for him to get to your place and keep your tanks topped off?

TURNING ON THE HEAT

Our place is totally electric. Everything is electric: heat, cooling, cooking, lights, and that toothbrush. Now, using electricity to generate heat can be an expensive and inefficient way of doing things, or about the most economical one you can get next to solar or wind. Our house is heated and cooled with a heat pump, which is for all the world like an air conditioner that works both ways. An air conditioner uses a compressor to take cool out of the outside air and move it inside while taking the heat from the inside air and discarding it outside. Well, a heat pump also does the same thing in reverse, taking heat from the outside and bringing it in. The problem with this kind of device is that when you need heat inside, it is usually pretty cold outside and therefore there's not a lot of spare heat floating around outdoors to bring in, and when you want to cool the air inside, it's hot outside and there's not a lot of cool to spare. Hmmm . . . what is cooler than outside air in the summer but warmer than outside air in the winter? Subsurface water! It stays the same temperature pretty much all the time, here about 62 degrees. That's exactly what our heat pump uses—the temperature borrowed from subsurface water. We pump water from deep in the ground—we have plenty of water, living on this sand and gravel dump, a large river about 500 yards to our south and a persistent creek about a thousand yards to the east and north. We take a few degrees of warmth from the water in the winter, which we then blow into the house, and the water simply runs down to a wet place in the sand below the house. The process in the summer is the reverse: we take a few degrees of cool from the water, put it into the house, and run the ever-so-slightly warmed water down to the same wet spot.

When we first read about this idea, we were excited about its obvious efficiency, especially for us here where we had ready and plenty of water. I was a bit concerned about the amount of water we would be putting down on the ground below the house, however: 6 to 10 gallons a minute when the heat pump was running. Man, 6 gallons a minute, maybe 400 gallons an hour, as much as 8,000 gallons on a really cold or hot day! Yikes! That is a *lot* of water. A friend and neighbor not far from us had installed the same kind of device in his home and saw the expelled water as a real resource: he built a large pond, lined it to hold the water, built a spillway for excess flow, put up duck boxes, and planned to stock the pond with fish. I wondered if I shouldn't consider doing the same thing, so I watched his progress closely as he finished his house and water pump arrangement. Eventually the problem was getting access to his "pond" because he, like so many people including me, drastically underestimated the efficiency of the device and there was never more than a small wet spot in the bottom center of his "pond," even during spring runoff and the rainy season! As a result, at the bottom of my heat-pump water outlet I buried an old bathtub, which provides ample recreation for the few frogs that enjoy limited swimming. It turns out that a heat pump using water is so incredibly efficient there is very little wastewater to worry about when all is said and done.

By way of backup heat in the event of a power failure—our water pump and therefore our heating and cooling system depends on electricity—we have a large fireplace as the centerpiece of our home. I love a fire, enjoy it, cook in it, and do appreciate the bit of heat it throws off. But the real secret is that our fireplace does have a Heatilator insert and closeable glass doors so it can very quickly and easily be converted from a source of comfort to a provider of heat. We never approach a winter without plenty of firewood cut and stacked where it is dry and easy to reach on our back porch. The few times we have had to resort for a day or two to our fireplace, emergency power packs for lights and radio, and the occasional kerosene lantern, we have wound up having more fun from the experience than distress.

If you are in an area of limited subsurface water availability, there is an even cleaner way of doing things with a heat pump, taking not water from the deep subsurface reserves but only a few degrees of temperature, thereby allowing you and your puny needs to make virtually no impact at all on the environment. This system uses a closed loop of a thermally efficient liquid like antifreeze that runs through a pipe down into the water reservoirs deep beneath the earth, picking up or dropping a few degrees of temperature while it is passing through in the closed pipes, then bringing that constant temperature back up to your house and your heat pump, dumping or subtracting those few degrees into the system and into your house. You don't use a drop of water in this system, just those few degrees of temperature. And that is way more efficient than trying to do the same thing from the uncooperative air flowing around the outside of your house that is trying to make you hot in the summer and cold in the winter!

SKID GREASING

About the only place our minor isolation has given us trouble was when we heard cable television was about to come to our community. (This was before television-receiving dishes made no place remote!) At the time we had a total of three television stations and those came in none too well because we live down in a river valley, separated from the broadcasters by hills and some considerable distance. So we were excited about television cable brought to within a quarter mile of our home and called the company doing the installation. I stressed that I would be willing to pay four or five years of bills in advance if that would make it worth the company's while to run cable out here. Well, the lady said, the cable would only be installed within the town's limits, but we could talk with the construction crew and let them figure out how much expense it would be to run cable out to our place. When the cable installation began I went up to town, located the crew, and talked with the foreman. I told him where we lived and he said he would look at the situation the next morning but couldn't be optimistic about our chances of getting cable all the way down to our place.

I told him I would appreciate the consideration, knew the situation he was in, understood the problems of expenses, profits and losses for the company, all that kind of thing. Then I went to the tavern, bought a cold case of beer, and put it in the cab of the foreman's truck shortly before quitting time, with a note explaining that I had done some telephone construction work in my youth and know what hot, dirty work it can be. I apologized for asking him to take the extra time to look at the poles and route down to our place and hoped the cold beer would make things easier.

We had cable down to our place first thing the next morning.

And that's not a bad plan for other things you need to have accomplished that might not fit into the usual protocol. On one of the first trips I made out here to my new land I hauled in a trailer with my smokehouse on the back. It was an early but hot spring day with lots of mud and I buried that trailer up to the axles in a hole down along my river bottoms. I walked out across the new bridge they were building across the river right here by my land and asked the boss of the job if there'd be any chance he could bring one of his big Caterpillar tractors down to the river road and drag my car and trailer out of the mud, and he said sure, he'd be right over. No big deal.

Well, it was a big deal because he didn't need to do that. Not to mention that I was about to ask him for an even bigger favor. After we'd pulled the car, trailer, and smokehouse out of the mud, we stopped to unhook the chains and I asked him what the chances would be as they finished off the approach to the bridge of putting in a culvert to let me get onto my land off the highway without having to exit the highway and enter our place by driving through the ditch. It looked to me like that was going to get to be a major problem since I'd already buried the car in this mud hole that wasn't even part of the ditch.

He said, well, the specs for this job didn't call for any culverts along my side of the bridge approach so there wasn't much he could do about that. Again, I said I understood his situation and certainly didn't want to ask the impossible or get him into trouble doing something out of the ordinary. I had already seen the bridge crew washing the dirt out of their mouths at the tavern after work earlier in the week, and this was Friday, so I knew they would be wetting their whistles right after five o'clock. And so I was there too. And for an hour I made sure no one on that crew paid for his or her own beers. I thanked them for dragging my car and trailer out of the mud earlier in the day but didn't mention anything else I needed. But the next time I came out to the land from Lincoln, I had a new culvert in place at the very spot where I'd been driving through the ditch.

Sometimes it's a matter of I-scratch-your-back-and-you-scratch-mine but more often when it comes to country living and hard work, the bottom line is, I'll set them up for you and you set them up for me.

WALKING THE WALK

At some point—before you buy, if possible, after purchase, for dang sure—you will want to get to know your ground like the back of your hand . . . literally. Cover it on foot, foot by foot. Yes, even if it is a full section of land, one mile by one mile, walk it slowly, watching, listening, and feeling for everything. Thoreau said he would walk for miles to visit a tree that was a friend, and that he knew them all by name, and I recommend the same for the new landowner. Get to know what you have and where it is. Make a map and/or notebook of observations of what is going on with the real residents of your acquisition: the plants and animals. Watch for animal trails and scat, scratchings on trees from porcupines, deer, bear, or big cats. Look down in the grass for mouse trails, mushroom remnants, discarded deer antlers, bones. Look up for nests, dried nuts and fruits still on the stem, damage and growth on vines and trees.

And then, a week or month later, do it again. You'll be amazed at how much has changed in even a short period of time and how much new information you'll need to record. My favorite time of the year on my land is winter when there is snow on the ground. And the very best time is immediately after the snow falls because before long the traffic in our river bottom ground will trample the snow into a hard pack. It is simply astonishing how much traffic there is: deer, coons, skunks, coyotes, turkeys, crows, voles and mice, and now and then even a mountain lion or wolf. Sketches of where the trails are and notes of who made them may be invaluable for you eventually as you plan further changes of your own on the land but whatever else might be the case, there is enormous fascination (at least for us!) in going back over the years to see how things have changed. Where can we expect snowdrifts after blizzards? Where does water settle after a rain, or run off if there is enough to saturate? Where are the currents in the river from year to year and season to season? When the water is high, what ground is most likely to be inundated? Where do we find the best mushrooms? Where did I see that white mulberry tree last spring and when exactly is its fruit ripe?

I knew about microclimates before I came out here thirty years ago from my work with viticulture, the growing of wine grapes. For one thing, grapes and their products are affected by the smallest changes in their environment: a bit more or less rain, the slightest variations in temperature or

light. And vineyards tend to be small and therefore more easily observed in close detail, so grape growers make a point of
keeping track of their ground and the nature of its produce
square yard by square yard, if not square foot by square foot.
But I was nonetheless surprised when I walked my own new
ground because as I stepped down a small draw on my way
from my cabin site to the river I found one area only a couple
yards across where I felt a distinct chill in the air. And I felt
it every time I walked through the dip in the ground. That's a
microclimate, a site with its own distinctive climatic charac-
teristic(s). I found places here where the ground is inevitably
and inexplicably moist, and others that are forever parched
and dry. As I planted various wild plants (for more about this
kind of environmental shaping, see my book *Weed 'Em and
Reap*), I needed this kind of information because different
plants have different requirements to thrive, some as small as
the kinds of difference I found even on my small plot of 60
acres of Nebraska river ground. Are the conditions consistent over the time of a year? Or several decades? Only our
journals, maps, weather diary, and records will tell us that.

There is, in fact, microgeography too (I think I just made
that word up). This place of ours has some considerable definition since it runs from upland Sandhills down to a river
bottom; it therefore ranges from dry-blowing sand to wet-
land bogs, and everything in between, sometimes in very
small parcels. Topographical and soil-type maps from our
Soil Conservation and Natural Resource District tell us the
very broad picture of what we're dealing with but in all honesty, you can pretty much tell that by looking at it from the
bordering highway. If you drive the ground, or better yet,
walk it, you get a much more detailed idea of what your

ground looks like, and we were amazed to find that the ground, soil, botany, and moisture character varies from yard to yard, even foot to foot, and probably inch to inch.

I can understand how that happens in the bottom ground where there are old (even ancient), buried riverbeds, sinkholes, and sandbars. But even in the uplands we find areas as small as a couple feet across where the grass is green earlier or later than elsewhere, where plants requiring more—or less—moisture thrive. It isn't simply where there is a depression in the ground, either; I imagine that there are places where an old tree has been buried and rotted and so more moisture is retained, or maybe where a buffalo died—or was killed—and made the soil better at holding moisture, or maybe more porous and therefore less likely to hold water. I'm not a soil scientist so I don't know the dynamics but I can tell you for a solid fact that there are substantial and important differences. And that it pays to find those differences, note them, and take advantage of them.

This is not good tree country. I know that, but I love trees. And this is a tree farm. I have in some cases planted trees willy-nilly, in some cases with a machine pulled behind a tractor. A tree was put into the ground every couple feet no matter what the soil looked like or what had been growing there before. Sometimes that has to be done because there isn't time to be more careful. But on other occasions I have dug holes one by one with a shovel—many hundreds over days and days—and in situations like that it is my opinion that it pays to look more closely at where you are digging those holes because in those places where the grass is greener, so are the trees. And in those places where scouring reed or cattails spring up and survive, you can bet that it's going to drown out any trees other than water lovers like cotton-woods, willows, or silver maples. I have ash trees planted on the dry, crispy places where the grass is never green and they are for all the world like bonsai trees, not even six feet tall, gnarled and twisted, even after thirty years of struggling to survive. And I have ash not twenty feet away, planted the very same day, that are now forty feet high, dark green, and happy as hogs at a self-feeder, as the locals say around here. Bottom line? Get to know your ground before deciding what you are going to plant, where. You will save yourself a lot of work, time, and money in your plantings. Unless you are thinking of establishing a bonsai farm.

WEATHER WATCHING

Meteorology—weather science—is a relatively new study, and the ground that we are on is relatively newly settled, just over a century, so we don't have a lot of data to look at even now as the science develops. When the pioneers came to Nebraska they had no idea what to expect by way of weather. They planted cotton, and tobacco, and fruit orchards, hoping to learn by experience. And man, did they ever learn from experience! The weather out here on the central Plains is brutally extreme, from Saharan heat to arctic cold. That we are still learning what to expect can be seen from the fact that scarcely a month goes by without new records being set. The bottom line is, we simply don't know what the boundaries of the climate are out here. Not to mention that there is plenty of evidence that the climate changes from time to time, from the Dirty Thirties, for example, to the Pleistocene Ice Age. While you should certainly take advantage of weather records for your site provided by libraries, government services, and the media, the best source of what the specifics are for your little spot on this huge globe is your own observations and records. If you bother to keep them.

In my case I never had much of a choice; I saw this piece of land, fell totally in love with it, and bought it on the spot, at the asking price. It was almost two months later that I finally came out to scout the place for the first time. I buried the car in a snowdrift, not having any idea what the ground under it was like, stumbled around through the drifts in a giddy ecstasy of delight at what I had done for myself in acquiring this prize, showed it off to a couple friends who joined us at the nearest settlement qualifying as a city, and then we decided to go into town for something to eat. Having never yet so much as driven down the main street of the town, a village of 322, eventually our home.

And since we had had to dig our way back out of that snow drift, it was dark by the time we got to the town, which to my surprise was at the very top of my piece of ground, just over the crest of the hill in fact. We didn't see anything that looked like a tavern or eatery (later learning that at that time all it needed, since everyone knew what and where the tavern was, was a sign saying "Open," later changed when a friend of mine took proprietorship to "Sorry . . . We're Open") so we went to the next town over, where my friend heard there was a steakhouse of some reputation. (And indeed there was, and is. The Gold Nugget in the next town over became a second home for me eventually, as did the town tavern at the top of the hill, The Silver Dollar.)

The point is, once again, I was lucky. There could have been some nasty surprises after all when I got around to looking at the town. It could have been way too little, or way too big. And I'm not sure I would have known or even thought about the distinction between those two extremes. I suppose I wouldn't have wanted a town really on the move because then I would have had to worry about being engulfed by it, and my point in buying this place was that I was trying to get away from towns and neighbors within arm's reach. Or it could have been too far, out of reach of any sort of convenience commerce, grocery buying, tavern visiting, and fuel purchases, the sorts of things that make life comfortable and happy. From our back door we can just see the top of the town's water tower but since the town itself is over the hill from us we aren't bothered by anything else of the town's hubbub aside from an occasional really talented dog howler. I can walk into town if I need to, and it is a very short tractor drive if I need to fight my way through the snow to get groceries.

WHAT IS A TOWN?

And there are the basics in our town: a grocery store, a bank, a gas station, a café, an excellent mechanic, and most important, a post office, and a few extras: a beauty shop, a flower shop, a lumberyard, a gift shop, a custom meats shop. Within 15 miles is our county seat with all the other things we might need, including an excellent retirement home where we have since moved my mother so we can enjoy her company (and cooking!). And 25 miles in another direction is what passes for a city in Nebraska, a town of 45,000, with theaters, upscale restaurants, excellent medical services, car dealers— everything, in fact, that Lincoln offers but with less traffic, less crime, less pollution, less congestion, and less expense. When we moved out here I presumed I would be running the 120 miles to our old home town, Nebraska's capital city, every month or so to take care of all the things that can only be done there but I quickly learned what everyone else here already knows: there is nothing in the city that we need out here. Today it is eight months since I have been to Lincoln. When I go to Lincoln again, it will be only a lark.

There was a time as short as twenty years ago when I could also say with some pride that there was less crime here in the rural countryside too, but that is no longer the case, if it ever was. Part of the growing and persistent problem of crime is a result of drugs and the increasing mobility and possible anonymity of the population. On the other hand, as usual, it is also caused by what is apparently the fairly consistent percentage of idiots and jerks you find in any population.

In fact, in some ways the problems of crime are worse in the rural countryside. For one thing, there is a tradition of trust and honesty out here, and it hurts all the more when those principles are breached. Secondly, it is far more likely in the thinner population that when you read about crime in the newspapers, you are going to know 1) the victim; and 2) the perpetrator. And their families. So, while you may feel perfectly comfortable snarling at the stupid idiot who is arrested for methamphetamine possession and is caught with a house full of stolen goods and a neglected child, the complication is that his sister is the wife of one of your very best friends. Then it becomes almost like a family problem after all—*your* family.

At any rate you are going to want to take some time and care in looking at the nearest community to the land you are considering, and the nearest town larger or smaller, and the closest metropolitan area (although if you are in the real boondocks, as I am, in a huge area where the population density is fewer than two people per square mile, you may have to adjust your definition of "metropolitan" quite a bit. An aunt of mine in Montana wrote to us that she had to adjust quite a bit to "city life," having moved from the ranch where she had spent her entire life to a town of 3,000. On the other hand, when my mother moved from Lincoln, a city of 200,000 that many would consider only a town, to St. Paul, Nebraska, a community of 2,500, she spoke of moving into "the country." Myself, I like the perspective of being a part of my little village, where I can honestly say when asked how big it is, "352−351 because right now I'm not there."

When you look at any town near your prospective new location, try to determine which way the town is growing (if it is indeed growing) or which way it is likely to grow. Look for where the new homes are being built, or how active the road is that passes by your gate. As I've noted, we live on a state highway, which gives us easy access to the outside world (and lamentably, the reverse) but since the highway doesn't really go anywhere but our town, few people pass through on their way to somewhere else. If you go through Dannebrog, you meant to go to Dannebrog. That keeps the level of traffic just about right for us. You will have to consider your own needs and tastes. There is one guy not far from here who built his house right on a curve in a major, divided, four-lane highway so he can look right down the line of traffic from his front-room picture window. I guess that's his idea of entertainment. Maybe he was a truck driver during his working days.

Chapter 3

THE SETUP:

Now That You've Considered What You Have, What Are You Going to Do with It?

INNOCENT DOESN'T NECESSARILY EQUAL STUPID

S o you have taken the plunge and are the proud owner of your own ranch . . . of ten acres. Now what? Where to go from here? I'll presume you are a wide-eyed innocent, or worse yet, a rosy-hued, myopic romantic, like me, and while you are sodden with good intentions, when it comes to having any idea what you are doing, you are as arid as the Mojave Desert. As ridiculous as this may seem, this is also in my experience the most common position for the urban-to-rural migrant. The idea of moving out here seemed great at the time, but now that we are down to the actual dirt and tool level, things tend to complicate. Well, there is help.

And you're going to need it. I'd laugh at the cosmic idiocy of people buying land with totally stupid ideas of what to do with it except that I did exactly the same thing. When I looked over my newly purchased land under four feet of snow, I saw wide, open meadows where I would play ball with my children, only later figuring out that under all that snow was a field infested with some of the nastiest cactus known to man. I imagined planting peanuts near a sandy pond where I could pump water to irrigate them, never guessing that by the time the weather turned dry, so did the pond. I imagined rows of walnut trees—where the water table was way too high for taproot trees and drowned out the first one hundred trees I planted in the first year—and maples in the uplands—where the water table is so deep nothing but lizards survived.

I know some Germans who wanted to be ranchers and so tried to grow cattle on fifty acres of Texas scrub using a golf cart as their only piece of equipment, on land where there is just about enough grazing for one goat on a seasonal basis. I talked a woman out of starting up a vineyard and winery on her twenty acres simply by mentioning the potential investment costs for equipment, the time needed for the vines to come to fruit, and the necessity for some fair sophistication in chemistry and botany. The idea that she might have to know something about 1) grapes or 2) wine, as well as 3) business or 4a) long hours and 4b) hard work, simply had never crossed her mind. Her understanding consists entirely of 1) you plant grape trees, or whatever, 2) you pick off the fruit and dance in it with bare feet, and 3) Here's to your health!

If you know what you're going to do and have the knowledge to do it, then you can move on to the next section of this book, but I'm betting you don't or you wouldn't have bought a book to answer questions because you didn't have any questions. If you're reading this book, chances are you aren't experienced enough yet to know what the questions are, much less know the answers to those questions. What's really important is that if you don't know what you're doing, you need to know that. And you do need to ask questions.

But when you get around to having those questions, who do you ask? Aye, there's the rub! Mercifully, there are more resources for boobs like us than you can imagine. Various parts of the country have various agencies and offices with a wide variety of programs to help people struggling to restore, occupy, improve, or enjoy the rural countryside.

Look in the phone book for Natural Resource District, Soil Conservation, AG Extension Service, State Forester, Game and Parks, the state and federal roads and highway departments, water services, etc. Go visit with these folks and ask them to help you ask the right questions. Check websites. Write letters. Go to the exhibits, fairs, and workshops. Pick up brochures. Contact private resources like Ducks Unlimited, Pheasants Forever, the Wildlife Federation, and the Wildlife Defense Fund. Whether you are a hunter or fisherman, or not, these organizations are concerned about conservation and may be helpful. In almost all cases they will not only be helpful but will probably want to come to your ground, look it over, and even develop a plan to suit your needs (and theirs), help you achieve those goals, and perhaps even find the finances to get the job done.

Speaking of which, if you do need to develop an income quickly but don't know where you are headed, don't have the equipment to deal with crops or livestock, or have more land than you can quickly use or afford, an option worth considering right up front is renting out ground suitable for farming or grazing to someone who needs the land and does have the resources to deal with it. You will need an agreement regarding the price, the amount of livestock to be put on the land, the kind of cropping to be done, access to the land, the cost or profit sharing, that kind of thing, but an arrangement of this kind can give a new land owner a cushion of time and financing to learn to know the land and to put well-considered plans in place for later development.

BIOLOGY 101

If you haven't already done a careful inventory of what you are considering buying or what you have already acquired by way of land, you sure want to get that done now. I've already suggested that you survey, inventory, and map what is there now, but is also the time to start considering where you might want things to be. Including trees. Linda and I marvel at people who move double-wide housing units out on the Nebraska Plains, sometimes cutting down the few trees already on the site, and then let that building sit there baking in the sun and shuddering in blizzard winds without planting a single tree or bush, sometimes for years, sometimes forever. Forget the cosmetics! Think about the economy of the matter! Just a little shade on that house will slash air conditioning costs and a windbreak will within a few years cut deeply into heating bills. I imagine the thinking of these people goes: "I'm only going to live here a couple years until I can get out and move to someplace where someone else has already planted trees, so why should I do something smart and decent?" I think the question answers itself.

If the rural ground you have purchased already has a dwelling on it, take a look at what you have by way of trees and bushes already in place around it. Need more? Need less? Maybe something different? And even if—especially if—you plan to build a home on this site sometime in the future, the

time to get trees into place is *right now*. Okay, once again I've
followed my own advice in such matters and well, it didn't
work out. Early on—twenty-five years ago—I found the spot
on my acreage where I imagined I would build a house eventually and I planted a wonderful, heavy windbreak around
the site: ponderosa pines, chokecherries, and wild plum. But
when the time came to build our home, well, that site was no
longer right for us. The place I chose so many years before is
too far back from the road, and the site was too small to
begin with and I planted the trees in too tight a circle for
easy construction or use for a house site. So, we had to put
our house elsewhere on the ground.

Now, what exactly did this mistake cost me? It took me
maybe an hour to plant the seedlings three decades ago, and
I suppose I hauled buckets of water to them three or four
times when they were young. The dozen trees cost me less
than two dollars. In return, I now have a beautiful grove of
large ponderosas and Douglas fir a couple hundred yards
west of where we did wind up setting down a house, constantly used by deer as an overnighting location. I visit the
spot sometimes just to listen to the wind move through those
big trees with their long needles. I don't see that as much of
a loss even if things didn't work out as I once dreamed.

This ground had been heavily grazed when I got it and
not a tree had ever been planted. Even when I had only a
cabin down by the river, however, I wanted to shelter it from
the view and noise of the highway, and even from my neighbor's beef herd in the other direction. So I hand-planted
rows of junipers around the cabin and had the Natural
Resource District and Soil Conservation people help me with
deep, long, thick windbreaks along the highway, and a year

later along a half-mile-long fence on my boundary with the neighbor. It seemed pretty futile, if not silly, at the time, these tiny little sprouts that didn't even stick up above the furrows I plowed for them, but now they are dense, towering walls that protect us not only from the intrusion of human noise and interruption but also from wind, snow, and even the noise of the highway. It was murderously hard work planting all those trees, digging each hole with a shovel, dropping in a tiny tree, filling in the hole, and stomping it solid, and even worse hauling water to them in 5-gallon buckets summer after summer. So was it worth it? The question is crazy. They are now our finest resource. Other trees we planted—hackberries, maples, ash, cottonwood—have now aged to the point where one occasionally is knocked down by wind or snow weight, and we harvest it for firewood to heat our home. Are we happy we planted those trees so many years ago? Shut up and toss another log on the fire! Take it from me—plant those trees, and don't wait until you need them. Plant them *now*! (Also, you will be astonished how cheaply you can buy large numbers of trees through offices like Soil Conservation, your State Forester, or a Natural Resource District. In fact, they may even offer to put them in the ground for you at a price you simply cannot match with your own labor, machinery, and supplies.)

Windbreaks, woodlots, and woods are always an asset, and can be a valuable one depending on the kind of trees you find or plant. Whatever you have, natural shelters are always good for all residents—wild and domestic—providing the joys of life; perhaps groceries for your table in the form of fruits, nuts, and other plants; perhaps heating your home or outbuildings by providing firewood, or cooling it with their shade. Some timber can be harvested and used or sold but such culling should always be done with care and consideration of what you will lose when the trees come down and how long it will take to replace them. It is my contention that no one should ever cut down a tree without immediately compensating for the damage by planting another. Wood is a renewable energy resource, but only if we renew it.

ARCHITECTURE

You probably think that the most important feature of any farmstead is the house. And for some it probably is. In fact, there are many homesteads around here with nothing but a house. It hasn't always been that way. It was understood a century ago that human beings could live almost anywhere; the first consideration was the welfare of the livestock, which provided the food and the income. It was the barn that was the major expenditure, the biggest and most important building on any farm. That isn't the case any more but the fact of the matter is, you probably know pretty much everything you need to know about a house. At least for you and your purposes. So I'm going to spend no time at all here talking about what to look for by way of a house. That depends on your means, your needs, what's available, what your family is, how it functions, the climate—on, and on, and on. You're on your own when it comes to finding a suitable house. The following considerations are not all that obvious to everyone.

AQUA . . . HYDRO . . . UH . . .WATER . . .

It's obvious that you need to know what your water situation is above ground: ponds, lakes, rivers, ditches, and even runoff patterns. At our place we have a very large river as one of our property boundaries, a couple sloughs in old riverbeds that can run water in the spring but are more often and more likely only wet areas most of the year, and a pond that was dug during the process of building a bridge across the river that gives us an idea how our ground water is doing but most delightfully is our single best bed of calamus plants and a source of wonderful night music when the frogs are in a courting mode.

In many places you will also want to give serious consideration not only to surface water features but also to what the water is doing beneath your feet. Too much water? Does what seems like a perfect house site turn into a swamp every spring or at every two-inch rain? How about runoff? Are you going to have to put in a drawbridge to get from the house to the road with every spring shower? Or is there too little water? How deep are you going to have to go for a clean well? Is it even possible to dig a clean well? Is the ground water contaminated? And don't just think of industrial pollutants! These days an even worse threat is nitrate poisoning from agricultural recklessness.

Can you even get to water? In many places water is naturally far, far below the surface, if it is there at all, and in others the water table is dropping because of agriculture exploitation. It's hard to establish a home where you can't get water to cook, drink, or bathe!

One of the first friends I made out here was the local dowser, or water witch. (Scoff if you will!) He gave us useful information about his own long history with water in the area and we used him to help us locate and drill our first well. We later added another because we use a water-based heat pump to heat and cool our water along with supplying all our household water needs. When we began watering all of the trees and plantings around the house during severe drought periods, it was a considerable strain on our one well, so we had another drilled farther out behind our yard dedicated to watering plants. We were lucky—our well water is sweet, clear, and pure. It is a gift for which we are thankful every day. Water is a factor in establishing a rural home that simply cannot be neglected. Put it high on your list of priorities.

While it is most assuredly not the case where I live, there are areas of this world, nation, and state where the problem is getting rid of water. High water tables, impervious soils or substrata, and various other hydraulic anomalies make too much water a problem for some rural areas. There are ways to deal with this too: drainage ditches, sumps, even tiling fields—that is, burying a system of perforated clay or plastic pipes to drain and carry off excess water are commonly used not four hours east of here. Your water problem—whether too much or too little—clearly depends on where you are. The chances of everything being just hunkydamndory when it comes to water are slim. Life just doesn't work that way.

If you are really lucky, you may find that your farmstead, if it is already in place, also has a windmill already in place. A windmill is a wonderful machine. It's hard now to imagine the sense of freedom and independence something as simple as the windmill brought to homesteaders and pioneers. You know, there was a time when you had to locate your frontier home close to surface water if you had any intentions of surviving, or hand dig a huge hole in the ground at the risk of your life and then haul water up with a rope, winch, and bucket, a gallon or two at a time. And then along came this wonderful invention that brought water up at a continual rate hour after hour, day after day if you wanted, as you wanted. It was in fact so abundant that you could cool your butter and eggs with it! The sound of that thing whirring and banging out in the yard must have been like music to the ears of many an isolated farmer and his family.

I can never conjure up that image without thinking of my old buddy Co-op George's story. He once told me it was his job as a kid to be sure the pump jack hooking the rotating fan to the vertical well pump was turned off every night—no sense in wearing out parts pumping water when it wasn't needed to water the family or livestock, after all. Well, one night George woke up and heard that jack grinding and squeaking away, so he crawled out from the warm covers and headed out to turn off the windmill. He no more than got to the screen door however when the sound of that rotating jack stopped. Hmmm. Maybe he had just imagined it. He headed back to bed. But he no sooner got there than once again the rhythmic squeaking started. Again he got up and went to the door whereupon he heard his mother whisper, "Shhhh . . . I think one of the kids is up. . . ."

If you have a working windmill, even if you don't need it, I strongly recommend that you get it put into order by your local windmill mechanic and keep it in order, servicing it, greasing it, replacing parts on a regular basis. You never know when that cold clean water drawn for you by the wind from the depths of the earth might be welcome or even necessary. Besides, it makes nice music. We have a windmill set up in our farmstead and there's not even a well under it. Linda grew up hearing the sounds of a windmill turning in the summer breeze and the music continues to soothe. Besides, it reminds us of George's story. . . .

USED WATER

Once you figure out where the water is going to come from to support your tenancy, you then have to figure out where it's going to go next. That is to say, where are you going to get rid of your wastes. Already some city slickers are going to be puzzled by this conversation: "Water comes out of the faucet. And peepee goes away when you flush the toilet."

Well, yes, sort of. But things become a lot more immediate when you live in the country. Just as you have to find water, get down to it, and set up a system to bring it up and into your house, you have to devise a system to get rid of it and take it away from the house after you've used it; that is, a septic system. I'm not going to get into the technicalities of this—there are entire books about that process, including my own *Outhouses*, a sort of hymn of praise to the venerated and in some cases like mine, treasured mechanisms by which you carry your waste products out of the house and dispose of them in the simplest of septic disposal systems: a hole in the ground. (Even simpler of course but increasingly subject to feminine objections about it being discriminatory and disgusting is the male preference for simply stepping out the door and peeing in the yard. I consider this one of the true joys of rural living; Linda says it sets me back in time and human development to approximately the period of pre-Cro-Magnon man.)

These days probably the most common civilized form of waste disposal in rural country is a septic tank and waste field. Briefly, your wastes go down the toilet, into a big plastic or concrete holding tank where various bacteria digest them (I know—eeeuuuugh!), and they then drain out a pattern of perforated pipes to seep harmlessly back into the soil. We have two septic tanks here, one for the house and one for an addition, which turns out to be my bathroom. The one for the house enjoys special fragility because it is used almost exclusively by women who apparently delight in clogging toilets and poisoning septic-loving bacteria. I have no idea why the ladies' septic tank has to be emptied, treated, and stared into almost annually at great expense and disgust while mine functions along for decades and probably generations without the slightest problems. It may have something to do with that previous mention about me peeing in the yard but I'm not going to suggest that even if it truly is the answer.

Women hate outhouses; some men also hate outhouses, but most men appreciate them. For generations outhouses have not only been a male refuge from indoor bathrooms filled with drying panty hose, racks of powders, lotions, salves, emoluments, and God knows what else women use to work their wiles, a place to contemplate at leisure the lingerie section of the Sears catalog, a safe repository for bottles not otherwise allowed in the house, and a complaint-free zone for relieving those pressures native to a man who eats well, but also a quiet guarantee of the solitude necessary for serious thought. The first building I moved onto this ground was an outhouse, given to me by a kind friend who didn't have the heart to destroy the one behind his farm home. It didn't take much to clean it up, fancy it a bit, and install a large window that permitted me a view of my realm from the comfort of my throne. It still stands within a short walk of our back door and to this day, thirty years later, serves me faithfully in a house full of women where I sometimes go for months without seeing porcelain.

Because our house is heated and cooled with a heat pump using water as its thermal source, we have more than a usual amount of wastewater, although I hesitate to call it "waste" because it exits the house pretty much the same as it entered with just a degree or two more or less temperature in it. Rather than run this water through the septic system, we set up a separate drain to run it out into a very small dry slough about 50 yards away from the house where it disappears harmlessly and most of the year invisibly into the sand. A couple particularly happy willows and a clump of elderberries are the only evidence of it being where it is.

AND OTHER OUTBUILDINGS

A real farmstead is a compound, a complex of many buildings functioning as a single community, not just a house, or a house and a barn. You may have or eventually want a barn, although those buildings are on the decline because agriculture products have changed dramatically over the past century in everything from crop storage to livestock maintenance. More likely, you'll need a building in which to store your machinery, even if that amounts to nothing more than an automobile garage. On our farmstead we have, besides our house, a large metal building in which we park our cars, store things, and in which there is a room serving as the office where I write these words. We also have a machine shed for parking tractors, a large shop where I do repair work including major rebuilding of tractors and machinery, an old henhouse that now functions as a lawn-equipment storage shed, a summer kitchen where I do my cooking, and a second house we moved in to serve as Linda's art studio. Down by the river I have the old log cabin, a couple more outhouses, a smokehouse, and a camper shack that is little more than a lean-to—four poles in the ground sided on three sides with corrugated steel and with a steel roof, open to the river, and an old iron Franklin stove serving as a campfire site. It is furnished with the springs from a couple old iron hospital beds.

Not a single structure was here when I bought this place. We built them all, or had them built, or more likely, moved them in from somewhere else, often as far as a hundred miles. And believe me, if I had it to do over again, I would have put each and every one of those buildings on a different spot. Not once with all eleven of my buildings did I pick the perfect location for it. My only consolation is that even with a second chance I'd probably still not put down the buildings in exactly the best place.

Not only should you think where to place any new buildings at your rural home, I think it's a good idea to look around at what other people have done, especially old-timers. They often know things from long experience that we might not think of. For example, have you ever noticed that barns on older farmsteads are almost never immediately to the side or rear of the house? A barn is usually set off from a rear *corner* of the house on a traditional farmstead. This way the larger building does not block the view or breeze, or worse yet, direct breezes from the animal residence into the house's back door! You can see the barn from the house but setting it off one corner does give you some options.

Probably the smartest arrangement for outbuildings, at least in a climate that has winters, are the long strings of buildings all tacked together that one sees in the American Northeast. This arrangement made it possible to tend to all the chores, animals, and machinery without so much as stepping foot into snow and cold. As I mention elsewhere, in Europe and in some European parts of this country, it was the custom to house animals in the same building as the living quarters, "barn-breaking" the animals to cut down on the more unpleasant consequences of sharing. I still think it would be a good idea to have important, often-entered buildings connected to the house somehow, even if just by a passageway, where winters are severe.

One of the things we have learned the hard way is that you need to consider a lot of very important things when you plunk a building down around a house. We cleverly placed my machine sheds on the north entry road to our farmstead, thus ensuring that any time it snows and the wind blows from the north—pretty much a given in Nebraska—there is an enormous drift all the way smack down the middle of our lane from the highway right to the garage and the house. Terrific.

And it's not just buildings you need to think about when you start tossing things into the mix. The picket fence between my office and the house runs directly along the north of the sidewalk, which again means that when it snows and blows, there is a deep drift running precisely where I need to walk to get to the cars, the shop, or in and out of the house for anything else. I did do some decent thinking when it came to facing my shop with its big doors and large front toward the south and out of the north wind. The garage faces west which means that it can accumulate some snow and wind—we lost one of the additions to a small tornado that came through many years ago—and fortunately my machine shed, where I park the tractors we use to plow the drive or get us to town when the weather is really bad, does face south so it collects some warmth from the sun even in the deepest winter. While a drift accumulates in front of it, at least the snow is not blowing into the open front and onto the tractors.

I wish we had given more thought to where we put trees; a couple are too close to the house for comfort. You'd be surprised how fast trees get really big, even in drought and sand here on the Plains, and drop leaves into house gutters, block satellite reception, and drop branches onto the porch during windstorms. One lilac bush is in a perfect spot to catch south breezes in the spring and direct its wonderful perfume to the house; I wish we had planted others there too. And maybe some wild plum and elderberry bushes, although their perfume is strong enough that we catch some of that even from where they are more than a hundred yards away in the river bottoms. We are close to animal routes, especially deer and turkey, and too close to tourist routes on the highway. I wish we had a better view of the river, but am glad we're below the brow of an enormous hill to our north and west that protects us from the incessant winds of the Plains. See how complicated it can get? Believe me, you're going to make mistakes no matter what, but with a little foresight and a lot of luck you will make as few as possible. You can do that by taking your time, doing some major thinking before building or planting, looking at what other people have done in the area, and staying current with your arrangements with God.

I wish I'd had a book like this to inform me when I built up our yard, but I didn't. And certainly there are a few things

I wish had been in place when we arrived, but they weren't. For example, we are in an area painfully prone to tornados, one of the few things in this world I am genuinely afraid of and hope never to see. Older farmsteads always featured a storm cellar, the pioneers being a good deal wiser than are we modern dwellers who have no qualms about living in a trailer house anchored down with four concrete blocks. Of course in those days of limited refrigeration, or none, the cellar also served as a food larder as well as a shelter from the storm. (One of the fascinating customs of those days was that the first person into the cellar was required to bring in the family ax. That is, no one went into the cellar until someone had the ax in hand, in case trees, or for that matter the house or barn, landed on the cellar door and the family had to chop its way out. How's that for an unlikely rural survival technique?)

We rely on a space under our sturdy stairs in the bottom floor of our house, which is below ground level, for protection from severe weather, and I suppose that's not bad shelter from a storm. A friend of ours who has a factory-built home (read: double wide) bought a ready-made storm cellar and had it buried under the concrete slab of his shop, which in turn is connected to the house. It is cramped but it is safe, and I do envy him that. I have also heard of septic tanks— new, I hasten to note—being installed underground or near a country home as storm shelters. Even if such a cellar weren't used as a haven from the storm, it would be darn handy as a safe storage area for valuables, like back-up computer discs from my office, which sits out here above the ground like a tin box kite.

You know what I wish we had on this farmstead that we don't have? A tile silo. Tiles are like hollow concrete blocks but thinner and harder, shinier, and prettier, being red or yellow and quite handsome. Silos are not used much in modern agriculture so these days they mostly are abandoned and falling into ruins. If I had a silo—and there are several within shouting distance of our land, which makes the pain even more acute—I'd convert it into my study. Wouldn't that be neat? Five or six stories for books and supplies and then a round room right at the top with windows in every direction, looking out across the countryside. A workplace like that, my theory goes, would inspire the writing of great literature.

You would, in fact, be surprised at how adaptable old buildings can be, so don't dismiss what may initially look to you like architectural liabilities on your land. Barns can be the sturdiest and most interesting buildings on a farmstead, easily the base for a study, shop, or even a home. I have seen structures as lowly as ancient chicken houses cleaned out, freshened, insulated, floored, roofed, windowed, and converted into really nice studies with wonderful southern exposures; chicken houses were often oriented to take advantage of a warming sun.

Shops and sheds may appear shaky on the surface, but adapting them to modern use is almost certainly less expensive than building from scratch, although using old buildings also carries with it restrictions based on things like the small size of doors and windows, limited floor area, and poor location. However, all of this can be remedied with a bit of work and ingenuity, and probably a certain amount of cash. Take some time and give some thought before you raze any old building, no matter how terrible its condition may seem. Consider adaptive use. And if there is no other course but destruction, do what you can to salvage lumber and hardware from it. Don't be too quick to set fire to that old wood (and don't forget to check with local fire authorities before you do any burning at all or you may find yourself in big trouble and paying substantial fines for burning without a permit!). These days, for example, old barn siding brings astonishing prices from chichi interior decorators.

My favorite buildings on our land are the old ones I have moved in—our home, the outhouses, the log cabin, Linda's studio—and some of my least favorite are new ones we built. Now, to be sure, that's partly because we've never had the money to do anything right, or didn't suspect what we were going to need down the line. A small four-stall machine shed was just fine when I had two tractors, and a one-bay shop was more than enough. Then I caught the old-iron bug, bought up old junked tractors like they were going out of style (because they are), started writing about tractors and shops and tools, and as a result, we tacked on lean-tos, additions, bays, and extensions, building more buildings, all of which were almost immediately also inadequate, not to mention in the wrong place. The moral is, if you can (read: if you have a rear-end full of nickels) give your building needs a lot of thought and then build a lot more than you think you're going to need. If not, well, you're just going to have to do the best you can with how things fall into place. That's the way life has gone around here. It hasn't killed me; it won't kill you.

UNWANTED BUILDINGS

There is every likelihood that some buildings on any site are no longer useful but still need to be dealt with. Don't forget that buildings can be moved off a farmstead as well as on. Buildings can be dismantled and salvaged for reusable lumber, hardware, and elements like windows and doors. (More about this below!)

Buildings that are literally of no use however can still be dangerous, to pets, children, and even you, if they wind up harboring things like rabid skunks, hantavirus-bearing mouse dust, dangerous snakes, scorpions, or other varmints. In a case like that, you may have to consider tearing the building down and hauling off the rubble or burning it, in which case you will for darn sure want to check with the local law authorities about burning permits. In fact, the best thing may be to contact the nearest fire department about burning down the building for you. In most cases, a rural fire department will do this as a free service, perhaps using the exercise as practice in using their equipment or skills. In that case, it is always a good idea to acknowledge gratitude with a donation to the people doing the work and to provide as much comfort as you can during the work they do: cold drinks, food, shelter from the heat and smoke.

GATES AND FENCES

As a city slicker, I would have never considered one rural construction that is an essential item but not one that hits you in the face (like the house or a barn): fences. Even if you are not going to be fencing in livestock, you may very well find yourself needing to fence out livestock. There is a certain amount of natural estraying—the legal and rural term for wandering cows, horses, goats, and pigs—but you also don't want to discount people who make a habit of ignoring their fencing obligations and thereby enjoy a few days—or weeks—of free pasture for their animals at your expense. I have had the bad fortune to have a couple neighbors with this system of cutting their costs, and it can be damn discouraging to see your own work and investment going down the gullet of someone else's animals and then even worse to find that no matter how exorcised you get about their invading your land with their livestock, they simply don't care. One way (and I can tell you from experience the most legal and eventually least expensive way) to deal with this is to keep the fences in good repair yourself, even if the legal obligation is for the livestock owner to keep his animals on his own property. Good fences and gates and maintenance can avoid a lot of problems despite being a lot of hard work. Your fences are in fact one of the major constructions on your land; look them over carefully and consider how much work you're going to have to do to bring them up to snuff.

In addition to a fence along your larger boundaries, consider a yard fence, too, not just to keep in things like pets and children, but also to keep out things like stray livestock and wild critters. A good fence won't stop everything. We have a fairly good, tight, "hog wire" fence around our substantial yard to keep our dogs from straying and while I am sure it also keeps out a lot of wild animals—some dangerous, like rabid skunks or porcupines that can wreak havoc with dogs—some always manage to make their way in and that's just another matter of dealing with what nature and rural living deal out to those who live there.

Gates may be nothing more than two poles with barbed wire or a discarded headboard from an old wrought-iron bed, and a stile little more than an old ladder leaning on the fence, but you can be sure it's there for a reason and whatever little attention it takes to keep it in order might just be worth the trouble. Of course, gates, fences, and locks rarely keep anyone out who has a notion to come on in, but they are a statement worth making. Same with signage: you may not like putting up signs saying "No Hunting" or hanging old tires over a fence post saying "Keep Out," but if you don't do that, there are people who interpret the absence of same as an invitation to come on in and help themselves.

ROADS, LANES, AND PATHS

I have mentioned the importance of roads around a parcel of land and going to and coming from it, but roads within boundaries and on the plot are also important—all the more so because they are completely the owner's responsibility. Consider the condition of the road coming into your property, and those that let you move around on it. What is their condition? Do they need grading? More rock or gravel? Paving? Do new roads need to be built? In our case it was Chris, my son from my previous marriage, who once looked at our ground and said, "You know, Dad, we have too many roads on this place." I considered his opinion and decided he was right. We had way too many roads, not just for maintenance but also for the damage we were doing to our plantings and wildlife. I closed a gate at the top of our ground and planted trees that effectively shut off the road there. I closed another road that crossed the uplands and then dropped down toward the cabin, leaving the bottom road, on which we had spread some cobble rock (stones larger than gravel) to make it more serviceable in wet weather. When we built our home, we invested in more cobble rock and gravel to ensure a solid, mud-free approach to the house from the highway and eventually paved a small slab in the yard near the house to allow easy parking and mud-free foot traffic to our vehicles and back. I keep a pile of both gravel and cobble rock near our entry so I can touch up any puddles or soft places that might develop on the road, especially during the spring thaw. Now that the road has been well stabilized, we rarely even need to haul a tractor load of gravel or rock to low spots, a hand-carried 5-gallon bucket being usually plenty to touch up problems.

MINOR SALVAGE

You'd be surprised by the number of people I know who have acquired rural property and got to looking around the buildings, finding things of remarkable interest, and sometimes even substantial value. I have gotten permission now and again to salvage the contents of old buildings that have been donated to fire departments for burning or are within a short time of being demolished and I can't believe what has been left behind. Sometimes it's no more than iron window weights that are useful for holding tarps and covers down over firewood and machinery but in other cases I have found and rescued gorgeous old glass and ceramic ceiling and wall lights (which we have in our home now at this very moment), maple and oak cupboards, walnut shelving, antique furniture (in one case, a fine old kitchen table and even an ancient churn), crockery, a beautiful old iron baby bed, woodwork, doors, paneling, windows, tools. . . . It's amazing.

No less treasure can be found in sheds, outbuildings, and barns: Horse tack and harness, tools, bottles and jars, hardware. I can understand how such things might be forgotten or put away or even discarded, but how have they escaped scavenging before I came along? I can't imagine. One of the first dates I had with Lovely Linda was a visit into the brush and tangle behind which her ancient and long-abandoned family homestead lay. Inside we found plenty of ruin: the ravages of time, weather, and raccoons. In fact, the house was on the ragged edge of collapse. But inside we also found some very old iron beds, jars, and perhaps most moving, an ancient crucifix hanging beside one of the beds. We asked the current owner if we could take one of the beds and he said we sure could because he was about to burn down the buildings to be rid of them anyway. As we hauled the most ornate of the beds out, he said, "You picked yourself a good one there. That was your great-grandfather's bed." The mystery is not even why no one had taken such treasures before but why the owner didn't seem to understand the profound meaning that bed would have on a great-grandchild like Linda. Or for that matter, on both of us eventually. While we barely knew each other during this adventure, that bed became ours.

A word of caution: even abandoned buildings are private property and taking anything from them is theft. Even *exploring* without permission may get you into a world of trouble. As rural thievery becomes ever more common, even innocent curiosity can be downright dangerous. But if you have bought the buildings, well then, you also bought the contents, I guess.

My ancestors on my mother's side were garbage men, a point of constant agitation for her, not least of which is the family story about the time the family minister came visiting and asked me what I wanted to be when I grew up. What else? I wanted to be a garbage man. And as I still remind Mom, that's pretty much the way it worked out. And that's why one of the first things I looked for when I bought this ground and the snow melted away was any sign of a dump. I used to haul our own garbage when we lived in Lincoln. One problem associated with this was that I sometimes came home from the dump with more than I took there in the first place. And eventually one of the joys of farm life out here was loading up a trailer with our garbage and trash, hooking it to my old 1937 Allis Chalmers WC tractor, and hauling the load the four miles to the dump on the other side of town— rescuing whatever treasures I found while there and bringing them home to a disapproving woman, now Linda instead of my mother.

I did find some salvageable refuse here—not much, but some. There was an old logging chain not far from the high-way—probably fell off a passing truck and skipped across the ditch and into the snow. Some cable was attached to a tree down along the river, perhaps a remnant from the construction of the new bridge. And there was a small old farm dump where I found an interesting piece of crockery and an antique thermometer still in working condition. The moral of which is, before you get too hasty about tearing down or burning down an old building, take a look around inside it. You may be surprised at what you find.

The ultimate treasure for many guys like me is the discovery of old machinery in a barn or shed or tucked behind some brambles in a woodlot. A tooth harrow or plow is nice. An old car would be a treasure. Perhaps even more likely since we are talking about rural property would be an ancient tractor, a true treasure, and perhaps the most valuable item on the whole place. I look at a lot of old farms, cluttered with rusting agricultural iron and marvel that probably the most valuable crop on the whole place is the stuff falling apart out there behind the barn or in the wind-break, and probably considered useless clutter by the owner. Take a look at what comes with your land purchase by way of rusty iron and consider its restoration value (check with someone who knows about such things) or for your own use. Later on I'm going to tell you that you are going to need a tractor and some implements; it would be nice to find that you have already acquired them as a bonus with the deed.

NEIGHBORLY NEIGHBORS

If you haven't already checked out and met your new neighbors, now is the time, and not just for social reasons. In rural settings everyone depends on everyone else, and the closer they are to you, the quicker and more surely they will be there to help you when you need it. Moreover, now would be a time for them to check *you* out and gain some confidence in you and your intentions. That's not always a positive response: I haven't heard anything about the issue now for a couple decades but when I first came out here there was considerable discussion and some disapproval that I had taken a piece of ground—as unproductive as it had been—out of any sort of agricultural production and was just letting it sit and "go to weeds"—that is, trees, native grass, and wildlife. This first encounter with those who may wind up being lifelong neighbors, even friends—or enemies—is not the time to get huffy about things like straying cattle, bad fences, noises or smells, clutter or contamination, but it will give you a chance to look things and folks over and get some idea what kind of problems you might face in the future.

Look over the crops and livestock you are going to be living next to, and downwind from, the next few years. Exchange names and telephone numbers, express whatever interest you have in cooperation or concerns about possible problems, including those you might be causing your new neighbors. We have occasionally had to rely on our neighbors for help in snow removal when my own tractor was down, for information about who could help us with other problems, even for things like corn for our chickens. And our neighbors are very active in the volunteer fire department and emergency medical team, two resources we also have had occasion to be grateful are so close.

It works both ways: If you have something to offer— extra garden produce, for example—a nice way to meet the new neighbors is with a gift in your hands. Please note that such generosity does *not* include whatever monopoly you might think you hold in religious truth. If you really want to make yourself a pariah, go around with the notion of disabusing your new neighbors of their religious ignorance!

MEDICAL SERVICES

For years we tried to convince my elderly parents they should move out here closer to us—I am an only child, after all—but one of the things they were concerned about was that my father had had a stroke and several cardiac "incidents." In Lincoln they had topnotch hospitals, emergency services, specialists, all within easy driving distance. At least that's what it looked like and that was what they thought. The facts of the matter are that even our volunteer services here on the remote Plains are extremely well trained, and within minutes of our call, without a single concern about fighting rush-hour traffic, they get to us when and if we need them. Moreover, they are all our friends and neighbors. They care about us, and we trust them. I have spent time in Big

City hospitals and with some of the top doctors in this country (you'd recognize the name of the clinic) and frankly, I
wouldn't trade the whole pack for the doctors within fifteen
minutes of us or the emergency services only seconds away
from our door out here in the boondocks.

And sometimes, well, we are still surprised by exactly the
medical tech excellence we enjoy for all our isolation. I have
always insisted that the doctors in my life consider themselves and behave like human beings; their educations are no
better than mine, they are mortals just like me, and however
dependent I may be on them for whatever dangers I am in,
they are nonetheless mortals. But sometimes the easy infor-
mality of rural America's social arrangements still surprises
me. I recently needed to go the 20 miles into our nearby city
cancer clinic on a daily basis for radiation treatments. The
doctor stressed the importance of me being there every day
without fail. The projected period of the treatments extended
into the time when everything on the Plains can be brought
to a dead stop by ferocious winter storms and so I wondered
aloud to the oncologist what would happen if during a blizzard, Wife Linda, who was serving as my driver, wouldn't be
able to get out of our drive and onto the highway, especially
if I wasn't up to clearing our way out with my tractor. "Oh,
that's easy enough," he shrugged. "I live on a farm just down
the road from you and I'll come over and pick you up." Yes, he
is a doctor, but out here he is also a neighbor and fellow
struggler against all the problems that come with rural life.
That's not just an unlikely anomaly either — it's the way
things are done in rural America. This kind of thing is the
rule, not the exception out here. My mother now lives in a
retirement home in the nearby county seat. She is having to

adjust to small-town living and is encountering the same kind of remarkable experiences. A few weeks ago a friend of hers at the retirement center spent some time in the hospital but when the day came that she was released, she realized she had no way to get back to her apartment. The distance from the hospital to the retirement center is only a half mile or so but this lady certainly wasn't up to hoofing even that distance and you don't get taxi or limo service in a remote Nebraska farm town. So, what was this elderly lady to do? Not to worry! The doctor—not the receptionist or a nurse, the *doctor*—said, "I've got a few minutes before my next appointment. Just wait here. I'll go get my car and run you back over to your place." Let's see you get a house call like that in the city!

Chapter 4

SELF-RELIANCE:

Where Can You Get Help?
What Can You Do by Yourself?

O
kay, so you're not moving to a desert island in the Southern Pacific or a treetop aerie somewhere in the Brazilian jungle. Believe me, there are plumbers, electricians, auto mechanics, and insurance salesmen everywhere. Especially insurance salesmen. You may have to check the yellow pages for another town near you but sooner or later, you'll find someone with the expertise you need no matter what that might be. But one of the reasons you may very well have moved into the country in the first place is to gain some modest level of control over your own life and surroundings. It's true; you may actually have to learn how to do some things on your own to avoid major problems. If power lines go down in a ferocious blizzard or if you are isolated when a flood takes out a bridge, you may need to get off the couch and figure out what to do about heat, light, water, and communications on your own. It's not that big a deal and you may actually find a lot of satisfaction in even that small degree of self-reliance.

TOOLS

To do such things you need more than native intelligence and ingenuity. You need tools. Most men and a lot of women love good tools anyway so this again may be little more than a good excuse to get yourself some good tools but I think it's going to be unlikely that you can live in a rural setting for very long without pretty much having to have some basic equipment to make that life possible and to keep it bearable.

To avoid overwhelming you, I'll start with small hand tools and work my way up to the big stuff. You need a toolbox, maybe not much more than a 5-gallon plastic bucket you can throw a few things in and carry wherever you need them around the place. Some tools are so basic to any home, rural or urban, the following list might seem pretty silly, but from what I have heard and seen, I can't start too basic. Some folks think they are prepared to move to the country equipped with nothing more than a copy of the Whole Earth Catalog and a sharp stick.

I'm going to divide my suggestions into household tools, emergency equipment, and larger, implement-type equipment. In each category I'll start with the most basic and necessary and trickle down to items that are important but probably not critical. If you've ever talked with someone who lives in the country or is at all serious about self-reliance, you will quickly find that you are going to need a lot more than what I suggest below. If you want to do your own construction, well, then the world of tools opens up and swallows you. Carpentry, cement work, gardening, masonry, roofing—each process has and requires its own tools and this book is not the place for that kind of thoroughness. If you want to get into this kind of thing but are not now active in a trade craft, I suggest that you go to someplace like Menard's, Home Depot, or Lowe's and do two things. First, go to the section of the store where they have do-it-yourself books, and believe me, you will find a book on absolutely everything, no matter how unusual or obscure. Read that, figure out what you are going to need by way of tools, and then go back to the store and get some help in setting yourself up to tear into pond building, chicken farming, or bonsai pruning. Even when you are in the store the first time looking at books, drift on over to the section of items, supplies, and tools designed for the activity you are thinking about and do some browsing. That may help you understand what you read in the book. This would also be a chance to look at some prices. That may determine how far you want to go in this direction. Getting some notion of what various items cost new can also be a guide if you go shopping for tools in a pawnshop, junk store, or auction sale. Finally, start accumulating tool catalogs. They are fun to browse through even when you are not buying. The most common are Harbor Freight [www.harborfreight.com, 1-800-423-2567, or 3491 Mission Oaks Blvd., Camarillo, CA 93011-6010] and Northern Hydraulics [www.NorthernTool.com, 1-800-533-5545, PO Box 1499, Burnsville, MN 55337-0499]. Both have given me excellent service in my own search and acquisition of tools.

HOME AND YARD

Obviously you need a decent claw hammer, pliers, screwdrivers, and wrenches. These are absolutely fundamental. You will need them every week for the rest of your life, so don't go cheap here. Spend good money and get good tools. You can pass them along to children generations later, and when you figure out what they cost you per day or per use, it's a joke. Get a hammer heavy enough to do the job but light enough that you are comfortable swinging it, especially if you are going to have that thing in your hands for hours and days at a time. Cheap pliers are worse than no pliers at all; I like Channellock for some sentimental reasons but they are pretty solid tools with the added advantage of adjustability. You must have both straight blade and Phillips blade screwdrivers (Phillips are the kind that make a plus sign if you press them into wood). While I have accumulated dozens of both, in the house, in the shop, in the garage, in the office— they're everywhere—again I am particularly fond of a model from Channellock that has a large and small version of both the straight and Phillips points, easily changed and firmly held by a comfortable handle. Look for the bright blue handle. In the shop I use combination and socket wrenches but in the home you need the much-disdained crescent wrench and a pipe wrench, both of average size, although I also keep a small one of each under the sink, which has saved me a lot of trips out to my shop over time. Cheap crescent wrenches tend to loosen up and slip, so again, if you are going to spend the money anyway, instead of spending it small-time ten times on ten cheap examples, spend it once big-time for a good tool. What's the difference? Well, you'll see it in the price, but do ask someone who knows, even if it's a salesman at the store. I once convinced Linda to let me buy a top-of-the-line set of combination wrenches by taking three into the house from the shop: a truly crummy piece of junk made in India, a serviceable but still shoddy one made in Japan, and one of the finely made tools I wanted to buy a set of. All she had to do was hold each example a moment to know what the difference is and why I would want to work with the good tools rather than the junk. Look at the tools and feel them. You'll know the difference.

I can't imagine getting along in or out of the house without an electric drill, so we have one in the house and one in the shop. Both of them are cordless, able to be charged up and then carried to a job even if it is too far out into the yard to drag an extension cord. In the shop I also keep a corded drill for heavier work or jobs that require a long spell of drilling. In our household toolbox we have a couple tape measures and a small level. A longer one hangs in the garage with the larger tools. In all of our various tool locations we have tool knives (also notoriously known as "box cutters") with replaceable blades. I like the kind that lets you easily retract the blade into the handle. These things are murderously sharp and having them lying around open not only ruins the blades but is downright dangerous when I reach into the toolbox in the dark.

What about a toolbox? I have never been very happy with toolboxes. I put stuff in there and then never see it again. I like open storage, hanging a tool on a nail on a wall so I can see it. Then when I need it, I take it down and put it into a plastic 5-gallon bucket that I can carry to the job, again making it easier for me to see and find the tool when I need it and giving me a place to throw old nails, scraps of wood, and other bits and pieces to be sorted out later when the job is done.

My buddy Dan the Plumber drives a service truck with about four tons of tools and supplies in it and he still carries most of the tools he needs for any one job in a 5-gallon plastic bucket. The real excitement starts when we are out in a canoe fishing or in the tavern eating a burger and a job pops up. That's when Dan dives into his pockets and amazes us all over again no matter how often we've seen the routine; there simply isn't a job that needs a tool he doesn't have in his pockets, up to and including a 60-gallon air compressor. Linda has a small, open, wooden box with a handle she keeps under the sink with her own set of tools. You might just as well face it now—sooner or later you are going to need at least a special room for your tools and repair work; more than likely you'll need an entire building—a shop. A farm isn't complete without a shop, and neither is a man. Maybe a woman isn't either, but I don't know about such things.

As long as you are going to be handling tools, especially now that we are headed toward larger tools and harder exertion, be sure you have some good gloves too. I like cotton gloves that I don't feel bad about discarding when they are worn or sticky or set up with cement or epoxy. We keep a supply of gloves under the stairs.

Out and about the yard and farm you will need other, larger tools, and a place to keep them. We hang ours on nails in the entry to the garage. We also have a small outbuilding for some lawn equipment and tools.

There's not a doubt in my mind that the single most important tool in our outdoor and yard inventory is a good shovel. Actually, several good shovels. We prefer the long, straight-handled kind as opposed to those with short, loop-handled handles. We find we absolutely need two kinds, one with a rounded-nose blade for digging holes and another with a flat-nose blade for scraping and edging. Both garden rakes and leaf rakes are of modest value to us because we mulch our leaves with the mower and don't keep a garden. On the other hand, we go through both push and sweep brooms around here as if we were in the sweeping business. That could be because we are in a land of wind and sand.

We do no carpentry so we've never had a carpenter's saw around the place but we do a lot of sawing—pruning trees, cutting brush, cutting kindling, and cleaning up branches blown down in storms—so we find that a bow saw is a crucial tool for our place. It seems I have use for one every week. And if I need to cut a board, I do what I can with a bow saw. I probably shouldn't admit it but I've even cut the hocks off of hams with a bow saw before putting them into a curing tank. Ten years ago I would have put "chain saw" way up on the list of crucial household tools but as I get older I am less and less inclined to move logs, cut wood, haul it, or stack it. Throw in the noise, stink, and vibration—and that's only me cussing when the damned things won't start—and the chain saw has moved down the list of my most important tools. I still have a couple around in running shape, but when I need to do some small work around the farmyard I have a much quieter and lighter electric chain saw I can drag out. In my dotage, however, I've resorted to a much lighter and easier tool: the telephone. I call one of the neighbor kids and have him cut, haul, and stack a couple loads of firewood onto the back porch for the winter while I supervise. I was cut out for that kind of supervisory position, I think.

Both in the shop and the house we have large and small pry bars, the thin, tough steel kind used for prying or pulling nails. Believe me, they are handy for a lot more than that. Out in the shop I have a couple 6-foot heavy pry bars—I was once told that mine were made out of an old Model T axle, one end ground down or beaten down to a kind of blade—I can't imagine doing without. I have broken my share of bones (always my own, I should note) and have acquired a respectable inventory of hernias so these days I try to save myself some hospital time and money by using tools that even the ancient Egyptians used: levers, wedges, and rollers. They weren't so dumb, you know.

I'm not even sure what the formal name is for a come-along—cable winch maybe? —but I'll bet I have gone through fifty of them over the last thirty years and still have ten hanging around here and there ready to be thrown into the breech when I need to move something big, up to and including dead tractors. A come-along is a portable winch with a hook on each end, one on a length of cable, and a handle by which you can roll up that cable and bring the two hooks closer together. I know I've said it before, and you are getting sick of my nagging, but when you get ready to buy a come-along, buy a big, good one. This is no place to save a few bucks because you will wind up spending more in the long run on cheesy ones that fall apart than on one good one that will last a lifetime.

With your new come-along you will need plenty of chains and ropes. I can't go into the various kinds and lays of ropes here or the strengths of chains or varieties of hooks. You'll have to find that information on your own and hopefully find someone who can help you get what you need for your jobs and your geography. I have made a point of buying just about every length of chain I've ever seen come up at a farm auction and I've never been sorry. You can't have too much chain.

If you are planning on moving stuff around, you're going to need a cart or wheelbarrow, too. Make sure the handles are long enough for you to walk upright while using it and that the body of the cart or barrow clears the ground so you aren't constantly banging the front or bottom into clods or stumps and pitching yourself over the front. Can you tell I've had that trouble? You will also want to be sure the tires and wheels are strong and large enough to carry a load without sinking into soft ground.

On the back of my machine shed a variety of ladders hang on large spikes. I prefer aluminum and fiberglass ladders; they are more expensive than wood, but they are also lighter. I have both extension ladders—the straight kind with two parts so you can slide one up and make the ladder longer—and stepladders, the free-standing kind that open up. I have both large and small ones. I'm not a house painter or carpenter but there seems to be no end of places I need to get up to; ladders are the answer but there's no sense in hauling a 40-foot extension ladder to a job where a 6-foot stepladder will do the job.

If you want a whole tool kit in one, rivaling the contents of my pal Dan's pockets, you should get yourself a fencing tool. It's pliers, hammer, pry bar, wire cutters, staple puller, bottle opener, and who knows what else, all in one. At each of our various toolboxes and stations, we have a fencing tool even though it's been many years since we've used one for fencing.

Two tools we do have and use for fencing are a posthole digger and a fence-post driver. (These days we rarely stretch barbwire, or bobwahr, as it's called, but we do on occasion put up a length of hog wire, or woven wire of narrower weave at the bottom than the top for the dog yard, etc.) I far prefer the kind of hole digger you turn into the ground and then pull out when the screw-bottom bucket is full, but then our place is sandy and the soil tends to be loose. I've never taken to the two-handle kind you slam into the hole, pull out a teaspoonfull of dirt, and then tie splints on your shattered elbows. A driver for metal posts is not much more than a heavy pipe closed at one end; you slide it over a fence post, stand the post straight up and down, and then slide and slam the driver down onto the top until the post is as deep as you want it. Around here this device works perfectly. It is simple to make and cheap to buy—my idea of a great tool.

There was a day when every farm had to have a high-lift utility jack but I get the feeling that may not be the case now. I don't know if the jobs to be done have changed that much or the jeopardy of things like tractors and cars sliding over and falling off these man-killers has led to their diminished popularity. Perhaps the tendency of their handles to suddenly rattle up and down with the speed and murderous force of a machine gun, or the failure of their locks dropping loads suddenly without warning discouraged folks from using them, but I still have one here and still use it. As with any tool, you need to use caution and common sense, blocking up anything you intend to get under, bracing things so they don't drift to one side or the other, keeping an eye and a hand on that handle. When you need to lift something, you need to lift something and a handyman jack or high-lift jack, whatever you care to call it, is one darn convenient way to lift something.

I realize I'm getting down to the bottom of my list and coming dangerously close to those specialty tools I said I didn't have room to discuss, but even here on the relatively treeless Plains we are down along a river, have trees in our yard, have a fireplace in the house and a woodstove in the shop, and call ourselves a tree farm, so we have some items that wouldn't be all that useful, I suppose, on a swamp or desert estate. I have a couple hatchets for splitting kindling in the shop and house and a splitting maul and a couple wedges for splitting wood. I have never found an ax to be all that useful, especially for splitting wood; a splitting maul is the right tool for the job. I don't even have an ax on the place. I have a machete for chopping through willows down to the river and for cutting thistles, although increasingly I simply don welder's gloves and walk my ground pulling up thistles before they bloom; and I have almost completely eradicated the problem.

Because we have a lot of trees in our yard and around the farm, often growing into our driveway and the road down to the river, we have scissor-type pruners to lop off branches that grow to the point where they scratch up our vehicles. These days they make terrific, leveraged pruners that will slice through a two-inch branch with hardly any force at all and have light fiberglass handles, leaving me no excuse but to get down there and get to pruning.

No, I haven't forgotten the most important of rural do-everythings. Even though I said I was working my way down to items of less importance, actually I have saved the most important for the end of my list. That's right: duct tape and baling wire. Okay, and baling twine. I know what's going to happen because I've been there myself. You're going to go into a farm supply store and look at a spool of baling wire, or a roll of binder twine, or a package of twelve rolls of duct tape, and you're going to think, "Man, I'll be working on this same spool, roll, and package way into my golden years. I ain't *ever* gonna use up all that stuff. Does Welsch really think I'm going to spend twenty dollars on a quarter-mile roll of baling wire (electric fencing wire will do just as well, by the way) when I can just pick up this cute little spool of craft wire in the hobby section, let's see, yep, twenty-five feet ... that should be plenty, and it's only five dollars? And one roll of plastic wrapping tape, and fifty feet of store string should be more than enough."

Look, you are now on the *farm* and you are going to be using duct tape, baling wire, and twine like you used toilet paper and Scotch tape in the city. You simply can't imagine all the uses you are going to find for these three items. Even if you do what I tell you and buy the big rolls, the full lots, the most you can get in one piece, in less than a year you'll look at the almost empty spools hanging on the shed wall and make a note to get back to the supply store soon and renew your supply. You'll be looking for even bigger spools and longer lengths than you got last time. And then you can also write a note to me thanking me for smarting you up before you went too far wrong.

EQUIPMENT

Hopefully you haven't gotten too far without giving some serious thought to buying some real equipment. When I got a letter from a friend whose cousin had settled down to raise himself some cattle in East Texas and sniffed at the notion of needing a tractor and/or pickup truck, getting instead—God, I hope I can get through this without falling onto the floor in laughter—a golf cart—just a minute—I'll be okay—I took it up to town and read it to some friends at the tavern. The ones who didn't wind up blowing beer through their noses with explosive laughter sat slack jawed and glassy-eyed in wonder, which turned slowly to dismay. Anyone dumb enough to live in a rural setting and buy a friggin' golf cart for a utility vehicle instead of a tractor is destined for quick extinction anyway. If you see someone headed in this direction, you might want to make a note because there'll be some cheap land up for sale real soon.

Try throwing a couple rolls of barbed wire, fencing tools, and fifty fence posts into the back of a—Sweet Jesus—golf cart! The single most basic piece of large equipment on any piece of rural property, farm operation or not, is a pickup truck. And make it one you can use, not one you have to worry about scratching or dirtying up. You need a *working* pickup truck, and not one of what my mother calls "those cute little trucks." You may want a big fancy painted up pickup for going to town but for working on the farm you want a truck you can use. If you are moving to the country and have no plans to acquire a pickup truck (or don't already have one), you might just as well throw in the towel now. Four-wheel drive is handy but I've never had one myself (although Linda does have one so she can get in and out of here when the weather is bad and the roads are muddy or snowbound). I purposely go shopping for a solid, well-running, full-size pickup that I'm comfortable in, because I'm going to be spending a lot of time in it. I don't necessarily look for one that has low mileage or is in tiptop highway shape because my Blue Thunder rarely goes farther than the post office or lumberyard up in town. We have our traveling vehicles. But my pickup is a working tool and doesn't have to be pretty or speedy, just tough and reliable. And comfortable.

TRACTORS!

And now for the really fun part. You need a tractor. I had this place for three years and got along fine without a tractor until a friend came visiting, took one look, and said, "It's not a farm until you have a tractor. You gotta get yourself a tractor. In fact, I have one that's been parked back in some trees a few years and I'll just give it to you if you can get it out here." I got a friend to help me haul this battered old 1937 Allis Chalmers WC tractor—exactly the same age as I am—out here and my life has never been the same. He was right: you can't have a farm without a tractor. For another ten years I got along with just Sweet Allis, pulling a road scraper, harrow, wagon, or plow, running a corn grinder or buzz saw, taking me to town and back through blizzards or through muck and mud up to the highway, hauling water to new trees, pulling sleds full of screaming friends through the snow at midnight on New Year's Eve, sparks flying from her exhaust stack.

Then we moved out here and there was no doubt that I needed more of a tractor, if for nothing else just for the jobs associated with construction of the house. I needed hydraulics (a much-later development than for what my 1937 Allis was built). I needed a blade to clear the roads of snow, and a bucket to haul sand, rock, lumber, fencing supplies, block, bricks, even just to move our household goods from the storage building into the house. At that point, for $3,500 I bought an International 300 utility tractor, not a big tractor, but also not a garden toy. It came with a huge front bucket and blade on the back. Later I picked up a posthole digger. That fine but tired old girl served me well for another fifteen years and has since moved on to be another man's darling, and I am sure they are happy together.

Just as I was astonished when I went from no tractor to Sweet Allis and realized how helpless I had been without that essential tool of a tractor, I was excited and pleased when I got my International 300 and realized how much more I could get done with the hydraulics and power of this larger machine. And then, just a year ago as of this writing, I faced conditions that made it clear I needed a different, probably newer tractor for new tasks and new demands in my life. And I got an AGCO ST-55, brand spanking new, the only new vehicle I have had since I got a new Ford Falcon station wagon in 1963. It's as if I have once again jumped from the Middle Ages and an oxcart into the space age.

Yes, this tractor costs as much as I paid for the entire farm thirty years ago, but my conclusion still has to be, 1) you cannot get by in a rural setting without a tractor and 2) while you don't want a tractor too big for your needs, do what you can to get one that comes as close to meeting your needs as possible. You definitely need a tractor with a working PTO (power take-off, a whirling shaft that is used to power lots of other equipment), and hydraulics (for lifting various parts attached to it or operating equipment associated with it). Insofar as possible get a tractor in good working condition with safety features like a roll bar and operable lights. Farm accidents are horrible, way too frequent, and even more of a threat to those of us who aren't used to working with farm equipment.

This attitude constitutes a real change for me. I never thought I'd write words like those in the paragraph above. The thing is, I love *old* tractors and I knew that old things acquire value rather than losing it. You buy a new car and it is worth thousands of dollars less the moment you drive it off the lot; you buy a Model A Ford or even a 1947 Nash 600 and each day it becomes worth more. Same with old tractors. What I didn't realize until fairly recently is that tractors and farm equipment don't work quite that same way. While a new tractor diminishes in value with each additional hour you put on it, it doesn't lose much value, certainly not as much as an automobile. And fairly quickly, after only modest depreciation, a tractor simply keeps its value steady. As it turned out, I sold my International 300 after twenty years of use for very little less than I bought it for. Which means, whatever you spend on your tractor is not money down the drain; you are likely to get a substantial proportion of it back when you sell or trade it for another tractor. And in the meanwhile you have gotten an incredible amount of work and pleasure out of it. That's not unreasonable: a good tractor is indeed like a good tool, built strongly for long hard service. Those of us who have and use tractors in a rural setting but not for farming put little wear or strain on our machines so they last incredible amounts of time, and are usually in pretty good condition when we are ready to pass them along. Moreover, unlike cars tractors are built for utility. They are pretty to some of us but more importantly they are strong, solid, and meant to operate under tough conditions, so they don't wear out. That sixty-nine-year-old Allis Chalmers tractor of mine still runs after all. In fact, it runs better than its sixty-nine-year-old owner most of the time.

I'm not going to try to advise you what kind of tractor to buy—what color or even gas or diesel, or what size. That depends on your wants and needs, but I will recommend that you buy one with a dealer close by for parts, service, repairs, advice, and sympathy. If it's hard getting a crippled automobile to a service garage, it's even tougher with a tractor. And please, *please* do make sure it's a tractor. A *farm* tractor. A dear friend of mine is at this very moment in the process of buying some rural ground. He is wondering, wisely, about getting a tractor. Less wisely he is letting a boneheaded kid talk him into get-ting—sweet mother of pearl—a *backhoe*!

Now, a backhoe is a mighty useful machine, not just for digging ditches but also for moving trees, filling holes, land-scaping, and even building roads. If you need a backhoe, you probably do indeed need a *backhoe*, and the thing to do in a situation like that is go to the nearest place where they rent construction equipment and rent one for a half day or so to get done the specialized jobs only a backhoe can do. A back-hoe, however, will not:

Pull a plow

Dig postholes

Pull a seeder

Mow firebreaks

Plow snow

Run a buzz saw

Cultivate

Grind feed

Drag logs

Grade roads

Pull a manure spreader

Run a pump

Pull a wagon

On and on and on and on and on. . . .

The backhoe is designed for one specific job when the occasion arises; a tractor is meant to do any job day after day after day. The first major tool you need in the rural countryside after your pickup truck is a tractor. Not a back-hoe. Not a lawn mower. Not a trencher. Not an armored personnel carrier. A *tractor*.

IMPLEMENTS

Now you need to consider implements for that tractor. For sure you want a bucket on the front and a blade on the back. I consider those bare essentials. You should be able to pick up a serviceable trailer somewhere. There's someone in every community welding up pretty nice trailers from the beds of wrecked or salvaged pickup trucks and that will serve you fine. I find that in almost all cases I haul whatever I need in the bucket of my AGCO ST-55. I have made a couple improvements that account for that to some degree. I bolted two plates with chain hooks welded on them to the top of the bucket right above where the hydraulic arms attach so I can throw a chain around any load and quickly and securely fasten it to the bucket. And I invested a big $125 into two ingenious bars—welded up by a helpful welding shop—that slide onto the bottom of the bucket, held firmly in place with chains passed around the bucket and tightened with turnbuckles at any point on the bucket. The two points extend 6 feet out in front of the bucket and can be used to haul fence posts, brush, or anything else that can be set on a pallet. The two bucket forks (as they are formally called) used in that case are like the forks of a front end loader.

The next most important implement for us has been our shredder, or mower. Ours attaches to the hydraulic lift system on the back of the tractor with a three-point hitch—two lower arms that are static and a top hitch attached to the top of the mower with a "top-link" screw device. This top link

operates hydraulically with levers operated from the tractor's operator seat to raise or lower the mower, which
consists of a monstrous horizontal blade spinning on an axle
turned by another link connecting it to the tractor's PTO.
This mower is truly more of a shredder, turning too slow and
never being sharp enough to actually *cut* grass or scrub
brush but mostly flailing it and tearing it down. We use ours
to cut wide firebreaks in the tall grass surrounding our home
late in the summer or early in the fall to reduce the threat of
fire. Since we use it for little else, it doesn't have to perform
cosmetically on the ten or twelve acres I want to cut, just
knock it down.

A posthole digger attached to the back of a tractor so it
can be raised and lowered, turned by a shaft connected to the
PTO, is a labor and life saver if you are going to be sinking a
lot of posts, especially in hard ground. Linda and I have
driven steel posts with the tractor bucket, putting the post
vertically under the bucket, one person holding it in place at
arm's length while the operator very slowly and carefully
lowers the bucket, pushing the post into the ground. It's not
a good idea to have someone out there in front of that heavy
bucket, especially putting an arm under it, but with caution
and without hurrying it can be done safely. Of course, a tractor bucket is precisely the thing for removing fence posts: a
chain is thrown around the post and over the bucket into one
of those hooks I mentioned above. Then you simply raise the
bucket and the post comes out of the ground, ready to be
tossed into the bucket or across the bucket forks.

I have always had a plow for my tractors but not actually
had much use for it since I don't grow crops. I have a pull-
behind plow (as opposed to one that mounts to the hydraulic

lift system, two- or three-point, on the back of the tractor). I cut one blade off, leaving a single blade. It is on wheels and rigged so that a cord running from a lift catch comes to the tractor. I can tow the plow to where I want to begin a furrow and, while moving, pull the catch and drop the blade, plow a single furrow as long as I want, and then pull the cord again to lift the blade. This is a very useful tool for planting trees in a row since it gets down below the grass and brush and clears weeds and cover. The trees are then planted by hand and shoveled down in the furrow, giving them a much better chance to survive their first summer.

While I don't have any crops other than my trees, I do plant an acre or two wildlife patch down in the river bottoms. There was a time when our State Game and Parks office distributed free packets of seed for such plantings but when they ended that program, I continued, simply hand sowing some packaged birdseed—millet and sunflower mostly—for my turkeys, doves, pheasants, and other wild birds. When I had a plow for my International 300 I dutifully turned the ground in the spring but the plow was a two-point arrangement (without the top link) and so when I sold the tractor I gave the plow (and the posthole borer) to a friend who also had a two-point International. Such things tend to work out, however, in rural life because I no sooner went through those transactions than a couple friends noted that I was now without a plow and contacted me about harrows they had and would be glad to give me. So I didn't even go a full day without equipment to get my wildlife planting accomplished.

Fewer and fewer farmers plow these days. Plowing causes wind erosion of topsoil and compaction of the soil layer under the broken surface, so more and more real farmers do low-till or no-till planting, putting seeds right down in the stubble from the previous year, saving a couple trips over the ground, and thus not only time but increasingly expensive fuel and soil damage. So that's what I do now, too. I have both an 8-foot-wide disk plow and a small 4-foot tooth harrow. I use the bigger, heavier harrow for breaking up the ground and burying the stubble and then the smaller, lighter harrow for covering the strewn seed. That seems to work well.

Getting the smaller tooth harrow was easy enough; my friend brought it on a trailer and we simply lifted it off and put it on the ground. The disk harrow was another story. I should have known better because after my friend Lyle told me I could have it and described where I would find it, Woodrow offered to go with his service truck to pick it up. So I crawled into the cluttered cab and we lit out for Lyle's ground to retrieve the implement while the offer was still good. When we arrived and I realized the size and weight of my prize, it occurred to me—how are we going to load this large, heavy piece of equipment up onto this truck? Woodrow said, "We're not going to load it." Well, what *were* we going to do?

Silly me. We simply hitched it to the bumper hitch of the truck and pulled it five miles across the country on county roads and then down the highway to my place. A disk harrow: That means a dozen steel disks were in contact with whatever we were driving on. The noise was deafening on gravel, as we threw rocks and pebbles thirty feet to either side of the road, leaving deep furrows behind us. "I sure hope the sheriff doesn't see us tearing up this road," I said, utterly chagrined, since everyone within ten miles could see and hear us.

"He'll never spot us through all this dust," Woodrow reassured me.

Then we got to the paved highway through town. My concerns about the noise and damage we caused on the gravel with that harrow now faded into utter insignificance as the whirling discs threw fiery sparks off the pavement and the incredible noise reached a level where dogs no longer barked at us as we passed but ran for their lives from what they had every reason to believe was the first sign of the Apocalypse. When we finally reached my gate, the disks were too hot to touch but as Woodrow helpfully pointed out "They sure are nice and sharp now!" And so they were.

Given some time and asking around you are almost certain to acquire what tools you need, large or small, for whatever you intend or need to do on your new ground. But a word of advice from a veteran: give some thought about how exactly you are going to get it all back to your place. As with your tractor, whatever cost you have in obtaining implements is not so much an expenditure as an investment. You are almost certain to get back whatever you spend on them when you dispose of them . . . especially when you got them free in the first place!

I have some other items sitting around that I have acquired at auctions at rock-bottom prices, as gifts from friends, or salvaged from junkyards. They are mostly sitting there accumulating rust. I have a buzz saw that mounts on my old Allis WC tractor and is turned by a huge, flailing belt run around a revolving drum extending from the tractor's transmission. It is loud and absolutely hideously dangerous, however. While I used it often in my derring-do youth, these days I take my mortality more seriously, so the buzz saw sits behind the shed. I imagine that someday I'll give it to a friend and try to make room on my calendar to drop by and comfort the widow.

EVERYTHING ELSE

You already know how much I hate four-wheel ATVs but do note, my contempt is only for their use—or rather, mis-use—for recreation. On rural ground an ATV can be the handiest tool on the place. I would not only like to see horrendous tax fees put on ATVs used for ecological destruction, I would like to see some of the money accumulated from this fee applied to the cost of the same machines for farmers and ranchers who use them in their work. A real-work ATV is not a silly little gas-eater and smoke-spewer but a real workhorse. On an acreage or orchard they can serve many of the same functions as a small tractor and are worth your consideration as a primary work vehicle.

You can't imagine how it pains me to start this paragraph. See, when I was a kid, my father earned the money to send me eventually to college and to keep me in meat and potatoes by augmenting his factory work with lawn-care services for rich folks in our town. And of course he expected me, reasonably enough, to work with him. And thus, I came to loathe anything smacking of lawn care. I'm sure that's one of the reasons, in fact, that I came out to the rural countryside—it's wild out here. The grasses are natural. There are wild flowers, wild bushes, wild trees, and wild everything. I figured that when I moved in our house, we'd continue in that mode: just wild stuff.

I had forgotten that people like Linda who did not grow up trimming bluegrass lawn edges and picking leaves out of flower beds not only don't hate lawn care; they consider it necessary. I did what I could to make it as clear as possible as early as possible to Linda that when it came to lawn care (and as she would learn soon enough, a lot of other things) I was adamantly insistent on being out of the loop. I will not mow a lawn. I will not care for a lawn. I will not rake a lawn. I will not water a lawn. I like grasses and flowers that know how to take care of themselves.

Nonetheless because I am married to Linda and because I love her we have a lawn mower. I have justified this obscene expenditure to myself by doing what I can to make the machine useful in as many other ways as possible, and I will admit, it is that. I got a good mower with lights because I wanted her to do her mowing at night so the neighbors wouldn't see that she does all the work around here, for one thing. But not long after we got it (it's a Sears Craftsman model) I broke a foot and wound up taking the mower deck off and using it to get around for most of a winter. As with our tractor, the most useful implement we have for the mower—actually the only implement we have for it—is a small trailer we can use for hauling firewood, brush, dirt, gravel, fertilizer, that kind of thing. We use it for most work inside the yard fence and on what passes for our lawn because the bigger, heavier AGCO ST-55 with its new tires cuts pretty deeply into the sod while the wide, soft tires of the mower tractor and trailer (no matter how heavily loaded) make not a mark. We have come to think of our lawn mower as our small tractor—close to an ATV—that supplements the more heavy-duty industrial-grade workload of our tractor.

A word of advice and caution: as with all tools and information in print that you obtain for your projects, put together a library. Keep all operating manuals and instruction sheets for all your equipment, supplies, and projects. That's one of the reasons you moved to the country and have acquired the tools, machines, and implements—to do things for yourself, to be self-reliant, to be directly involved with the mechanics of your own existence. To do that, you need information. Talk with the people around you in your new community about how to do such things as keep a septic system healthy, or adjust a well's reservoir pressure, or fix a windmill, adjust a tractor carburetor, correct a bad case of the pips in your chickens, and sight in a rifle. The real pleasure of life is not so much knowing as learning, and if you don't enjoy learning, you have no business moving into a dramatically new and demanding context like rural living. Be prepared to forget what you knew—or thought you knew—and to learn new ways of doing things, with new tools and problems. Yes, the right tools are crucial to doing the job but even more important is knowing how to use them.

Chapter 5

TAKING CARE OF BUSINESS:

How Things Are Done
in Rural America,
and How You Can Do Things
in Rural America

HOW IT WORKS

W hen we started this discussion I said your adventures in rural life were going to be anthropological, a trip into another culture; this is where we move from tricks of nature to the nature of your fellow man. And take it from me, this is where things get tricky because you are about to find out that what you have come to think of as "the way things are done" is actually just another arbitrary complex of customs, irrational and unpredictable. Say you want a dog. That's something that surely might come up when you move to the country, right? Our good ol' boy Thud died a few months ago and as I have stated elsewhere and quite firmly in this marriage, no man should ever put himself in the situation where he has only one big black dog; that is, finding himself without a back-up black dog. Because if something happens to that dog, where are you? That's right, without a big black dog, that's where! No man should ever find himself in the country without a big black dog.

If you were in the city and wanted a big black dog, what would you do? Look in the papers, I imagine. Check at the Humane Society, go through the normal channels of dog acquisition. That is, normal channels of dog acquisition in the city. That's not what you do in the country. You may not even have to do anything at all in the country to find that requisite big black dog. Within hours everyone in a 20-mile radius is going to know you lost your good ol' buddy Thud just as surely as they'll know when your wife loses you. Moreover, all your friends know your feelings about big black dogs, in part because that's the way they feel too. And they're not about to let you go for long in need. I am not kidding you, it was not two days after Thud left us and went to Dog Heaven that we started getting calls on our answering machine. "Hey, Rog, this is Dan. I hear you're looking for a pup . . ." "This is Ray Farquhar over in St Paul. I heard up at the tavern last night that you're looking for a dog. We got a litter of lab-poodle mix here and . . ." "Welsch, I got a puppy with me up here at the co-op for you. Should I bring him down or do you want to come up here and look at him?"

You're probably saying "Well, sure, everyone loves dogs and so everyone thinks you should have a dog and every dog deserves a good home, so. . . ." But no, it's not just dogs. When we were looking for a used house to move in here, we didn't go to a used house lot or advertise for an abandoned house or go driving around the countryside. No, we just mentioned it to our friend who owned the tavern up in town and the next time we came out, a couple weeks later, he had seven houses lined up for us to look at.

Despite the fact that I've worked within this marketing system for thirty years now, its speed and efficiency still amaze me. I get a new tractor and now have a forty-year-old battered tractor I've been using for twenty years, to unload. How do you sell a tractor? Having never sold a working tractor before (I did once sell an antique tractor I'd restored in my shop but that's a different matter), I had no idea what to do next. Drag it to the next nearby farm auction? Find someone to haul it to an implement dealer? That's where I had bought it originally. Maybe that's the thing to do. I sure hated the notion of putting an ad in the papers in the nearby city and having to deal with shoppers coming by to kick tires.

What I did was mention that I needed to sell my International 300 up at the tavern to a friend one day. Within the week he called to tell me he knew of two people looking for a machine like the one I wanted to sell and would it be okay for him to bring them down to look it over? The next thing I knew they were loading up my old International 300 and handing me a check for the asking price.

I can't even recall all the deals I've gone through exactly like this. "I heard someone say you're looking for a disk harrow. I got an old one down by my pasture I'd like to get rid of. If you can haul it off, you can have it." "Dennis said you need some big round bales of soybean stubble. I got a bunch of 'em not a mile from your place. I'll deliver them for $13 apiece." "Were you looking for a calico mouser? Loosey up at the lumberyard just brought her latest litter down from the rafters and Bobby is about to hand them out. If you hurry up there, you can get the calico." And that would be our beloved Hairball, now eighteen years managing matters feline around here.

RURAL DOES *NOT* EQUAL RUBE

You can get square deals out in the country. You can even get great deals out in the country. But you do not for a single moment want to think you're dealing with hicks who can be skinned because once you start thinking like that, nothing in your life is going to go right. There is an old folktale called the Arkansas Traveler that is instructive. It was often told at rural fairs, gatherings, festivals, medicine shows, pageants, that kind of thing. And it is important to note that it was a rural favorite because it spoke to rural life.

The scene was usually set that an old-timer was sitting on the front porch of his shanty playing his fiddle, and he was playing the catchy jig called the "Arkansas Traveler," which is coincidentally about a traveler in Arkansas! Down the road comes the Traveler, a city slicker identified by his inappropriate clothing and carpetbag, clearly a *tourist*. The Traveler stops at the front gate of the cabin where the old man is playing and shouts, "Howdy!"

"Howdy yourself!" responds the resident.

TRAVELER: Say, Farmer, the corn looks mighty yeller in these parts.

FARMER: We planted the yeller kind.

TRAVELER: Well then, how'd your potaters turn out this year?

FARMER: Didn't turn out. We had to dig 'em.

TRAVELER: Farmer, can I take this road to Little Rock?

FARMER: No need to. They already have one.

TRAVELER: No, I mean does this road go to Little Rock?

FARMER: Well, I've lived here sixty years now and it hasn't gone anywhere.

TRAVELER: Lived here all your life, have you, Farmer?

FARMER: Not yet!

TRAVELER: Farmer, there's not much difference between you and a fool, is there?

FARMER: Only the front yard and the fence.

TRAVELER [Now exasperated] : No, I mean you're not very smart, are ya?!

FARMER: I ain't lost!

At first blush you might think this is a stereotype of the ignorant backwoodsman; that is, the farmer. But take another look at the exchange. Who exactly *is* the dupe in this dialogue? Who thinks he's smart and who actually *is* smart? That is precisely the reason I moved out here from the city. I often tell people I came to the remote Sandhills of the Plains to get an education, and that is the exact truth. Don't fool yourself for a moment. The highly touted assets of city street-smarts are nothing but shallow and hollow fiddle-faddle in rural America, as useless as crinoline skirts or an ascot necktie. The lessons may be subtle in the rural countryside's School of Hard Knocks, but the lessons are nonetheless there.

I am reminded of the time when I noticed a twenty-acre parcel of ground for sale not far from mine. I thought it might make a nice addition to my own river bottom ground so I stopped by the banker's office and asked him if he had any idea how much the owner might be asking for it. "If you can guess within $20,000 I'll buy you a case of beer," he said.

Hmmm. This seemed like a sure bet to me. Twenty acres would cost at a minimum $500 an acre around here at that time. That would be a rock-bottom price of $10,000. Add

$20,000 and you get $30,000, which raises the top limit of my already cooling case of beer to $50,000, or $2,500 an acre, an utterly absurd price. Confidently therefore I guessed, "$30,000," already tasting that cold beer. "You lose," the banker said laconically. "He wants $75,000."

Staggered by the obscenity, the idiocy of this price I went into the Chew 'n' Chat Café where the usual cast of cronies was sitting around playing cards. I sat down next to my old buddy Bumps, still dazzled by what I had just learned from the banker. After some conversational preliminaries I said to Bumps, "You know that piece of river bottom down by my place they have the "For Sale" sign on? Do you know what they are asking for that?"

Of course he did: "$75,000."

"All I can figure," I said, "is that they think some half-wit with more money than brains is going to come along without the faintest idea what land is worth around here, never check about the flooding down there, and pay the asking price without so much as putting in a bid."

Without looking up from his cards, Bumps said, "Worked on the other side of the road."

I had just been Arkansas Travelered.

FIELD-SMARTS VERSUS STREET-SMARTS

One of the themes I tried to emphasize repeatedly during my thirteen years with Charles Kuralt when I was doing my "Postcard from Nebraska" essays on *CBS News Sunday Morning* was the unavoidable truth that the American farmer is with few exceptions a good deal shrewder than his city cousin, and always has been. Moreover, he is likely to be more highly educated, more technologically sophisticated, and more challenged in his daily work by a wider variety of intellectual demands than the city boy working in an insurance office or radiator hose factory.

One of my favorite CBS News essays was about a young farmer working land homesteaded by his great-grandfather, living in a house built by his grandfather. When I drove into his yard with my television crew, his wife was baking cookies and making lemonade for us, his father was in the yard welding on some equipment, and he was out along the fields on his tractor mowing weeds. My point was that looking at this traditional young man, the hardy yeoman, the man of the soil, you might expect that you were dealing with a rube, a hick, a yokel.

The truth of course is that any farmer can't survive without being very sophisticated about economics, meteorology, botany, zoology, geology, chemistry, physics, and sociology and skilled in manual arts ranging from welding to automotive mechanics, from posthole digging to building construction. In this case our story was even more dramatic because the young farmer donned a helmet and g-suit on weekends and flew F-16 fighter planes with the National Guard, having returned from combat in the first Gulf War. And his wife, she had been a mechanic in the same war theater. You want to be real careful about assumptions when you deal with American farmers!

WHAT THE YELLOW PAGES DON'T TELL YOU

In Chapter 2 we discussed what exactly constitutes a town. Obviously, it is a commercial hub, but no one seems to have any rules about what is necessary for a place to rise to the distinction of being called a "town." What's a village then? Or a crossroads? As you cross America, population densities change. For that matter as you cross Nebraska population densities change. Half of my state's population lives within fifty miles of its eastern border, the Missouri River. And then you see fewer and fewer people as you go westward the rest of the 400 miles to the Wyoming or Colorado borders. That means that "towns" in eastern Nebraska may only be suburbs of Lincoln or Omaha, or will be suburbs within a couple years. Towns a hundred miles east of where I am now sitting, smack in the middle of Nebraska and America, may have ten or twenty thousand people.

Wow. When you get out here in the official Middle of Nowhere a community of ten thousand peoples is pretty much a city. I think of my little town of Dannebrog, population 352, as a town—okay, a village—but there are other towns and villages within an hour's drive of here that have fewer than fifty people.

Same with businesses. My buddy, Plumber Dan, lives in the village of Nysted. There are precisely no businesses there. Not one. Just a cluster of residences at a crossroads where there was once a grocery store and church camp. There is still a church but even it is struggling to stay alive. The population of Dan's "town" is less than two dozen, of which at least a dozen are his kids. In Dannebrog, I calculate roughly that we have seventeen businesses. Our main street of businesses is less than a full block long, on one side of the street. On that street and scattered in what could generously be referred to as our "business district" is:

Auto mechanic shop

Co-op filling station and mechanic shop (with an
   adjunct fertilizer plant)

Grocery store

Two cafés

Tavern

Bank

Beauty shop

Post office

Lumberyard

Electrician's shop

Gift shop

Two bed-and-breakfasts

Two churches

Fitness center (The Healthy Woman, which I once got
    into real trouble for calling The Hefty Woman, by
    the way)

When our bank went belly-up twenty years ago, everyone lamented that that would pretty much kill the town, but then the same complaint was heard when the schools were consolidated and the town lost its school. The town pulled together and started a credit union and then a bank from another town came in and picked up the business and now we seem to be on track again. There is some dynamic in what succeeds and what fails. The town's Danish heritage and small fame from television exposure brings in enough tourism to support the gift shop, but again it seems unlikely to me that the average town of 352 people needs a gift shop. I wonder how our grocery man keeps things going; folks tend to drive the 25 miles to the city's supermarket for their food purchases, not only because the wares are cheaper but also because they are fresher and in wider variety. Same with the lumberyard. These seem to be businesses of convenience: if you need a sheet of quarter-inch plywood, it isn't worth driving to Grand Island, so you pay the extra couple dollars and just get it at the town lumberyard. If we lost either however the town would take a serious economic hit so some people like me patronize these businesses with an eye toward keeping them open.

Too few rural Americans recognize that strategic view of local commerce. They prefer to save a few cents to buy from larger stores in larger cities removed from their own small towns, not considering the damage that would come to their communities if the local enterprises fail. Do we really want to have to drive 25 miles *every* time we need a sheet of plywood or head of lettuce? Wouldn't it be a good idea to pay a little bit more with each purchase to keep the businesses in your own town in operation even if you could get the same item for a dollar less twenty miles away at a K-Mart? Not to mention other external pressures against all businesses these days: prohibitive costs of maintaining, or worse, replacing subsurface fuel tanks, the problems of finding suppliers to haul in small lots of hardware or lumber now that we have stupidly let our rail system fall into disrepair or total ruin. As new technologies like the World Wide Web and e-mail develop and the national tax hysteria burgeons, small-town post offices are being closed and it's hard to mail Christmas presents or get mail-order tractor parts through your computer modem.

MORE THAN THEY SEEM

I'm sure the religious zealots in town would disagree with me, but as usual they are wrong: the town tavern is not simply an important part of the economic and social structure of our town (about which more later), it is a crucial element. A small-town tavern is not a cocktail lounge or a Wild West saloon. It is not a place to get drunk and start a fight. In fact, you may find that even the language limits in a small-town tavern are a good deal more restrictive than in your own front room, especially during election times. A town tavern is a social center, a *family* social center. Families go to town taverns to eat, converse, do business, relax, learn the news of the town, and compare notes. There are people who refuse to cross the threshold into a tavern, and that's fine for them. I hear there are also people who refuse to use their opposing thumbs. I can't imagine that either one of them gets much done.

Actually, most businesses in a small town are this kind of "portmanteau" operation; that is, while going under one descriptive name, they actually encompass far more activity than that name suggests on the surface. Schroeder's Café on our Main Street is actually more of an Old Gents Club House than simply a place to get a good breakfast or great pizza. The windows of our grocery store are the bulletin board on the busiest corner of the community so that's where you find sale bills for auctions taped up, and announcements of school activities, litters of puppies for sale, and babysitting or lawn-mowing services. When a freight line semi comes into town and has trouble locating the farm where a package or pallet is to be delivered, everyone pretty much accepts that Kerry is a good guy and he'll sign for it at the grocery store and hold it until you can come to town and retrieve it for yourself, whether it is a one-ton load of books or a quarter-ton load of uncured hams, which he will even hold in his cooler until your smokehouse is ready for them. (As you can tell, the situations I use as illustrations are not hypothetical!) All of the businesses in a small town form one fabric, overlapping, augmenting, filling in, substituting. When the smoke clears, there really isn't much that needs doing or is left missing. I guess that's why they call it a "community."

I sure wouldn't abuse the privilege but on a few occasions when I have had a genuine emergency and needed fuel, food, cooking equipment, or just about anything else I didn't have, but knew would have been available in a commercial outlet in Dannebrog if it were open, I have called the proprietor and asked if he or she would be willing to open up the store or shop and let me get what I need. I have never been turned down, or even gotten a hint of discontent. In fact, in cases where the businessman or woman could not open up for me, I was given the key to the business so I could let myself in and take what I needed, being trusted to pay what I owed another time, when the place was open for business.

I don't know how often I have done business with someone here in town and left after a conversation with some friends I've encountered, forgetting in the fuss to pay my bill—for food, groceries, gas, lumber—It doesn't matter. They know who I am and where I live. They just mention it to me the next time I am in their business, unless I remember the lapse myself when I get home and make a frantic and chagrined phone call to head off a call from the sheriff's office. Similarly, I know that I can always, in every business in town other than the bank, which is to be expected, get whatever I need off the shelf and announce as I go out the door. "I don't have my billfold with me and I need to get this job finished. I'll get back to you tomorrow on this," and get a wave signifying that there's no problem. Tomorrow will be plenty soon enough. Trust like that generates a powerful amount of good-will and gratitude in my heart.

In any small town—probably in any town of any size—there are businesses that don't have signs out front or special buildings where business is conducted. Everyone around here knows who the best person is to contact when you need a fence built, or who sews up clothes or repairs a torn sports coat sleeve, or who sharpens chain saw chains. There is no specific business in my town that caters meals or prepares specialty foods like wedding cakes but there are several women who do precisely that kind of thing out of their own kitchens, meaning that their products are also particularly good and notably inexpensive. Around town such things are clearly understood: Jeri makes wedding cakes, Lola caters parties, Harriett does Danish specialties, Dee makes the best pirogies outside of the Ukraine.

EATING IT UP

Small town food is often underestimated; some of the best restaurants I've ever been in were in tiny towns, perhaps the only place to eat anywhere in the neighborhood. So much for competition! But there are also hidden gastronomical agendas in the rural countryside. At another point I will comment on special occasion meals, feeds, and foods, but while we are talking about underground business activities, I have to tell you that when we want really special pastries, cookies, or breads, we go to Phyllis's place on the other side of the creek. Krispy Kreme has absolutely nothing on her doughnuts fresh from the deep fat on her stove. While Phyllis's baked goods can also be purchased at the town grocery store—if you get there quick enough after she makes her delivery and everything she's left with Kerry is already sold—you can also submit requests to her. Linda likes big, soft, oatmeal cookies. There's no way in hell I'm ever going to figure out how to make cookies, and no way I'm ever going to get close to making anything in the world as good as Phyllis's cookies, so I just give her a call a few weeks ahead of Linda's birthday or Christmas or Valentine's Day, put in an order for a couple dozen of her famous, soft, oatmeal cookies, tell her they're a surprise for Linda so she doesn't spill the beans if they should run into each other in town, and then go to Phyllis's to pick them up . . . hopefully just as she takes something else out of the oven so I can put on a pitiful, starving sort of look and get a freebie.

I've done the same with Dee and her famous pirogies. I ask her to make up a big batch for some special occasion, argue her into taking money for the meal, and in her case she delivers the meal here to the house and I can treat Linda to a night out without the going out part.

There are only three places to get meals in our village: a small café that is open only for breakfast and noon meals, a bakery which really isn't a bakery at all except on Thursday nights which is pizza night, and the tavern, where you can get noon and evening meals of usual tavern fare—burgers, fries, that kind of thing. But it's not all that simple either. On Wednesdays (fried chicken days) and Sundays (when everyone in driving range brings their families to Harriett's café) you can't just walk into the small café and order up a meal; Harriett's cooking is so famed for so many miles in all directions that you may have to take a number and stand around outside until someone finishes a meal and leaves room at one of the tables. It's even worse at Schroeder's Bakery on pizza night; you may be the thirtieth or fortieth in line for a pizza unless you've called in your order ahead of time. If a busload of diners has come in from Lincoln or Omaha, you may just be out of luck this week. (On the other hand, if the geezerly accordion player has set up shop in Schroeder's and is blasting polkas three feet from your table in the tiny facility, you may be glad you have to seek refuge down the street at the tavern, with or without your pizza.) We only have Schroeder's pizza on Thursdays and Harriett's fried chicken on Wednesdays, but since it's better than any other pizza or chicken made anywhere in the known world, we consider ourselves lucky to have even that.

On the other hand, the tavern menu is pretty much available any time, noons or evenings except Sundays. Sometimes they have specials on steaks or chicken baskets, but who wants a steak or chicken when you can have the best burgers you had in a long, long time, with the buns crisped up on the greasy grill, and a draft root beer that is simply out of this world? I am not being a booster for my own little town. I don't lie about things like food. Dannebrog is a small town but here we eat big.

Within a few minutes down the highway there are several produce stands, little more than open sheds with some tables, counters, and bins. They are closed most of the year but sometime in June we start watching for the first signs that they are getting ready to open up. That means the sweet corn will be coming along pretty soon. The people who operate the stands have truck farms where they grow radishes and peas that come along early in the season, and then the sweet corn, green beans, maybe some early potatoes. As the summer progresses there is watermelon, squash, pumpkins, peppers, and tomatoes. Honey, jams and jellies, even breads and cookies are sold there on consignment, and I'm willing to bet that no fancy food guy in New York City has a fresher choice of produce than we do. And somehow it all tastes better when you know that the money you spend isn't going for packaging, marketing, processing, or middle men but straight to the folks who did the work and harvested the food moments earlier from fields within sight of where you bought it.

I note that there are now two new vineyards just planted a few miles from here and so now I can start anticipating sitting among the vines sometime soon, enjoying a glass of wine from the soil that I love so much myself. Life is good when this kind of thing is happening.

GETTING RICH LOSING MONEY

Speaking of which, I probably should save the stories about my old and much lamented friend, Dick, for some other place in these pages but as I contemplate what I want to say about him, it's hard to know where to stick him. Now's as good as any time, I suppose. I truly loved Dick. He was a crusty, tough little guy who ran a steakhouse in a town not far down the road from my place. His story is instructive for all Americans. He was a laborer on the project paving the highway between here and his town and he noticed that there was no place for the workers on that big job to get a decent noon or evening meal or a couple cold brews when the day was over. So Dick borrowed enough money to get a small, basic business opened and he and his wife worked like dogs to cook up meals and tap kegs even while he continued to work on the construction job the rest of the day. And when the dust finally settled, Dick had become a millionaire.

Dick made no secret of his methods: He lost money on every meal he served. When I first came out here thirty years ago his huge T-bone steaks ran $2.50, $3.50, and $4.50 each, including a fresh salad with a superb blue cheese dressing of his own invention and hash brown spuds with melted cheese on top. The food and the menu were plain, simple, inexpensive, and excellent. And he did indeed lose money with every meal.

On the other hand he had his beer cooled down to just above freezing. His draws and pitchers were generous but not overpriced. When he poured from a bottle, it was a generous dollop. His idea of an after-dinner serving of Benedictine and Brandy was a tumbler full, easily four ounces. It was rare to be in his establishment for more than an hour without Dick treating everyone in the tavern to a free round. And it was rare that the place wasn't jammed, with us regulars but also with people driving fifty or a hundred miles to see if the stories about the big, delicious, tender, cheap steaks were true. And it was rare that his guests didn't have a drink or two. Or three. And buy a round now and then. And come to consider Dick's place one of their favorites, and to come back again, and bring guests. The restaurant added rooms, and then more rooms, and pretty soon you had to stand in line for a table on weekends, and thus, on money made almost entirely on drinks, the meals served at a loss, Dick became a millionaire.

Nor was the attraction simply Dick's food. Part of it was simply Dick. As I said, I loved the guy. He was my kind of person. Just a couple stories . . . When I was building my log house, I stumbled into Dick's one evening with my crew, dirty, tired, and ragged. That was okay at Dick's. When a farmer came in wearing overalls and asked if it was all right to come in and have a meal dressed like that, Dick's standard response was "If that's the way you earn your money, then that's the way you can spend it." At the end of a wonderful meal and enough cold beer to clear the dust out of our mouths and put some cobwebs into our heads, we started drifting up to the cash register to pay our tabs. One of the people in my contingent was a somewhat snooty guy who was a major editor for a very large newspaper. He eyed the sign behind the bar that said: "No out of town checks accepted," and said to Dick, "I have a check here from some writing I did for *Time* magazine"—he said it with the italics!—"and surely you'll accept a check from *Time* magazine." Dick didn't even look at the check. He just said no. "But ... but ... but ..." my friend sputtered, "it's from *Time magazine!*"

"Well lah-di-friggin'-dah," Dick said. "*Time* magazine lies to me once a week. Why should I believe their checks?"

While at the table I exploded with glee and pride and the editor fellow stood there flabbergasted. A young lady from our group stepped up, now a bit worried herself. She was a student, worked part time, was attractive and a lovely person, but certainly not in a class with the editor who had just had his check rejected. On this occasion, because we had been working at construction all day, she was in work clothes, with cement and sawdust in her hair. "I don't suppose you'll accept my personal check then either, huh?" she asked timidly, and just a little chagrined. That's all it took, of course. A bit of common humility was all Dick needed. He took her check, looked at it with a glance, and said, "Sure. Your check is fine." You just can't help but love a guy with an attitude like that.

If anyone ever deserved to be rich, it was Dick. The night he died, a little bit of me died too, and a lot of his community.

DON'T BE SURPRISED

Superior versatility, quality, and quantity at unlikely sources doesn't stop with food. Farmer Dennis is the best auto body man in the country. (The official motto posted on his shop door is "A city boy's price at a country boy's pace.") Plumber Dan prides himself on his excellent venison jerky. Not far from here one of the very best antique tractor restorers operates out of a small garage in the rural countryside. The best tractor mechanic's shop is an adjunct to his farmyard and farming operation. If you ask Mel what he does for a living, he'd probably say "I'm a farmer," but everyone who knows anything, especially those who use International tractors, think of Mel as a master mechanic.

Don't for a moment discount the commercial cultural offerings in the rural countryside. I am willing to bet that the density of the artistic population in my remote, rural village is many times that of New York City. I know of two talented and skilled artists within a mile of where I sit writing this, and maybe five more who are hobbyists or journeymen in the arts. There are musicians too, and for all I know, dancers. We have accumulated our limited art holdings from local artists, in one case a painting of a derelict shed on our land painted by a now very accomplished, even famous artist. He gave us the painting as a wedding gift because we are friends and because for many years when he lived in this area I trusted him with a key to the gate so he could paint at his leisure in our river bottoms.

There are many stories from pioneer America about the postmaster who carries his entire operation in the crown of his

beaver hat. There are businesses like that in small-town
America. And if the "businesses" in question are not entirely
contained in the entrepreneur's back pocket, it may be in the
trunk of his car or the back of his pickup truck. Big Don
Hochstetter died a couple years ago, leaving the town pretty
much in the lurch. Don had been the town's marshal and so
was our legal expert. He was a dowser and plumber, a
mechanic, machinist, welder, and farmer. He had been on the
village board, and in the fire department, and could be seen
just about any time on a backhoe set to digging a hole anywhere in town, so Don knew the location of every sewer, water,
and electrical line within the city limits. Don did everything.
The first time I met Don my car had died in town, where I was
a newcomer, and nothing would get it started. Big Don came
shambling along through the snow to see what all the fuss was
about and crawled into my old '69 Chevy van. He opened the
engine hatch and concurred with my assessment that the problem was fuel, probably the carburetor. "Yep," he said, "It's the
carbulator." That was Don—he never could say "carburetor"
[thus, carbulator], aluminum [alumium], or accretion [secre-
tion] right but he never apologized, just forging right ahead,
presuming (accurately) that we all knew what he meant.

"Do you have a hammer handy?" he asked.

A hammer? Now, I don't know how much you know
about carbulators . . . er, carburetors, but one doesn't nor-
mally consider a hammer a carb tool. But I did have a
hammer in the van and with some uneasiness handed it to
this huge new friend of mine. He gently rapped the center,
threaded post holding the air cleaner lid on. "Try it now," he
said. And the car started. What the hell was *that* all about?
He explained that over time when you tighten down the but-

terfly nut holding the air cleaner top on, you warp the alu-
mium casting of the carbulator and the butterfly valve no
longer moves freely in the casting. By tapping softly on the
shaft holding the lid on, you can reshape the casting just
enough to fix the problem. Which is what he did.

On another occasion I had driven my tractor into town
but when I was ready to back out of the parking place and
leave, I couldn't get it into gear. Thank goodness Don was
playing cards in the tavern, so I stepped in, bought him a red
beer, and asked him what the problem might be. This time he
had his own "toolbox" — a pair of pliers in the side pocket of
his overalls — with him, and within minutes he had opened
the gearbox of that tractor, spotted the problem, fixed it, and
gave me recommendations for repairs I could make to avoid
the problem in the future. Every town has at least one
resource like Big Don Hostettler, hopefully several. You'd be
nuts not to take advantage of them.

An old friend and high school classmate, Dick Cavett, once
invited me to go to New York to be on his show to talk about a
book I had authored, and he asked me why I prefer rural life to
the city. Well, of course there are a lot of reasons, but one certainly is the society of the matter. I noted during our on-air
conversation that when I was living in Lincoln, teaching at the
University, living in a neighborhood, my contacts were almost
totally with a very narrow range of people. All my colleagues
and neighbors shared my level of education, income, experience, politics, religion, history. But, as I told Dick, when I sat
down for a cup of coffee at the Chew 'n' Chat Café in
Dannebrog, I shared the table with the town drunk, a banker, a
farmer, a carpenter, the brightest guy in town, the village ne'er-
do-well. . . . Dick acknowledged that this might be the case.

But what he didn't know, what his audience in the studio didn't know, what a good proportion of his television audience didn't know but what everyone in Dannebrog understood— and probably was laughing about—was that I was talking about one and the same guy. He had at one time or another during his life in town filled all of those job descriptions: the town drunk, a banker, a farmer, a carpenter, the brightest guy in town, and the village ne'er-do-well.

The moral of the story is, when you live in a rural community, before you start thumbing through the nearby city's yellow pages for services or products, ask around for who does that kind of work or provides those kinds of products in your neighborhood. A good place to ask would be the town tavern.

MAKING A LIVING

I can't say that I would recommend trying to make a living in a small town. That's a tough go. For one thing, all of your customers know you and so the slightest social gaffe and suddenly you lose half your customers. Your kid drops a pass in the last minutes of the game that would have cinched the state championship, and who wants to do business with someone who has a kid that clumsy? I'd laugh, but it's not a joke. I am fortunate in that I have never had to make a living from the people who are my friends and neighbors in this village. I have loyal readers of my books and articles here but I could buy one meal from the profits I make from book sales to residents of my own town. Most are nonetheless kind to me. On the other hand, there are detractors who resent the traffic in town from tourists curious to see where the television shows for CBS were filmed, or where that guy who writes the books lives. Most of all, some resent the fact that I do not have to depend on the town for a living, which means that I am beholden to no one and can do pretty much what I want, without appropriate acknowledgment of the usual rules of small-town protocol. I can pal around with the "drunks, derelicts, and everybody nobody likes" (explanation to follow below when I tell another story about my buddy Dick) and pay no attention to opprobrium from the "proper" and influential elements of town. That doesn't make me popular with them. There are a lot of people who live in the town or near it but use it only as a bedroom community, commuting and working in the nearby city and having virtually no contact with the businesses or people in town. They're okay with the elitist elements (if you can imagine such a thing as a social "elite" in a tiny, rural, Nebraska community) because there's not the irritation of someone like me who has become intimately associated with the town but who doesn't fit what some think is the proper façade they want. Well . . . tough.

Frankly, I think the only way you can make a living with a business in a small town is if your business does not cater to trade from that town. These days that is not only easy to do, it's the easiest thing in the world to do. When I came out here to live twenty years ago I knew I was giving up some things in terms of my work. Even living in a major business area like Lincoln, a capital city, and working at a major university, it was clear that I was at a disadvantage when it came to dealing with publishers at major Eastern houses, magazine editors in Des Moines, or television producers in New York City. Modern technology has set many of those problems aside, however, and now the balance seems to be in favor of rural living. Sure, I can't pop into a CBS or Random House office for a visit, but communications are now so fast, easy, inexpensive, and convenient that I don't even bother with the telephone, and a fax machine seems as primitive as smoke signals.

About the telephone . . . Believe me, I understand what a wonderful convenience it was, and on occasion still can be. I call my mother almost every day, and we hear from our daughter at school in Lincoln just about that often. Hearing a voice can be comforting, and even useful in understanding the meaning of words. But as I grew older and deafer the value of the phone would diminish . . . if it hadn't lost its usefulness to me long ago. People frequently ask me how I get so much done: a book or two written a year, scripts, articles, tractor repair, family activities, charitable work, political activism, social obligations.

The answer is easy. First, I don't go to more than two meetings a year, and then only if they are absolutely essential and if food is being served. That way I can make sure something is accomplished, since in my experience nothing—nothing!—is ever accomplished in meetings. I had a gentle disagreement with an old and beloved comrade of mine a couple years ago about this issue. He is constantly in meetings, insists that they are a major way of getting things done in his life, and he was trying to convince me that I should come to Lincoln for a very, very, *very* important meeting, dealing with something of great interest to me. It sounded bogus. I listened patiently and even objectively to his pitch, but I wasn't convinced. So, I turned down the invitation, but asked him to let me know exactly what was accomplished in the full day's meeting to show me how wrong I'd been.

He called the day after the meeting, gloating about how wrong I'd been. The meeting had gone wonderfully, he reported. They had discussed important issues, exchanged ideas, looked over the situation, and evaluated possible solutions. "But what was the final product of the meeting?" I interrupted.

"We made detailed plans for another meeting!" he exulted triumphantly. And of course I was invited. I said that I sure hoped they would serve a meal.

The second way I've gotten a lot done over the past three decades is that I don't use the telephone for anything but entertainment. And while the telephone is wonderful for that, it really doesn't do much of anything productive, otherwise. I can answer maybe five or six postal letters in an hour. I can easily answer fifteen e-mail messages an hour (after sorting out the spam, the main reason I argue we should keep the death penalty). I can't get three phone messages dealt with in an hour. First, no one manages to convey a piece of information over the telephone in twenty words, the average length of an e-mail. No, it's a matter of: "Since I have you on the phone anyway, how's that AGCO tractor running? Getting any rain over your way? Have you heard that Tiffany Branchwater is pregnant by the Clarkson kid?" On and on and on. . . .

People telephone at their leisure and when the phone rings, you are expected to drop everything and talk, no matter where you are in your schedule or what you are doing. If you don't get that phone call right now, the message will be on your machine, if you have one, and then you call back . . . at your leisure. And the person who called originally is not at the other end. Or is busy. Or has another call. Or is in a meeting. Ten calls later you are still wasting money and time, all in an effort to establish a wire link so you waste more time and money. The telephone may have been a useful device at another age but now it is just a colossal pain in the ass.

Do note that an answering machine goes a long way toward eliminating the problems of the telephone. For one thing, if someone you don't want to or can't talk with calls, the machine intercepts and handles the call for you. Telephone solicitors simply hang up halfway through your message, hopefully in disgust for having wasted their own time rather than yours. And when all is said and done, now the burden of convenience is shifted by the answering machine: now you can call at your convenience and inconvenience the other person who was blithely willing to do the same to you. Every return call is an act of vengeance when you have an answering machine.

But I wanted to tell you about the *conveniences* of rural living when it comes to certain work. I'm a writer, and living with a touch of isolation in the countryside is absolutely perfect for this activity, which requires focus, uninterrupted periods of time, some sense of serenity and comfort, and—believe it or not—access to major information sources. When I started my writing career a lifetime ago—my first book was published in 1966—I had to make trips to libraries, newspaper archives, museums, and schools. While that sort of occasion still arises once or twice a year, if that, now the world is at my fingertips on this computer screen, through a common telephone wire now made magically useful again, with search engines, incredibly rapid communications, imaging, and consulting. Whereas three decades ago I had to hand-deliver a manuscript with irreplaceable illustrations to a publisher in New Jersey, flying there with the materials held on my lap in an airplane, now the very same kinds of products are sent with lightning speed over the World Wide Web, including the illustrations. Most publishers don't even want to fool with paper now, preferring an electronic package delivered instantly by e-mail and more conveniently edited on their own computer screens.

THE NICE AND THE ANNOYING

I can imagine that some businesses can't operate this way. I have asked my friends in town not to send visitors to my place because with the small notoriety I have acquired on television and in my writing people figure that when they are on vacation, they might just as well stop by and chat with me, having a cup of coffee or a beer, or maybe taking Linda and me out to supper, taking a look at my shop and tractors, spending a few hours learning how they can get their own books published. What they don't realize is that they aren't the only ones who came up with the idea. The Sunday that I was trying desperately to get something done in my office and twelve separate carloads of very nice, friendly but uninvited folks dropped by to chat "just a half hour, not more than an hour" was when we finally went ballistic and put all kinds of ugly signs at our gate warning people to get away fast before the daily blasting schedule started and the wild jackals were loosed from their pens to clean up carrion and stray children. Linda, who is an artist and also needs long hours of isolation and concentration, concurred. As she put it, "There's a reason there's a gate at Graceland." Elvis and Priscilla we're not, but nonetheless. . . .

As I explained to Tom, Al, Marna, Jim and Sue, Linda, Irma, Dawn, Harriett, Kerry, and Lola, while their businesses depend on people coming by, stopping in, and even doing that on a fairly regular basis, our business depends on people *not* doing that. And so my friends in town have been very helpful in heading off possible interruptions in our work. The moral is, you'll have to think about what you intend to do for a living. Can it be done with the distances and isolation of the rural countryside? The answer may be no. Or it maybe not only be yes, but yes indeedeedo!

Of course the web, computers, electronic writing and messaging, that kind of technology is not the only thing that has changed to make country living a good deal more easy than it might have been as shortly as a dozen years ago. When I was working with CBS News there was a constant need for rapidly exchanging printed materials. My producer in New York asked if we could get FedEx deliveries out here, and with a laugh I told him that we not only get them, we probably have better service than he does in his office at 524 West 57th! I simply make a call, walk fifteen steps to the box out by our gate, throw my package in, and within hours a guy I now consider a friend comes roaring into our drive, picks up the package, pets the dogs, tells me the latest jokes he's picked up on the route, and my package is on the way. Same with UPS, or any of the other delivery systems. Not only do we get doorstep service, pickup, and delivery, since these people are personal friends and acquaintances, our packages arrive in perfect condition, even when the address has us in the wrong city, the wrong state, or omits niceties, providing nothing more by way of a mailing address than something like "The fat guy in the overalls who writes the tractor books, lives someplace with a name something like 'Danebrog, Nebraska.'"

That kind of service is even more dramatic with our post office folks. You'd probably laugh at our post office. It's not as big as your garage. There are two employees: Phil the postmaster and Elaine the rural carrier. We have a box out by the highway and sometimes that's where the mail comes, but if it won't fit, the carrier comes into the yard and puts our stuff in the cab of my pickup so it won't get wet. If mail comes that looks even remotely like it might be for us, Phil takes the time and trouble to see if we're who it's meant for. That's not always the case in the post office, you know. I've had mail returned to me or not delivered to me for the merest error or omission in the address—that's big city stuff. You want their service then you damn well better be ready to do things their way. That's not a small-town post office. My zip code is 68831-4007. The 68831 is the code for Dannebrog, the surrounding area, and even little Nysted, the near-ghost town five miles to our west. The 4007 is the designation for our driveway. We have our own zip code. Our mailbox has its own zip code! Talk about feeling important.

Most of the time however, since I usually have outgoing packages, I don't wait for the rural carrier to bring the mail to our box; I drive up to town—sometimes on a tractor so I can feel the air in my hair and the bugs in my teeth—and pick up our mail first thing in the morning. Since it's a small-town post office, overnight delivery, as Phil reminds me every time I try to use overnight delivery, doesn't really mean overnight out here. That's okay; nothing I send is that important anyway.

When I first came out here I was so tickled with the notion of having a farm (even though it's only a "word farm") and living in the country, I got a mailbox up at the post office. At that time, the post office was a tiny room in the back of what is now the grocery store. My box number was 1111 and it was the kind that had two little dials on it and you opened it with a combination code. The postmaster (at the time not yet Phil, although Phil has now been here twenty-six years) pointed me toward my new address and I asked, "Uuuh, what's the combination for my box?" He said, giving me one of my first lessons in rural living, "It's scratched on the front of the box door just like all the others."

Amused, I asked, "You must not have much trouble with mail theft here, then, huh?"

"We could put the mail in baggies and hang it on the front doorknob," the postmaster said.

Just as the network of various delivery systems—electronic or physical—work for getting things out of the wilderness and back to hahahahahaha civilization, it works the other way around too. These days there's not much you can't buy by mail order or even more easily online. Sometimes it amazes me what we have had delivered here at our door at one time or another: pallets of books or parts, solvents weighing over a ton and requiring my tractor loader to take them off the semi, frozen foods, bees, wine, and last week, a pint of coyote urine. You don't want to know. Just trust me on this—contrary to what Mick Jagger would have you believe, you *can* always get what you want. Or darn near always anyway.

PUTTING IT ON THE MARKET

What about when you want to sell something? Word-of-mouth works the same way for the seller as the buyer, of course, but you will find too, that in every small town there is an information center somewhere—in the bank, at the co-op, on the door of the grocery store, at the entry of the café, on the wall of the tavern—where all sorts of notices are posted: notices for farm auctions; offers of free puppies; prairie hay in small, square bales; young goats; a bicycle lost; a baseball mitt found; a bake sale at the Baptist Church next

Saturday. One of the peculiarities it took us a while to get used to is the cardboard box sitting in the middle of a main street intersection with a notice on it reading something like "GARAGE SALE THIS AFTERNOON TWO BLOCKS NORTH" (or, more likely, "GARAG SAIL THIS AFTERNOON TOO BLOKS NORTH," rural protocols not being quite so fussy about spelling as a retired English professor might hope and prefer).

One note of caution: You can't expect business you do in a small town to remain confidential. If you do something real stupid like put water into your gas tank instead of the radiator, and you tow your tractor to the local mechanic to have the problem remedied, you are going to be known the rest of your life as Old Water Gas. If you inherit a goodly amount and deposit the loot in the bank, you'll be hit up for a loan by the local ne'er-do-well before the ink on the deposit slip dries. I am not joking about this one: If you indulge in a new and creative sexual activity, as one local lady did in my village, you can expect the feat to be recognized and saluted with a round of drinks and toasts at the tavern the next time you step through the door. In fact, if you do anything you would just as soon not have generally broadcast, the next time you hear a report of your actions, they will have been dramatically improved.

What you can't buy in a small town, you may enjoy for free. When the Halseys have a garden, for example, we enjoy fresh potatoes, huge heads of cabbage, and wonderful tomatoes. When Big Roy's corn crop was hailed out and he planted turnips for cattle forage, we had months of wonderfully sweet turnips. Sometimes zucchini, bread, or homemade wine is delivered to our door; sometimes we're invited to come up and get whatever we need or want; sometimes we return to our car or truck to find a box of goodies on the front seat; sometimes a box of anything from sweet corn to black lab–mix puppies, from venison jerky to snapping-turtle eggs is set on the bar at the tavern or displayed inside the door of the grocery store where everyone is invited to help himself. Even the post office serves as a distribution center for leftover birthday cake, cookies, or Danish pastries. It's not simply a matter of not wanting to waste things that are perfectly good but a genuine enthusiasm for sharing. It is not at all unusual to be sitting in the tavern when someone comes in, glowing with pride, with a load of fresh sausage, or a home-cured ham, or a bucket of mushrooms to share. "Here, try this," he'll say.

NEITHER A LENDER

While that sort of practice resonates with Christian charity and is rarely anything but altruistic, I have grown a good deal less sanguine about the constant practice of rural lending and borrowing. I have had friends borrow everything from my tractor to my shotgun, from my power washer to my pickup truck, and in each and every case the item in question was returned in worse condition than it left, sometimes ruined. Often it wasn't returned at all. My Dad made a determined point of never loaning or borrowing anything and pounded into my head that if I should ever borrow anything, it had to be returned in better condition than when I got it. That is definitely not the attitude around here, where the feeling prevails that if you could spare this item long enough to loan it out, you probably really don't need it much anyway. One good friend asked to borrow a relatively expensive car-top luggage carrier for his daughter to use on a trip to Florida, where she was going to live for a while, until she moved permanently . . . to Africa! I wondered aloud how he planned on getting the carrier back to me if this was a one-way journey? He looked at me in puzzlement and then indignation. Obviously, he considered it downright un-neighborly of me to clutter my mind—and his—with such a consideration. He wanted to borrow the carrier; returning it hadn't come into the mix yet, if it ever would.

To this day my favorite example was the time a friend who had become an in-law asked to borrow a couple expensive, heavy-duty house jacks from me to raise the corner of his sagging house. For those of you who might not know about such things, these heavy screw jacks are put under a building and turned to raise the building, or in this case, a corner of it. The element you are lifting is pushed just a trifle beyond where you want it and then a permanent foundation like concrete blocks, stones, or wood pilings are put under the building and the jack is eased back down until the house rests on its new base. A couple more turns and the jack can be removed to be used the next time you need to do some heavy lifting. But my friend and kin didn't bother with those last few steps. He just used my jacks to lift his house . . . and walled shut the bottom of his house, thus making the jacks the new permanent foundation of his home. Did he apologize? Did he replace the jacks? Did he even bother to tell me where my jacks had found a new home? Why would he want to do something like that? I loaned him the jacks, didn't I? So obviously, I didn't need them.

It seems unfriendly of me, I realize, and I am sure I've gained something of a reputation for being selfish, unreasonable, and snooty, but after years of replacing broken items that had been borrowed, having to go out around town to retrieve loaned items (borrowed things are blithely loaned to someone else, and even then to a third party, who doesn't even know from where it came originally and therefore couldn't return it to the owner even if he wanted to, and simply loses things no matter how expensive or irreplaceable they may be), I've had to make a policy of loaning nothing to anybody. On one occasion a really good friend needed a tool and wanted to borrow mine. I knew that once that thing went out the door of my shop, it was gone forever and I would have to buy a replacement. So instead of losing the expensive tool I was fond of, I just went ahead and bought a less expensive example of the same item and gave it to my friend as a gift, saving the trouble of getting all hepped up about him not returning the one I would have loaned him. I didn't get the impression that the irony of what I had done made a dent.

ALL THE NEWS

I've made it pretty clear that I am enthusiastic about new developments in communications, changes that have rendered old stereotypes about rural isolation and ignorance utterly inaccurate. On the other hand, some changes probably haven't been all that dramatic, or maybe even represent a certain degree of backsliding. Small-town newspapers are in serious decline. Costs of production have increased, the price of paper has risen dramatically, and the very rapidity and ease of other forms of communication I also mention above have made the immediacy and therefore importance of the printed word less important. Moreover, the unhappy condition of American politics and civility has decayed to the point where a small business like a newspaper toes the ideological lines set down by the powerful of the community or it is quickly without advertisers, readers, or a business. We get five newspapers at our home, all delivered by mail. That means they are all days behind the news. We get Lincoln's Saturday newspaper on Monday, the rest of the week's dailies one day late. The Grand Island paper is a daily, also a day late but in an edition meant for the day we get it. The Cairo newspaper is from a town about ten miles away but is important to us because it covers the news of the school where Dannebrog's children go. It is a weekly. And *Stjernen*, Danish for Star (but pronounced here as if it were the fish "sturgeon") is a monthly newsletter of the Dannebrog Booster Club, a village form of a Chamber of Commerce.

You'd be surprised how little you miss by getting a newspaper a day, or even days late. Actually, it doesn't make that much difference. You can get the news of the day, or hour, from television, the newspapers providing some depth to stories you want to know more about, but more importantly each covering in a narrower focus not covered by the newspapers of the next larger community. Things seem to mesh nicely and give us about everything we need to know—sometimes more than we need to know.

The important thing about local newspapers is to help you learn about your new community; for that reason, I strongly recommend that if you are contemplating moving to a new area, even if it is close to a city where you now live, you should subscribe to the smallest newspaper you can, closest to the area where you intend to move. At first the pages will seem to give you nothing by way of important information. For one thing, everything is school sports reports. Well, that tells you something about rural living too, doesn't it? And what about the report on the front page that Dexter Homesworth found a radish in his garden that looks exactly like a profile of Abraham Lincoln? You're laughing, but I have seen exactly that story when opening our own local papers. Do you know where you really find the news in such papers? In the legal reports. There you'll find who is doing what, both legal and illegal. It's one thing to read a big-city crime report about thugs, goons, miscreants, deadbeats, and thieves you hope never to encounter. It's quite another to read your local paper and find out that the thugs, goons, miscreants, deadbeats, and thieves are your neighbors and even your friends!

Of course you may not get much more than a few words about a credit company filing suit against someone whose name you've heard noised around before, or maybe your plumber being charged with assault . . . against his brother-in-law. Obviously you want to know more about the story, but where do you find the details? Well, again I would recommend the tavern—alcohol does make for juicy gossip—but we find that a beauty shop also is an excellent source. For one thing, almost all the women go to them, as well as many men—barbers are a dying breed. Women tend to congregate at beauty shops in small enough groups to make semi-confidential exchanges possible, and they are stuck in a dryer or chair long enough to tell the *whole* story. And you always wondered why every little burg seems to have at least one beauty shop!

A serious word of caution, however: Sit and listen, maybe even ask questions in innocence no matter how feigned. But be very careful about saying anything judgmental yourself, not until you've been a part of the community at least thirty years, maybe even more. I don't know for sure how long it takes. I've lived here thirty years and that's still not enough to know who is related to whom, I can tell you for a fact. And if you're as clumsy about such things as I am, the first time you remark on what a useless clod that half-wit Marvin Blenderworth is, you're going to find that the woman you always thought was a Jensen is actually a cousin of the Blenderworths, twice removed. And it ain't gonna be pretty.

Now, I mentioned above that television is a good place to get the news of the day. And that's true. But again, you have to understand that you are likely to be watching television news shows produced close to home, in a local or even small-town station. After all, do you want to know about the robberies and weather in a city three hours to the East, maybe in another climate, or even another time zone? Or do you want to know what to expect by way of icy roads tomorrow morning between your place and your doctor's office? Is it important to you to know what the sirens were up to in town about lunchtime or how traffic is moving on the beltway in the metroplex? If you want to know news that is relevant to you, you may find yourself watching a news program that is produced in a concrete block building at the base of a tower within sight of your outhouse.

If this is indeed the case, the first thing you are going to have to do is revise your understanding of what news is. In all likelihood, the news anchor who is two weeks out of broadcast school and didn't do all that well and so has had to settle for an assignment here in the Middle of Nowhere doesn't even know how to pronounce Caracas (one local newscaster here once made a stab at it with "carcasses," not getting past the first syllable in Venezuela), discussing the impact of the riots there on free-market trading and the exchange rate for the dollar. I don't know if it's a matter of haste, or mal de siècle, or something they learn in school about courage, but reporters at small stations appear to take enormous pride in never looking a word up or bothering to ask someone who might know, no matter how unfamiliar they are with it. In fact, the more bizarre the word seems to be, the more challenge its pronunciation promises, the more assuredly the reporter is not going to have gone to any authority to determine what someone else might think is an appropriate way to say the word. It's amazing. For this former English teacher it can be a bit depressing at times. But sooner or later you come to anticipate such wonderful gaffes, even relishing them. Sometimes the reporters stumble a bit but the really accomplished ones never hesitate, blustering right on through this combination of letters they have never seen before, blurting out the first impression they have of how this strange new formulation might be pronounced. You simply cannot imagine how interesting a report on the Lions Club having purchased a new set of all-weather tires for the senior-citizen center Handi-Van can be when "Wichita" comes out "wa-CHEE-ta" or Des Moines becomes "DESmonds." Maybe it takes a perverse sense of humor but I know this means a lot to Linda and me.

And then there are locally produced commercials, looking for all the world like something out of 1950s television. Often it is a local merchant, figuring that if he is going to pay fifty bucks for a television production, he by God is going to use the opportunity to get a shot at an advertising contract with a major network and so is going to be the on-camera talent to sell mobile homes from his lot himself. Or worse yet, let his granddaughter who is apparently in training to be the town tramp do the on-camera work. You will never be more grateful for public television—no matter how annoying the endless pledge drives—than when you move to rural America.

Chapter 6

RURAL ZEN:

The Philosophies of Rural Living; Yours and Theirs

YIN-YANG

Whether you want to believe it or not, living in rural America is not so much a matter of geographical location as it is philosophical orientation. No kidding. You know, like Zen, Yin-Yang, that kind of thing. You can live in the country and not buy into the whole rural mentality but if you choose that route, you'll never understand what's going on around you, or appreciate and enjoy it. My academic training was in anthropology and so I have always enjoyed moving into other cultures in a participatory way. There are people who are uncomfortable with the idea of becoming something other than what they were born—that is, what they've always been. But I figure you'll never know what you are unless you explore some things you aren't. I could have continued spending my weekends and vacations out here in Smalltown, America, but I really wanted to be a part of it, and have it be a part of me. To do that you have to at least consider the way people think, even if you don't want to adopt the mentality that prevails in your new environment.

I'm not at all sure we can ever actually become totally adapted to another culture, including rural or small-town life. I know for sure you can't learn how to be a farmer by taking classes, reading books, or attending workshops. Or simply by having good intentions. I know very few people who have successfully become working farmers without a life substantially grounded in agriculture from childhood on. That is, to be a farmer, you have to grow up being a farmer. That could be bad news for some of you, and maybe you can prove me wrong, but I'd be surprised. I know for sure that I can't do it. My place is a certified tree farm, but not a real working farm. I have planted tens of thousands of trees but never conducted a real harvest. Nonetheless, having planted trees that cost me next to nothing, done minimal mainte-nance—watering a couple times a year, doing some weed control and mowing, that kind of thing—I find that every time I discover one of my trees dying or dead, it breaks my heart. It's all the worse when it's a tree that has made it for a few years in the struggle against this ferocious geography, and then dies, from drought, wind damage, insect or animal damage, or simply dies from something I can't detect.

And yet not a thing in my life depends on that tree, on any of the trees, or for that matter on all of the trees. This is not tree country and I know that. Between fire and bison, trees were almost rarities on the native Plains, and it'll prob-ably eventually be that way again. So I know I am indulging myself in an idle fantasy putting a tree farm where grass is dominant. And yet, when they die. . . .

And then I try to imagine what it must be like to be a real farmer, to have one's very subsistence depend on a crop—an operation the wife needs, the kids' educations, the very ownership perhaps of a farm that has been in the family since great-great-great-grandfather homesteaded it 150 years ago—and see the storm clouds gather in the west. Is it hail that will pound the crop into bio-mulch in minutes? Or a blistering wind? Grasshoppers? Cinch bugs? A late snow, or early frost? I can't imagine how real farmers deal with that kind of constant jeopardy. I'm not up to it, I know it, and I admit it. So there.

I like to tell the story about a time twenty years ago when I was thinking about just that kind of thing. Linda and I were driving down the highway over to the neighboring town to enjoy a steak and some cold beer and along the way we met my old friend, Marv, coming toward us driving a grain truck. Kernels of corn were dropping occasionally from the bed of the truck and I figured Marv must have been hauling a load of his new harvest to the grain elevators. Not long after that I saw Marv's wife, Marlene, coming along the same road, also driving a grain truck, and then one of his sons. Yes, they were taking the harvest to market. And that meant they had won the gamble. They had faced all the hazards and uncertainties of farming and had brought in a crop this year.

I wondered what that must feel like to bring in the harvest after a long summer of struggle. You know, after all the work, risk, and doubt, what would it feel like to have beat the odds and won? Not being a farmer myself, I'd never had that feeling. Well, thank goodness I now had friends like Marv and Marlene, so I could just ask them. I knew that once they got their business done in the city, they'd almost certainly be back to the same steakhouse we were headed for, just down the road from their home, and maybe I could just ask them then.

And that's what I did. Sure enough, after an hour or so, just as we were enjoying dessert, Marv and Marlene came in. I invited them over to our table to have a beer with us and I explained my curiosity, just as I outlined it above for you, and asked them if they would share with this city boy what feelings they have during the triumph of harvest. Marv's answer was typical of farming philosophy, stunning in its implications, and instructive to me as an outsider. "What does it feel like to celebrate the victory of a harvest reaped and safely sold?" I asked.

Marv said, "I haven't cashed the check yet."

"But . . . but . . . but . . ." I sputtered, "when you *do* cash the check . . ."

"I have a combine stuck down in the soft bottoms over by the creek and I won't know where I am financially until I know I got it out without tearing it up or bending the frame."

"But once you have the combine out safely . . ."

Marv wouldn't relent. He simply would not declare victory. That would have been too risky. Arrogance like that only tempts the gods to crush mortals like ants. I doubt that Marv has ever heard and certainly never said the Greek word "hubris," but he sure as billyhell knows how it works. Declaring victory is a sure way to get your butt kicked in agriculture. Pride goeth before the fall, and all that. That is part of the Zen of Agriculture, and if you don't understand that, you don't have the single most important piece of armament needed to weather the storm.

WHOSE CULTURE?

When I first came to the rural countryside I thought the people out here didn't know much about city life. I thought it was curious that I was getting to know quite a bit about small-town and rural life but no one out here knew much about life in Lincoln. Or *wanted* to know much about life in Lincoln. There simply wasn't much curiosity about what my life was like no matter how interested and enthusiastic I might be about goings-on here. Once I was interviewing a craftsman who makes and plays a rare, traditional, folk music instrument in the western town of Scottsbluff, Nebraska. He worked primarily as a laborer and cement-truck driver but in his spare time had become a state, even national treasure, famed for his skill in making and playing the hammered dulcimer. "You know, Albert," I told him, "there are some really interesting and skilled dulcimer makers and players not far from here in Denver. And in Lincoln. In fact, I have been to dulcimer conventions in Grand Rapids, Michigan, and I think you would really enjoy traveling to one of these places and exchanging ideas with some other craftsmen."

He looked at me with amusement at my innocence and said, "Why would I want to go anywhere? I'm *in* Scottsbluff." Of course. If you are quite content where you are, and within your own skin, why would you want to be somewhere or something you aren't? That's not being provincial; that's confidence, and contentment. We could all use a good dose of that.

One of my favorite authors, Wright Morris, who grew up just a few miles east of here, down Ormsby Road in Central City, recognized and explored the rural mentality in many of his books, most expressively for me in his book *The Home Place*. He writes about the situation of a hometown boy returning to the farm with his city-bred wife, in the process examining the conflicts between rural and urban life, customs, and attitudes. At one point the city-bred wife touches on the contradiction between rural and urban attitudes toward each other. Morris' conclusions about the people living in the country demonstrate his own sophistication about both rural and city living: "'I'll tell you what it is I can't stand,' she said. 'It's all right for you to share their lives. That's fine. But they don't give a dam [sic] about yours.'"

Every time I have immersed myself in other cultures, I have learned about not simply the character of those cultures new and alien to me but even more importantly about my own native culture: Midwestern, middle class, European-born, mainstream, white American culture. The same is true of my experiences in rural America: what has struck me is not so much how strange life is in the countryside as how peculiar it makes life in population centers seem. I can now imagine that every contact the rural or small-town American has with his city cousins and their ways must be puzzling, if not downright disgusting. And yet not without its humor.

When I mention a steakhouse-tavern in a tiny town just a few miles west of my home, I am almost always referring to Dick's establishment, The Gold(en) Nugget in Boelus, Nebraska. Boelus is even smaller than Dannebrog, with a population of two hundred, if that. But the steakhouse is famous, pretty much dominating and supporting the town that otherwise has only a bank and grocery store surviving on its main street. Well, "famous" in the Plains, Nebraska, small-town, Howard County–sense of famous anyway. I just looked in a major road atlas to find the population of the town and find that Boelus isn't even listed as a town in Nebraska! It's pretty hard to imagine that a restaurant can be all that famous when the town it's in doesn't even exist according to some standards. If you are a tourist and decide to stop in Boelus and check out this place I prize and praise so highly, you may have some confusion because despite the fact that there are only a couple buildings still standing and occupied on the main street—which is wider than it is long—there is only a single blank door opening in a blank building façade.

Yes, there is a sign announcing that this is a tavern and they serve Budweiser beer, but even it has been modified in such a way that it is hard to figure out where exactly you are and what you are dealing with by way of a business. See, the thing is, while the establishment has been known for thirty years as The Golden Nugget (remember, now, this is in Boelus, Nebraska, a town of fewer than two hundred people), duct tape has been used to obscure some of the name. No, the duct tape is not to repair a wind-, storm-, or hail-damaged sign. The duct tape is a country bow to corporate, highly educated, very expensive, lame-brained, dirt dumb, big-city lawyers who composed and sent officious letters a couple years ago to the proprietors of the Gold(en) Nugget threatening legal action because of the illegal appropriation of the trademarked name of Golden Nugget in Las Vegas. The misuse of the name, they explained, could cause confusion with prospective customers and visitors.

Well, uh, sure, it would be mighty easy to confuse Las Vegas with Boelus. I mean, what with the glare of the neon when Gene leaves the night lights on in the grocery store window or someone's brake lights come on as they drift down the Boelus main street. And the gray, blank façade of the Gold(en) Nugget steakhouse with a single light-bulb sign saying "GOLDXX NUGGET DRINK BUDWEISER" is for all the world a clone of the Vegas Strip place of the same name.

Tourists planning a big blowout might easily confuse Nevada and Nebraska, what with them both beginning with the letters Ne. You can understand why these fancy city lawyers felt the need to land on the Boelus Gold(en) Nugget and bring an instant halt to the enormous potential for us siphoning off half the Vegas action here to Howard County, Nebraska!

Now, imagine the hilarity the pompous legal correspondence from these stupid clowns gave to the six or eight regulars sitting along the bar in the Gold(en) Nugget the day it arrived! Gene, Swede, Bobby, Marv, Neil, Larry, and Biology Bob could hardly wait till the next time I came in before they showed me yet another example of the crashing, cosmic, colossal stupidity of my city compatriots. What could I say? I shrugged and laughed along. No doubt about it, the cities do seem to be a constant source of useless ignorance, but even at that, rarely does an example this sublime come along. Thus, part of the rural philosophy is an understanding that in addition to there being little reason to have an interest in what goes on in the city, there is in addition considerable reason to hold such activities in contempt.

PUNISHING THE GUILTY

In town the motto is "caveat emptor"—buyer beware. In rural America, even though that mentality is slowly creeping into commerce there too, the standard among the elders is still "Your word is your bond. A handshake is as good as a contract. Do unto others . . ." I have always argued that the root of urban evil and modern inequity is anonymity—since no one knows who you are, since you are never going to see them again much less have to deal with them, you might just as well screw them before they screw you. People in rural communities still do know who you are. Sure, you can skip out on paying a bill with the small-town mechanic or tavern, but the next time your vehicle breaks down you're going to have to find someone to tow you ten miles to the next mechanic . . . and hope that your reputation hasn't preceded you. And ten miles can be a long way to travel for a cold beer after a hot summer day if you've stiffed the town barkeep.

But there is more to it than that. I think there is still a hope within the rural heart that you can trust people. Even those who look for all the world like they can't be trusted. In the first months that I was out here, when I was still virtually a mystery to everyone, I needed a heavy-duty trailer to haul buildings, two-ton loads of water, and the heavy oak and walnut logs of my log house. I had spotted a welding shop in a nearby town where some wagons of exactly the kind I had in mind were sitting, so I drifted into the shop one day to see if we could maybe do some business. As luck would have it, I spoke to the proprietor, a salty, grizzled old dog who had been a blacksmith before the days that occupation mutated into welding. His hair was about an eighth of an inch long and he was chewing on a cigar about an inch long. He was a small man compared to me but obviously a no-nonsense, tough S.O.B.

I on the other hand was a sallow kid-professor from the city. I was driving a battered Chevy van with bumper stickers for every liberal, tree-hugging, anti-war, gun-control cause you can think of. I had three kids of various ethnicities with me and a dog I tied to the bumper of the van. I was wearing shorts and a Hawaiian shirt. My hair was in a ponytail, possibly—I don't remember—with an eagle feather behind my left ear as I was wont to do.

Eddie, as I later learned is his name, looked me over with obvious doubt, if not contempt. I told him what I needed—one of his big, four-wheel trailers with adjustable length, heavy-duty hubs, wired for rear lights, with a ball hitch—all of which would have to be put on since the trailer was not outfitted in this way as it stood. Eddie did some fast calculating, came up with a figure that seemed fair enough, and I agreed to the bargain. He said it would take him a minute to make the alterations I wanted, and so I just sat around in the shade of the van with my kids and dog, probably causing something of a stir across the streets of the village. "The hippies are coming! The hippies are coming!" Well, what do I care? I'm a city guy. I'll pay for this trailer and I'll never see this little welder guy again, right? I don't need to please him. I'm paying him good money. It's just a business transaction.

Eddie finished the work, handed me the bill, precisely what he told me it would cost, and I said to my son, "Chris, get my billfold off the dash of the van, please." A moment later Chris came back and said, "Uuuh, Dad, there's no billfold there." Gulp. Did I forget my billfold? Hopefully I had the presence of mind then to throw in my checkbook. "Okay, uh, Chris, grab my checkbook out of the glove box." Moments later, "Dad, there's no checkbook in the glove box."

There I stood, having committed to a transaction of something like $600 and I not only didn't have the money, or a check with which to pay for it, I didn't even have any identification. Not so much as a name tag. "Uh, well, sir, uh, it seems that I have gone off without any way of paying for this work." At this point I am sweating more than Eddie, and he was the one who had done the welding. "All I can figure I can do is come back next week and pay you then if you will hold the trailer for me."

"Do you need the trailer this weekend?"

"I sure do, but that's okay. It'll just set me back a little ways and besides, it's my own damn fault."

"Go ahead and take the trailer. You can pay me next weekend when you get back."

I was stunned. Why would this guy trust anyone with a setup like this, much less me? I was a total stranger, and stranger is how I looked. I might as well have been an alien needing a trailer for my UFO. As I drove away from the welding shop with my new trailer, my embarrassment turned into something else, something I suspect is the very nature of this kind of dealing: I was buried, inundated, flooded with intense feelings of responsibility not to let this guy down. His trust of me was not his problem; it was mine. If I betrayed confidence in humanity like this, then I would be responsible for the downfall of mankind. And I am not exaggerating.

I sweated bullets all the way to my place, all that weekend while I worked, all the way home, and then the next three days after I found my checkbook and sent this guy a check. I simply did not want to disappoint him and his trust in humanity—even in the form of me—or maybe confirm what he suspected of people like me, by not paying him promptly and fully. I sent the check on Monday and called him on Wednesday to make sure he had received the payment and that it was right. He grunted that it was fine. It was obviously no big deal to him. This is the way he does business. This is the way everyone in small towns does business. And you'd have to be a first-class asshole, you should excuse the French, to betray that trust. I never do.

As you probably have guessed, I wound up doing a lot of business with Eddie until he retired. I still do a lot in the shop that bears his name even though he no longer works there. Now I consider him a real friend, and whenever I can I pick up a tab for his supper or breakfast when I run into him in a town café because he taught me something more important than just about any other lesson in life: Trust is a burden on the one who is trusted, not the one who trusts. And no matter what else you might think about someone, there's no harm in giving him a basic respect, presuming his integrity rather than a perfidy. Eddie is something of a hero to me.

Eddie and his approach to commerce are anything but unusual. Here's an ad from our local newspaper this past week: "Butternut squash, big and beautiful. $1 each. Leave money in container." This suggests not only that the merchant 1) trusts his customers to put their money in the jar, but even more remarkably, 2) trusts that they won't take out any money that is already in the jar. All America should be like this and anyone who violates such trust should be put to death. Sorry to be so harsh, but I'm just being honest here.

TOUGH BARGAINING

More often than not, I have found that in conducting business in rural America, you are more likely to come out better than you anticipated, than you are to come out worse. I go to a friend's farm to buy a hog for butchering on a day when hogs are going for forty-nine cents a pound. The farmer estimates that the hog in question weighs 240 pounds. I opine that, what the heck, let's just round it off at $120. The farmer says no, I saved him hauling the animal to market. Let's make it $110 even. We wind up settling at $115, both probably making out well in the exchange plus gaining a renewed faith in our fellow man and even feeling a bit smug about our own generous nature.

When I sit down with my buddies for a couple beers at the tavern, we don't order up and then carefully calculate what each person owes. No, one of us just says "This one's on me." The next round will be on someone else. If one of my friends is a bit short or forgot his wallet this night, it doesn't make any difference. He'll make up for it next time. At the end of the evening no one makes even a cursory check of who paid for what. It just isn't done. Of course if one person makes a habit of not picking up his share, sooner or later it is noticed and he finds himself pretty much on his own when it comes to fun at the tavern. But I have seen someone behave like that only two or three times in all my years out here. I like living life like that—not keeping track.

Which is not to say there isn't in every rural community—just like every urban community—at least one, perhaps several people who can't be trusted with a bucket of spit. I have been bilked twice by our own resident thief and flimflammer for a total of $550. I consider it tuition. It was expensive tuition, but 1) I learned not to trust this guy no matter how convincing his story and 2) I now have an iron-clad reason not to trust him again, ever, and so 3) he doesn't bother me any more with his schemes and thievery. So, if he's so dishonest, why isn't this miscreant in jail? Well, we don't even have a jail in this county, for one thing, and the law just works differently here than elsewhere. I think most people consider the punishment sufficient that this guy can't do any business anywhere within fifty miles of his home; he can't buy gas (even with cash, because he has stiffed every station and doesn't dare go back because he'd be dunned for previous debts), can't get a car repaired, can't buy groceries, can't get a haircut, can't . . . Well, you get the idea. He might just as well be in jail.

That strain of honesty is certainly one of the reasons I wanted to raise our daughter in a rural setting, and the reason I wanted to live my years here too. Life is too short to deal with dishonest people. Another prime reason was a feeling I got very early on as I acquired friends that are farmers and small-town people—a persistent mood of common sense and even wisdom. Of course there are rural fools and idiots—maybe even more than you'd find in the city—but it is my impression that there is definitely a higher proportion of wise elders in the country.

TEMPERING THE STEEL

My guess is that the rigors of agriculture, rural life, and proximity to nature, earth, and climate are like a blacksmith's hammer and anvil, making steel not only harder but sharper. Also a distinctive proportion of the population inherits, or learns—I don't know how they get it—a flair for expressing that wisdom with a diction that is the closest thing I have found to folk literature. Not long ago, for example, I saw a television report on a tornado-ravaged town not far from here. The cameras followed an elderly lady as she returned to her home—or at least the place where her home had been—and recorded her reactions for the news report. She looked over the utter wreckage and devastation of everything she had owned and been, and she said quietly, "Well, isn't that take just one heck of a note?" Good grief, this woman's life had just been destroyed by the fiercest weather phenomenon on earth! Everything she knew and loved had been lost. And her response? "Well, isn't that just one heck of a note!"

Her clear feeling and declaration was, "Okay, so let's not waste any more time moaning and groaning and feeling sorry for ourselves. Get me some gloves and a bucket and let's get busy cleaning up this mess." Isn't *that* just one heck of a note?!

As often as not, rural wisdom is expressed at the edges, or even the heart, of humor. I've spent my life studying the nature of folk humor and I think I have a pretty good idea how it works and why. I have always been interested especially in pioneer humor because once one understands the savagery, brutality, and misery of frontier life, humor becomes a puzzle. Why, in the middle of all this pain, would anyone joke about anything, much less precisely the conditions that are causing that misery: drought, flood, death, disease, starvation, isolation, beasts, and bugs? Make no mistake about it, those are precisely the foundation of pioneer and frontier humor. (If you would like to read more about humor as a strategy for dealing with historical hardship, see my books *Shingling the Fog and Other Plains Lies* (University of Nebraska Press, Lincoln) or *Catfish at the Pump: Humor of the Frontier* (University of Nebraska Press, Lincoln). Nowhere is the distinction between urban and rural cultures more clearly defined than in their respective humors. Urban humor is sledgehammer blunt, little more than a punch line, rarely with subtlety or nuance; rural humor tends to be narrative and funny in the telling rather than relying on some sort of punch line resolution. No one wonders if they've just been told a joke when an item of urban humor is delivered. On the other hand, sometimes you have to think twice to figure out whether something funny has just been said in a rural setting. There have been occasions when only days later have I realized the humor of something that has been said to me over breakfast at Harriett's or coffee at the co-op.

To be sure, part of that is the laconic, straight-faced delivery of rural humor but there is also an incredible subtlety in rural diction. For example, I was once in a conversation with several agricultural experts from the academic world and one farmer from the remote Nebraska Sandhills. One of the high-tech experts asked the farmer how his corn crop had turned out that year and he said, "Oh, it wasn't as good as expected . . . but then no one thought it would be." The conversation among the academics continued but my brain was having a hard time wrapping itself around the convoluted logic. Did the farmer know what he had just said? I looked at him and as the experts nattered on he smiled slightly and winked. He knew what he'd said.

Similarly, a city reporter recently interviewed a farmer about his impressions of the severe drought we have been enduring in this area for almost a decade now. What did he think about the drought? How long could he endure without sufficient rain for his crops? Did he see in any relief in the future? He said, "The way I see it, every day of drought is just one day closer to a good rain." I can't say for certain but I'm betting that farmers within reach of that broadcast all chuckled to themselves, and not one city boy out of a thousand saw anything ironical in it at all.

WHEN IS A DIRTY JOKE *NOT* A DIRTY JOKE?

I imagine an entire future book around the topic of what I call "civil ribaldry," a uniquely rural form of humor. My father and mother never cursed. They most certainly never told dirty jokes. And yet my father did tell a kind of joke that I then found to be common out in the rural countryside, a kind of earthy, slightly naughty story, but couched in such subtlety that the tales can be told in the presence of ladies and children without so much as a hint of disapproval from the prim and proper—like my mother and father. I think, for example, of one such story Butch Williams told the first time he met Linda and me. He noted that Linda was quite a bit younger than I am and said we reminded him of the old man who married his young hired girl, telling her that if she ever felt like she needed some lovin' while he was working out in the fields, she should just step out on the back steps and fire the shotgun and he'd come running. Butch paused dramatically as that scenario soaked in, and then said, "Poor old guy died two weeks into pheasant season."

Or when Bumps Nielsen told me that his Uncle Vic had been out on the main street of Dannebrog talking with a crony the first time an airplane ever flew over. "Imagine that," Bumps said. "All your life you've never seen anything up there in the sky but clouds and birds and now all at once there it is, a machine with a man in it, high in the sky over-head." He said that on that occasion, Vic's friend said, 'Why, look there, Vic. It's one of them mail planes!' "Nah," said Vic. "Them's just the wheels hanging down."

No urban humor club audience is going to have the patience to sit still while a stand-up comedian takes the time to spin a yarn like that.

As is the case in that last story, there is also a constant element in rural humor being a part of local folk history, which it truly often is. The jokes are not so much contrived situations of pure fancy: "A rabbi, a priest, and a Baptist minister all come into a bar and sit down, and the bartender says. . . ." Factually true or not, rural humor often has at least the air of legitimate history. Seminars of such narrative spring up totally unexpected at the drop of a story. Two or three or five people will be sitting around a table at Schroeder's in the morning playing cards, or three or four tired laborers will be having a cold beer after work at the tavern when someone mentions something—a big fish caught over at the reservoir, a fire at someone's farm, a fight the weekend before at the tavern—and the stories start. When that happens, I absolutely glow. I love storytelling sessions like that, and everyone knows it; after the first few lines of a story that promises to be great, someone will hand me a sheet of blank paper, or a bar napkin, because they know I'm going to be flailing around to find something to make some notes on. As Eric, the former bartender at the town tavern once said, "Rog, you know, so many people come in here and hear these stories, go home and forget them. You, you take 'em home and sell 'em." He said that—I like to think—with some admiration.

JOKES OR ORAL HISTORIES?

Even when a rural person moves to the city, the knack of recognizing and remembering such stories, and the inclination to retell them, persists. Just a few days ago I mentioned that I was working on this book and a friend who had been raised in a small town started telling her stories.

"Then you might want to hear about my Aunt Dorothy, the wife of the banker in my hometown. Anyway, Dorothy volunteered to help with the church social. It was decided to have a rather large watering tank filled with lemonade for sale. Each church lady was to bring chunks of ice made from water frozen in milk cartons. Of course, my aunt agreed to bring seven to eight, always an overachiever. The day of the social, several women start screeching soon after my aunt dumped her allotted chunks of ice into the tank. As her chunks melted in the hot July sun, several bullheads appeared. She'd grabbed the wrong milk cartons out the freezer. We still laugh about the day Dorothy soured the lemonade with bullheads."

You don't make stuff like that up. Nor do you ever live it down. That story will be told for generations, probably to Aunt Dorothy's chagrin . . . and Uncle Bob's amusement.

THE EXTENDED FAMILY

A lot is made about a small community being like a big family, and a lot of the people who make that noise don't really mean it or understand what it means. But it is true. When I lived in a city, when I am in a city now and hear sirens, I may notice them. On the other hand, I may not. I was once in a hotel in Philadelphia and heard lots of sirens. You can't get up and look out the window every time you hear sirens in the city. This time the sirens got louder, and closer. I still didn't bother to leave watching something inane on television to look out the window. But then there were more sirens, and they seemed to be shutting down fairly close to the hotel. So finally I got up and looked out the window. Good thing I did. The hotel I was in was on fire. After making my way down the hall and then down the stairs, I spent the night along with all the other hotel guests sitting up in an empty theater while the fire department made sure the fire was out and the smoke was cleared from the building. Characteristically, the hotel still tried to bill me for a night's stay.

When the sirens go off in a small town, however, not only does everyone wonder who of our neighbors, friends, and kin is in trouble, but half the room, whether at church or in the tavern, will jump to their feet and dash for the door because they are the firemen for whom that siren is blowing. We live about a mile from town and in most cases we can hear the fire siren when it goes off up there over the hill; if I wake at night and hear the siren, you can be sure I'll ask around the next morning to find out who had the problem and how much damage was done or who the EMTs hauled off to the hospital because the chances are almost one hundred percent that I will know who it is. What are the chances of knowing where or who the problem is when a city siren goes off? What's more, who cares? (In my office here as I write these words, one of the main communications items I have at my desk is a police scanner, keeping watch over all emergency calls for the county; it is my principal source of information for what's going on during the day, and rarely is there a call from the police or fire units in which I don't recognize the name or location. They say that all politics is local; well, I can tell you for a fact that in the case of a rural scanner, all news is local, for damn certain!)

There are reasons for not raising children in a rural or small-town setting—isolation, for example. And it doesn't help when you are, like my Antonia, Linda's and my only child, whose father is not much like any of the fathers of the other kids in her school. There is just as much opportunity for kids to get into trouble, maybe even more since there is clearly less to do in a small town and therefore a higher level of boredom. On the other hand, when you are in a school class with only thirty-five classmates, you are not about to avoid being into sports or other school activities. For one thing, the participation of every student is needed not just in each of the school activities from theater to sports, civic projects to speech contests, but they are necessary in all of them because there aren't enough kids to fill all the roles. (When Antonia's school produces a play, some actors have to play several roles!)

That's also why I believe a rural domestic setting is good for children. My children learned early how to drive a tractor and help me with jobs around the farm even though we aren't running a real agricultural operation. There are jobs I couldn't do without the help of another set or two of hands, and that meant I needed my kids, up to and including driving trucks and tractors. There's a big difference between a kid getting to drive to the city as a lark and needing to drive to get something important done on the farm. Same with jobs. There are make-do jobs where it is clear to the kids that they are not only not particularly important for it but frankly aren't particularly necessary for anything. Not on a farm. Out here, they are needed, and that is a good thing for even a child to know.

DRIVING US NUTS

As with so many things in life, that is also precisely the worst part of rural living for children, or more precisely, for the children's parents. While the school buses go to each and every farm and several corners in town to pick up students for our consolidated school, which is six miles from our gate, there are problems with busing. It's a long ride, what with having to crisscross the country and pick up so many kids living so far apart. There is a certain amount of chaos, even though our school-bus drivers out here are strict disciplinarians who take no crap from anybody. And as anguished as we were when Antonia announced she was done with the school bus, we did recognize and admit that it had to be tough to be maturing into a young woman and have to share a seat with some snot-nose third-grader for the half-hour ride it took to get to school.

That means that every parent's nightmare of children getting behind the wheel of an automobile happens even earlier in the rural countryside than it does in the city. Children can get permits to drive to school here when they are fourteen years old. I'm not enthusiastic about twenty-one-year-olds driving cars, or some full-fledged adults for that matter, and now suddenly I was seeing fourteen-year-old children just barely out of elementary school coming at me at sixty miles an hour on the highway, the misbegotten spawn of the very adults whose names I read listed for twelve separate traffic violations in last week's local newspaper. All you can do is cross your fingers and pray for God's mercy.

So our little girl at fourteen had a car and was driving to school on her own. You can bet I made her work for it. We had that car a month before she ever ventured out our gate. I made her parallel park between barrels, drive the half mile down to the cabin and back backwards, pass a twelve-page test on every part of an automobile, including crawling under the car and identifying all major components, knowing the difference between a fuel line, the wiring harness, and the brake lines. But then the time came when out the gate she went, and Linda and I held our breath.

With, it turned out, good reason. One morning I was getting ready to get into the shower to start the day. I had heard Antonia start her car and head off for school moments earlier. And I heard the town emergency siren go off. There wasn't a doubt in my mind or a moment's hesitation in what I did next. I grabbed my clothes and threw them back on and headed for the door even as the telephone rang and I could hear a neighbor's voice over the answering machine saying I better get to the curve between my place and town because Antonia had had an accident. I found her already with the EMTs, crying but not hurt, her car totaled. Her windshield had fogged over on the bad curve and she had hit an oncoming vehicle head-on. Thank goodness the other people saw her coming across the centerline, slowed down, and tried to avoid the collision.

There were probably more bad times for us raising a child in a rural setting than good times, and there were occasions when Antonia was not at all happy with her lot. But now she feels it was a good growing experience, and she shows every sign of having profited and prospered with her feet planted firmly in the soil instead of on the pavement.

I once was a student in one of those high-performance driving schools, learning first how to handle stock cars (Ford Mustangs set up for racing) at high speed and on a tortuous track (Sears Point, Sonoma), and then Formula Fords. It was a wonderful experience and even though I had been driving for 40 years at the time, I learned a lot, including a couple things that later probably saved my life. But some of the remarks made by the instructors (whom I later cheered on in Indy and Grand Prix races on television) that struck me most were not about driving on the track, but on the highway.

They said that almost certainly the most common tool Americans own—even beyond a hammer or screwdriver—is the automobile, and yet it is a complicated and dangerous device about which they know almost nothing. These guys who make a living driving in extremely dangerous situations at insane speeds, in heart-stopping congestion, said—each and every one—that they are far more afraid when they are on a freeway, surrounded by inept fools at 75 miles an hour than they ever are doing 175 going into a turn with two other cars within inches of them on either side, but driven by certified experts.

I wish I could tell you things are different in the country, but they aren't. In fact, it's probably worse. For one thing, there are those carloads of fourteen-year-olds acting like idiots behind the wheel of two-ton high-performance automobiles their parents somehow think will make them popular at school. Secondly, in the city you can at least take some comfort in the fact that some of the idiots in other cars will be observing 35- or even 25-miles-per-hour speed limits, whereas most of the roads in the country are high speed highways—two lane highways—and the idiots out here are about the same caliber as in the city. Unless you are on back roads, in which case you—and that idiot in question—are wrestling the wheel in mud, snow, gravel, or rock, and probably still going too fast.

I know the people in my village, I know where they have jobs in the city twenty-two minutes away, and I know—and they know—what time they need to be at their jobs. I can tell by the sounds of their vehicles on the highway at my gate, or I can see them as I cautiously approach leaving my drive to go into town for the mail, that they are leaving for their jobs precisely three minutes late. Every day. *Every* day, which means they have to speed every day. Especially when the weather is bad and their cars are slow to start, or they have trouble getting out their own drives. In no case do these half-wits think about leaving three minutes earlier and driving safely. In fact, you can pretty much tell exactly how important these people and their jobs are by how fast they drive: workers at the onion factory on their way to a day of sorting culls leave late and drive 85 miles per hour to get to the plant. The oncologist on his way to save lives at the cancer clinic leaves in plenty of time, goes 55, ten miles under the limit. It may be only Nebraska but drivers here feel they can save substantial amounts of money by cutting down on their automobiles' electric bills, so they don't turn on their lights until they can no longer see the front of their hoods. It never occurs to these Mensa cadets that lights might serve as a helpful way to let other drivers see *them* (and head for the ditches to avoid collisions, since they are little more than an accident looking for a place to happen).

Drinking and driving is considered an entitlement by many in the rural countryside. Distances are indeed measured by consumption: "How far is it over to the auction by Elba Saturday?" "Oh, about a six-pack. . . ." I once asked a Texan if it's really true that you can drink and drive in that benighted state. He answered simply, "S'posed to!"

At this writing I am sixty-eight years old. I sense a clear fade in my driving abilities, like not remembering where I am going, things like that. Seriously, I know I don't see as well as I once did, I am damn-near stone deaf, and my reaction time is getting slower. When I can, I mitigate the danger I might be to other drivers by having Linda do the driving (she is substantially younger than I am, does a lot more driving anyway, and I am not of the school of some geezers that men are the ones who kill bears and drive the car). Weather permitting, I drive a tractor into town, which means I am slower and more visible for other drivers.

That is not the common line of logic among aging rural drivers, or of aging urban drivers so far as I can tell. Again, however, it's the same situation as with children driving: it's one thing to have a disabled driver doing 25 or 35 miles an hour and having to stop at every corner, not counting stop signals ignored or missed, and quite another to have an ancient dwarf of a lady whose hair is taller than she is, crouched in a monstrous Cadillac El Grosso, peering through the steering wheel, flooring the accelerator when she is ready to go forward. Or backward, as the case may be depending on where the gearshift was last time she got around to operating it. You laugh. The very lady I am thinking about in this town is precisely this example. Not long ago she stepped out of her car in the drive-in beauty shop and . . . what? You've never heard of a drive-in beauty shop? Well, neither had we until she made Maxine's shop in town a drive-in by, well, driving in. She thought her battleship of a car was in reverse, so she floored it, and, uh, it wasn't. Took the whole front off Maxine's shop. Damage to car? Thirty-five dollars. Ah, they really knew how to make an assault Cadillac back in those days, didn't they?

Part of the problem, as it turns out, is that this beldame can't hear a thing, so she doesn't know when her car is running. Helpful local mechanics remedied this problem after replacing her seventeenth burned-out starting motor with a true rural solution: they took a machinist's hammer and

knocked the mufflers off the exhaust system. This turned out
to be a marvelous solution, since now she can hear the B-52-
like roar of her turbomonster and what's more, so can
everyone else within twelve miles of wherever she is when
she starts it. While this could be something of a problem for
anyone who works a night shift, it is a real boon for all the
rest of us because it gives us time to get off the streets before
this rural commando rolls onto the streets in her Bradley
fighting vehicle.

This is particularly important when she is parked in town.
She obviously can't see over the back of the front seat, even if
she stood up on it, and the rear-view mirror won't adjust for
that low an angle of reflection, so she just backs up until she
hits something—anything—and then puts it into a forward
gear—any forward gear—revs the engine until its scream is
loud enough to be heard through the open manifold pipes, and
again pops the clutch in a cougar-like lurch forward. The volume of her starting up, much more substantial than either the
whine or smell of a starting motor trying to keep up with an
engine already running at 4,200 rpms, warns everyone that
she has begun the launch sequence. Doors in businesses all up
and down Main Street fly open and people with cards still in
their hands, grocery carts only half full, or deposit slips only
half filled out quickly evaluate the situation to see what jeopardy their cars are in and if necessary to move them before
that ten-ton behemoth of battered steel with Yoda's wife at the
wheel begins its backward trajectory seeking something solid
to stop it. When the big engine of that car of hers lights up, the
streets fill with people standing by to watch the fun. I often
wonder what visitors to our town must think of this incredible flurry of utterly inexplicable chaos.

I presume that every small town has a driver or two like our little old lady because there is no shortage of other examples. My buddy Rod had the distinction of having two accidents in one day, both DUIs. And both involving school buses. Horror of child jeopardy aside, the real mystery is how you can hit even one huge yellow vehicle in a day, much less two. The only thing that made the two-school-bus collisions at all conceivable was his incident of only a year before when he ran into the bank, setting off the security alarm as well as dislocating the front wall. His excuse was that there was no bank-crossing warning sign at that corner.

Rod lost his driver's license for these transgressions, of course, which means that he was then reduced to driving his tractor to town, along with its permanently hitched disk harrow. Now, if Rod was a threat behind the wheel of his battle-scarred DeSoto, imagine the damage he could—and did—do with an International tractor dragging a disk cultivator when he drove into town for a few beers and parked on Main Street. His response was a common one: Everyone in that town—in that county—knew that at four o'clock every afternoon he would be headed to the tavern and so whose fault was it exactly when someone had the temerity to pull out into an intersection just because he had the right of way? A standard joke in town is that the village board finally had to take down the stop signs at our four-way-stop intersection because everyone got tired of sitting there waiting for three more vehicles to show up.

PEDESTRIAN STRAIN

If defensive driving is the rule on rural roads, then daring to be a pedestrian is next to playing Russian roulette with five of the six cylinders loaded. I used to walk in and out of town mornings to get my mail because I thought it was good for my health, but then one bright, clear day I was walking by the co-op fertilizer plant, being probably the only foot traffic in all of Howard County at the moment. I saw a huge John Deere tractor maneuvering around the yard, pulling a trailer with a bale buster—a big piece of machinery—on it, along with some bags of feed and supplement it front–bucket loaded with an enormous, wide feed bunker, a kind of heavy table from which to feed cattle, but I didn't think anything of it. One sees that kind of activity constantly in farming country, and this was well off the road on private property. Nothing to do with me, none of my business, normal traffic: I walked on, my mail bag over my shoulder, staying on the left-hand side of the road, a main street right in town, with no traffic in sight, nothing to obscure my vision.

I should have known. The next thing I knew I had been thrown to the gravel and looked up to see the gigantic green monster passing over me, its huge tires passing on either side of me, the bucket with its two-ton load just over my head. The driver had exited the co-op and jolted onto the gravel road; he was concerned about losing part of the bagged load on his trailer and had turned for just a second to see if he had lost anything. In that moment the tractor came all the way across to my side of the road and that monstrous iron bucket with the bunker in it had hit me square in the back, just below shoulder height. And thank God for that. If the bucket had been a bit higher, it would have hit me in the back of my head, probably tearing it off. A bit lower and it would have hit me right in the small of my back—insofar as anything about my back is small—probably crippling me for life.

The mail bag over my shoulder took a good deal of the blow but still I was pretty well knocked out while being nonetheless grateful that no other part of the machine had hit me or run over me. The driver, as scared as I was, I'm sure, ran back to the co-op and called the EMTs and since I was still in town, only a couple blocks from the firehouse, they were with me almost instantly.

As it turned out, I had some cracked ribs and a broken left hand, which puzzled the doctors because the X-rays showed that the hand had been broken before and left unrepaired, a mishap I couldn't even remember. I still have some painful echoes of that mishap but mostly in the occasional retelling of the story. For example, when the EMTs commented on the abrasions to my scalp and gravel embedded in my head, I explained that that was not anything to worry about since that damage was from the night before when I walked home from the tavern. There was talk in town that someone needed to put up a Deere-crossing warning sign at that spot in the road. Someone else said it was my own fault for not wearing a wide-load sign when I walk along that road. When the question came up who had been driving the tractor that ran over me, someone ventured that it was probably Linda. Two days later in the mail I was sent an orange vest with a slow-moving-vehicle symbol on the back. I was questioned several times on the extent of the damages . . . to the tractor.

City newspapers constantly publish letters from readers irritated about slow agricultural traffic on the public highways, noting that it is very dangerous having huge combines, harrows, and tractors hauling monstrous trailers of grain or bales on a highway at 35 miles per hour when someone else

is driving 65. Or how about 75, because that's the way it usually is. So, we have some bonehead doing 75 miles per hour,
ten over the speed limit, on his way to see a football game,
and in a hurry because he had to have one more drink for the
road before he left the party, already fifteen minutes too late
to get a really good parking place. And he comes up way too
fast behind a guy doing his best to make a living feeding the
world, going as fast as he can and being cautious because of
his load, with precisely as much right to be on this road as
anyone else. Or in my opinion, with far more right and purpose to be on this selfsame road.

I guess you can tell where my sympathies lie. When I
come up behind, or meet, a farmer on a road or highway on
or pulling farm machinery, far from complaining I offer up a
little prayer of gratitude for people willing to do this back-
breaking, dangerous, economically risky business to keep us
all well-fed and happy. I blink my lights or wave a thank-you
gesture to the man or woman behind the wheel and never for
an instant complain about having to slow down to give them
all the room and consideration they need. And if you don't
feel that way about it, well, I would like to be more polite,
but I can't: Tough shit. Deal with it.

An unexpected and mixed blessing/curse is what happens if you stop along the side of a country road. You can
count on one of the next two cars stopping to see if you need
help, and maybe ninety percent of all vehicles thereafter. The
more remote the road, the higher the percentage of
Samaritans. That is, if you break down on a rural highway,
even on a state or county two-laner well removed from anything resembling a city, you will get stoppers offering
assistance but not nearly as many as if you are stranded on a

gravel or rock road in the middle of nowhere. It's like a constant and reliable road assistance insurance system and can be a real lifesaver.

So what could be the downside of something like that, you ask? Well, let's say you've been on the road for a few hours after a big breakfast. You had a couple glasses of juice, three cups of coffee, and downed a couple glasses of ice water to wash down everything, especially the salty bacon that was crisp, just the way you like it, so you had three rashers. You are on a back road and hit a series of washboard bumps that kind of shake the breakfast down, especially all the liquids, if you catch what I mean, and you need to make a rest stop posthaste. You look ahead as you top a hill, and check the rearview mirror: nothing for miles. You pull over, walk around to the passenger side of the pickup to get out of the wind, open your fly, and just get a start at a really important valve relief, and sure as billyhell, here comes a grain truck over the hill in the distance. You calculate it will pass by you just about the time you are in full release, but that's okay because he'll just drive right on by, right?

Wrong. He is going to slow down and stop to make sure you are okay and don't need help changing a tire or getting to town for a mechanic. And you're going to have to shout a brief explanation, and he's going to laugh and wave, and about that time here comes a woman with a car full of kids headed toward school from the other direction, and she'll worry that you're being sick, and so she'll stop to check, and all the kids will be looking out the window at you, and, well, you get the idea.

Wife Linda is an artist and likes to paint *plein air*, which is fancy talk for "outdoors." A woman sitting alongside the road with some sort of peculiar device that could possibly be a jack and what looks like tools scattered around her can attract more attention than you can imagine. I keep thinking drivers in rural America should have a system of flags like they do on ships to communicate what is going on. Maybe a red flag could mean that the driver needs aid, and a white one could convey that he is giving up and taking a nap. Blue might mean that everything is fine; he's just looking at the scenery. A red heart could mean that a couple is enjoying a bit of privacy on this rural road, if you catch my drift. And a bright yellow sign could mean, well, you know. Hopefully you'll never have to use the brown flag . . .

HIGHWAY HOWDIES AND PARALLEL PARKING

To my mind, one of the most charming customs of rural life here on the central Plains—I have no idea if this is the habit elsewhere—is the finger wave, the "highway howdy" or "farmer's salute." Whenever you meet someone on a road or highway out here in the middle of nowhere—and the more remote the road you are driving, the more likely this is to happen—the driver coming at you will raise a finger or two in greeting. If anonymity is, as I have suggested, the source of most evil in the New America then this small effort to acknowledge another human being you may or may not know but recognize as a fellow traveler is as grand and beneficent a blessing as I can imagine. My friend Izzy Bleckman was from Chicago when he first came out here and was mystified by this tradition. At first he thought the other drivers were signaling that something was wrong with our vehicle, in fact. But once I explained that no, these folks were just waving to us, expressing a greeting, he made one of the most profound and complimentary comments on the rural Plains that I have ever heard. He asked, "Rog, what kind of country is this anyway, where people wave at people they've never seen and may never see again?"

Iz, it's that kind of country. That's why I love it and that's why I live here. When I leave the main highway from Lincoln or Omaha and get on a two-laner well beyond the suburbs, one of the first things I do is move one hand from the eight or four position on the steering wheel and move it to the top so I can participate in one of the most positive activities I know and love about rural America: the finger wave.

If rural driving offers its share of surprises to anyone accustomed to urban habits and requires some learning, then rural and small-town parking is the stuff of graduate seminars. When they built the tiny post office on our Main Street a few years ago, that was very nice and everyone was quite proud of our new facility. But what really caught everyone's attention was something the official government specifications obviously call for but which is about as arcane as parking meters would be: lines painted in front of the new building to designate parking slots. The new building got its share of appreciative glances, but the population's most ardent attention focused on those four lines painted on the pavement of Main Street, the only pavement in the entire town other than the highway. What's even more remarkable: one of the slots is designated for handicapped parking! As my friend Eric said upon first seeing these incredible urban items transplanted to this utterly inappropriate context, "How are we going to decide who in this town is more handicapped than the next?"

On the west side of Main Street we have diagonal parking and on the east, parallel. I don't know why. Neither does anyone else, but that's what we have. It is almost an act of faith, maybe even pride, to park in such a way that a normal vehicle occupies at least enough room for two vehicles. A three-space occupation is a coup. You'd think that everyone parking parallel on the east side of the street would be pointed north, but no, that's an urban ideal. If I swing around the corner headed south but am going to the grocery store on the east side of the street I simply veer across Main Street—there is after all no centerline—and park facing the "wrong way." It's only a nicety because in front of me may be a parked tractor, with a trailer behind it, thus taking up four of the parking places, which truly is something of a feat when dealing with a situation of parallel parking. There may be a huge grain truck sitting just about anywhere, or a pickup pulling a stock trailer full of hogs stopped and left sitting smack in the middle of Main Street. I once cursed my luck not to have a camera when a friend pulled into town with his truck and trailer and parked while he had lunch at the tavern. He was hauling a windmill tower. Between his truck and the trailer carrying a 60-foot tower he used up every parking place on the entire east side of Main Street. I was green with envy.

Parking is a matter of simply pulling your vehicle in a place where you wish to leave it and turning off the key. There is no worry about there being a parking slot open. There is always a parking slot open, more often than not directly in front of wherever it is you are going. You may want to leave the key in the ignition of your vehicle in case someone needs to move it. That's understood to be polite protocol. On the other hand, you may want to exercise some caution in leaving your vehicle sitting around in a small town with the doors unlocked because there is every chance you'll return to find that someone has left a box of tomatoes, fresh green beans, or zucchini in the passenger seat while you were gone. Or maybe a brand spanking new hunting puppy. It's happened here. Early on in my own small-town experience I was warned about leaving my venerable, battered, rusted-out old pickup truck, Blue Thunder, sitting on Main Street with the keys in it; I was told I should always be sure to leave it with a full tank of gas so that if someone should be dumb enough to steal it, they wouldn't run out of fuel before going far enough to give me time to file a claim on my theft insurance. Good advice!

And sometimes you don't even have to pull your vehicle into a place where you wish to leave it. It is not at all unusual in a small town to turn into a street you wish to travel—most often the main street—and find two pickup trucks side by side, driver's window to driver's window, both rolled down, the drivers leaning out each vehicle and conversing. In a situation like this, one does not approach the two stopped trucks and honk or yell. You can see they are busy, right? And since you are already rolling, why don't you just swing around them. On either side. If necessary you can drive through the parking lanes, or even bump up onto the sidewalk. Or stop your own truck, turn it off, and stroll up to lean on the hood of one of the already-cooling vehicles and join the conversation, which may go on for an hour or more without a thought of pulling the vehicles into designated parking slots and exiting them. If you expect otherwise, you just don't know how things are done in the country, and whose fault is that?

I can't say much about how stoplights are dealt with in the rural countryside because we don't have one in this town.

Or, for that matter, in this county. Not one stoplight in the entire county. I know there is one about twenty-five miles south of here but other than that. . . . As I have noted, our land lies on a highway where it crosses a substantial river, Nebraska's Middle Loup River. A couple years ago the State Roads Department re-decked the bridge. They closed one lane and worked until they finished it, and then moved traffic over to the newly paved lane and worked on the other. At each end of the bridge they put up a stoplight and the lights controlled traffic on the one-way bridge during construction, which took over a year. During that time we took some pride here in town that for once we did actually have that urban frippery of a stoplight. The joke was that for the first few months, some of the smarter guys in town made a fortune betting the slower citizens which color the light was going to turn next.

For months before the construction began, machinery was brought in, supplies and equipment was stockpiled and organized, and the posts and signs were erected for the stoplights. That meant everyone knew what was coming, and as I said, there was some anticipation. At the precise moment announced, the one lane of the bridge was closed and the stoplight was switched on. So help me God, I am telling you the righteous truth: It was not two minutes before someone honked at whoever was in front of him for not starting off briskly enough when the light turned green. I wish I had been there to record the moment. The honker had to be a city puke.

RURAL LIFE AND THE MARRIED LIFE

It's hard to say what effect country living has on marriage. There are so many dynamics in the changing nature of marriage everywhere—of men and women for that matter— within every marriage as it grows or withers, laughs or cries, it's hard for me to determine what might be different for any particular union if it were in the country or not in the country. On one hand, I sense a new air of equity in the rural countryside, in that farming is so tough a business that women have to do the work of a man. It is not in the least bit unusual to see a woman in heavy coveralls doing any kind of farm work from scooping steaming manure with a tractor to wielding a prod and pushing cattle from one side of a pen to the other. I guess that's good. There seems, however, to be the same inequity in who does household work like cooking (at least in our household) and the far-too-common disjunction between men and their world, women and theirs (thank God, not in our household). I don't know what to do about that but I've tried to make my contribution (see *Everything I Know About Women I Learned from My Tractor* [Motorbooks, St. Paul, MN]). Divorce is as common here, I feel, as in the city, and probably deserved more than it occurs. There is a tragic lack of regard between married couples and frequent, public incivility, another reflection of growing American incivility to everyone. If the men I know around here just treated the women in their lives as well as they treat their vehicles, dogs, and buddies, life would be a lot easier for everyone. Well, I've dealt with those issues in other pages and I suspect that the problems of human relationships don't depend all that much on geography and don't vary all that much from the city to the country and back.

PETS AND OTHER LIVESTOCK

Maybe all mankind's problems are basically the same everywhere but with slightly different degrees and intensities.

When we lived in the city we had plenty of animal problems, for example. Our neighbor had cats. I'm not all that fond of cats anyway and these cats went a long way toward setting in cement my antagonism toward felines. They took special delight in killing not just birds, but songbirds: cardinals, goldfinches, wrens. And they didn't just kill and gut them but, as cats will do in an effort to make themselves even more obnoxious to their detractors, they deposited their victims on our doorstep so we could appreciate their particular skill in removing the good and beautiful from our lives while inflicting their own miserable wretchedness on the neighborhood.

I suppose they could have explored the joys of sex just about anywhere since they roamed the neighborhood at will day and night, but they took a particular fancy to the area immediately below our bedroom window, in the very narrow and resonant area between our house and another neighbor's, probably because it was for them all the world like singing in a shower, the howls and moans of their ecstasy echoing and re-echoing off the walls in rolling, irritating, infant-violin-lesson screams.

This neighbor's cats—I know they were her cats because I caught them occasionally *in flagrante poopicto*—chose of all the square blocks of area open to them, two places to bless with their disgusting eliminations: our daughter's sandbox and our garage floor, right in front of the area where I stacked firewood in the winter to keep it dry and clean and to put it in easy reach, where I could get to it without going out into the snow and cold, and where—oh yes—I could go in my stocking feet without having to put on shoes or boots. Socks—or bare feet—and soft, gooey, disgusting cat shit is a combination that brings this dog lover's blood to a full boil, believe me.

Finally, after a night full of these cats' ardor, on a day when I found a cardinal dead at our back door, the very evening I stepped out to get firewood in my best socks and stepped into a huge, gooey pile of feline stink, I snarled in full honesty to my wife Linda, a picture of gentility and compassion, "That does it! Tomorrow first chance I'm going to shoot those goddamn cats." She knew I meant it. Even discharging pellet guns in the city is illegal, I think, but I'd done it before and really don't care about the niceties of the law when it comes to situations like this. I had a good pellet gun in my office, looking out over the neighbor's yard and the lounging area of these cats when they were resting up from their previous night's debauchery and girding their loins to wreak havoc throughout the rest of the neighborhood with the arrival of this night's sundown. The neighbor was gone all day—which I suppose is why she turned responsibility for her miserable animals over to all the rest of us—and I figured all I had to do was lean out my office window the next day the first chance I had at a clean shot and make the world a better place.

Tears welled in Linda's eyes. Aw jeez, I could see it coming. "Just give me one chance to take care of this in a civilized way," she said softly. "I'll talk with Betty and I think we can clear this up without hurting the cats. Just give me a chance."

Okay. I'm not unreasonable. So, Linda wrote out a long, kind, understanding note about the problems we had been having with these cats and took it over to put on the lady's door to find when she got home that evening. We saw her car come into her drive. Heard the door slam. And not long thereafter, there was the expected knock at our door. It was this lady. She had Linda's note in her hand. Linda answered the door while I tried to look like I was reading the newspapers while actually listening in on the conversation. They talked a bit about the problem and then the lady said, "The thing is, it is not my cats you are having trouble with. First, they are the sweetest kitty-snookums you have ever seen and they would never ever *never* hurt a birdie. Second, they have their own stinky box on the back porch so they wouldn't need to do their duty anywhere else, and certainly not in your garage, which isn't even their property! But most of all, whatever happens under your windows by way of romance is definitely not *my* kitties because *my* kitties are brothers and sisters!"

That was the end of the conversation. The lady turned and left. Linda closed the door, turned to me, and quietly said, "Shoot the cats."

Well, rural life can be a lot like that too. I imagine that some of our problems are that we live on a river and at a bridge. That means that when loose livestock—cows, goats, horses, sheep—gets through a broken fence or open gate, it naturally comes down along the river and stops at the bridge, which is to say, our place. That's okay. A certain amount of that kind of thing is to be expected. It's the nature of rural living. And I want to be a good neighbor. And try to fit in. So when we wind up with a herd of five or six horses or cows racing up and down across our backyard tearing up the ground and bringing our dogs to a fevered snarl, or maybe hogs turning our neatly appointed garden into a total shambles, we simply try to identify the animals as best we can (not knowing a thing about horses or cows) and notify the sheriff's office so he can help us find the owners and deal with the problem.

But it's not as simple as that. While many—even most of the people we have dealt with in situations like this—quickly and without further damage do what they can to get their animals off our ground, some like the idea of free pasturage for their livestock for a couple days—or a couple weeks—and don't bother to round up their animals, or repair the fences, or shut the gates. Any one visit of stray animals in cases like this can drag out to weeks, and even worse, happen again and again and again. Then things get serious. One reason our sheriff may have trouble getting animals off our ground is that no one reports their livestock missing because they don't pay enough attention to their stock to even notice that it hasn't been around for a week or two.

The standard remedy for a situation like this is to round up the animals, impound them, feed and water them, and then charge the owner when he or she eventually comes around to pick them up. But newcomers to the rural areas are only rarely set up with holding pens or corrals, horses or vehicles to herd the strays, or ropes and feeding equipment. So then what? Well, you still want to report the problem to the sheriff so he or she can start to keep a file on the problem. If the situation is truly egregious and constant, then you need to contact a lawyer and have him or her contact the owner. Even that may not help but that's the appropriate route. If that doesn't work, then there are more drastic remedies that may not be legal but also may be the only things that work. I am not about to provide you with information that might get us both in trouble but let me leave you with two words in regard to neighbors who don't see any particular reason to keep their livestock off your land: Bon appetit!

As if the irresponsibility of not caring for livestock or pets weren't enough, there are people who violate all principles of humanity and neighborliness and dump animals. I can understand a dog or cat or certainly large livestock straying. If anything, we feel absolute agony when we wind up with a sad, lost, hungry, tired, cockle-burred dog at our gate begging for a drink and a friendly voice. They can count on shelter here. We feed them, water them, do what we can to make them comfortable and then put a major effort into finding the owner. As often as not, we know the owner is already out there looking for the lost pet (or, again, livestock) and we are likely to meet them on the road, yelling out a name like Blackie or Goldie, and we can quickly unite them with their lost friend.

But the fact remains, there are heartless, ugly criminals who bring puppies, kittens, even adult animals, even family pets they no longer want, and simply turn them loose in the rural countryside, dumping them in ditches or farmyards—often at bridges like ours for some reason—to starve, fend for themselves, maybe find a new home. I am not an enthusiast for the death penalty but people who behave like this bring me back to the reality that there are those human beings who simply do not deserve to live. (One rotten-to-the-core wretch left a tiny puppy freezing at our garage door one Christmas Eve. Fortunately, he did this at several homes in this area and was spotted. He was visited by some people like me, except a lot nicer apparently because they didn't beat him to death when they went to his home and confronted him with his disgusting subhuman behavior.)

The problem is worse than an inconvenience for us and a cruelty to the pets. Dogs and cats go feral, that is, revert to the wild. Then we have a real problem. Packs of wild dogs can be dangerous to game and human beings alike, especially the children who come down to our river to fish and swim.

Wild cats are, to my mind, even worse. They are devastating to wildlife and raise all kinds of hell with our own domestic pets. It's not a matter of taking these animals to the Humane Society so they can be reintroduced to homes as pets. They are feral. They are not nice animals. They are in fact ferocious, never acquiring the natural timidity of truly wild animals. There is no choice: feral animals have to be destroyed. And the truly tragic part is that they have to be destroyed by innocent guys like me while the really guilty parties continue to let their pets breed irresponsibly in the city, confident that what the hell, they can always dump the litters in rural ditches or farmyards. Every time I have to destroy a feral animal, in my heart I curse the person responsible and wish there were laws letting me shoot the truly guilty parties instead of these innocents.

FEATHERED FRIENDS

Some of the most interesting strays we have had wander through here were some peacocks. I have no idea where they came from; like guinea hens, peacocks are close to their wild origins and have a tendency to wander, so we never had a chance to corner and pen these or even find out where they came from in the first place. They came, and they left. But while they were here, they had an interesting impact, one I cannot convey in print on these pages. The next time you visit a zoo or exotics park, listen for the sound of a peacock. Now imagine that sound in the middle of the summer night through an open bedroom window. See?

I was once the generator of my own problems in a matter like this. We had a lot of burs in the yard and I had heard that geese or ducks are good for cleaning up that kind of thing. And I love ducks. Nothing is cuter than a duck. So my buddy Dan offered to take me to a nearby auction—the place, truly, where you buy things like geese, ducks, guineas, turkeys, goats, rabbits, small livestock—and guide me in buying what I need for our new place. Great. Nothing like local experts in matters where you know nothing at all. So, one Wednesday evening we headed down Ormsby Road to the weekly auction. We had a little time so Dan took me to a really neat little tavern in a small town right on the way and we had a few beers. And then a few more. We were in no hurry, Dan said. They would be auctioning off a lot of other stuff before they got to things like ducks, geese, goats, and rabbits. We had a couple more beers.

He was right. We got there in plenty of time. They were still auctioning off junk but eventually a box of baby ducks came up—Dan said that's what I needed, right there—for fifty cents apiece. He prodded me into raising my hand to bid. Another guy bid once, I bid again, and then I was declared the winning bidder. Wow. I couldn't believe my good luck! Just like that, I had my ducks.

As I went to the front area and picked up my box of baby ducks, the auctioneer leaned over and said, "I have another box here. You want them at the same price?" What could I say? Wow, if the first buy was a good deal, wouldn't the second chance be a bonus? "Sure," I said. "Put me down for that box too."

I couldn't believe how well things were turning out. Then the auctioneer held up a box of Pekins. "What are Pekins?" I asked Dan. He said, "Man, I wish I had seen that they had some Pekins. They are truly fine ducks, much bigger than regular ducks. Actually, they are what you should have gotten. Maybe you ought to bid on them. . . ."

So I did. And again I won. And I bought a second box at the same price. And I picked up some geese at a really good price too. Quite a few geese in fact. By the time we were headed back home and stopped at the same neat little town tavern to talk about our triumph at the auction, I had 120 birds peeping in the back of my pickup truck. And the reality of what we had done was dawning over me. Linda didn't talk to me for a week, and that was fine with me because what I said to myself was enough punishment. Briefly, duck poop everywhere. If I had trouble with a couple cats, now I had inflicted on myself a constant decoration of our porch and patio with great gooey gobs of goose and duck poop.

Moreover, I didn't understand that ducks don't go into a coop to roost at night and sleep quietly until the breakfast bell rings. As it turned out, all 120 ducks and geese preferred most of all sleeping right under our bedroom window, again making me eat my words about our previous neighbor's cats and reciting an hourly litany of excuses to Linda. And, for that matter, to curse my own gullibility and vices. Eventually foxes, coyotes, chicken hawks, and bald eagles relieved us of our duck problems and we got a considerably more moderate portion of chickens instead to help us with a grasshopper problem. Grasshoppers ate into the ground everything we owned except the mortgage. Our friend Claudia told us we needed a biddy hen with her chicks and that would do it. And it did. Before long grasshoppers became an endangered species around here and those few chickens were having to travel well outside the yard to find the occasional, stray grasshopper.

Chickens roost at night, so they retreated to their house, and even though the roosters crowed in the early—*early!*—

morning, they were inside their own house and the faint call was darn near inspiration to us in our bedroom on the other side of the house. I loved our chickens. I loved the brilliant yoke of their free-run eggs. I loved the ferocity of the hens' protectiveness of their eggs and chicks. I loved seeing them constantly at work cleaning our yard. It was a curious cycle I never figured out: chickens ate all the dog poop—dogs ate all the chicken poop. So there was never any poop in our yard! So where did all that poop eventually go? Isn't there some law of physics that says no poop is ever really lost or gained in this universe? I simply dismissed it all as one of the mysteries of God.

The tough part of the Chicken Era at Primrose Farm was that the burden of keeping, as usual, fell to Linda. She was the one who hauled water out to them in blizzards and turned on the heating lamps when I was gone. She waded through spring's muck and mud to be sure they had food, and when I was gone, she collected and cleaned the eggs. I never lamented the departure of the ducks but damn, I do some-times, quite often, actually, miss those chickens. Again it was our neighbors the predators that finished off our poultry problems, and to some degree I understand that. I watched a bald eagle carry off a prized fat orange hen with feathery legs and while I felt very bad for her, I thought that when my time comes, I can only hope that I have the good fortune to be carried off in just that way by eagles.

There's no explaining people's taste in animals. My friends Dick and Deb wrote me the other day that they had been to the local Humane Society to find a dog—the perfect and only thing to do—and learned that nothing is harder to place than a black dog. On the other hand, I can't imagine having a higher priority than a black dog. We had a golden retriever, and Linda loved her more than anything, and I did adore her, but given a choice, well. . . . That goes for rural life too. Don't judge other people's spouses and don't comment on their pets. I think of the time I was going into the back door of the grocery store and passed Kerry's little dog in its pen. I said something civil to the dog and it may have growled or something, I don't know, but jeez, it's a little dog, so I went about my business.

And so did the dog. It grabbed my leg, tore open my shin, ripped my overall leg to shreds, and generally went into a feeding frenzy that would do credit to a piranha. I made a major detour around the building, avoiding the back door and that miserable cur altogether this time, and marched up to Kerry at the counter. "Your goddamn dog just about tore my leg off!" I sputtered. "Look at this! He tore the entire leg off my overalls, and I was just standing there! There's blood everywhere. I hope to God that miserable goddamn dog has his shots up to date! How do I know he hasn't given me rabies?"

Now, I love Kerry. He's a great guy, a really good man. I don't know what I expected. Maybe an apology? I don't know. I didn't expect an offer to replace my overalls or take me to the emergency ward. Nor did I expect what I got. Kerry said, "Oh, I think you'll be all right. That damn dog of mine has bitten six or eight other people already this month and none of them got sick, so I don't imagine you'll have any problems." And I didn't.

Once again, rural logic prevailed.

Chapter 7

THE VERY NATURE OF RURAL LIVING —

Rural Living Is Close to Nature

THE PEACE AND QUIET OF IT

The most common comment we get when we talk about where we live at the edge of the Nebraska Sandhills, on the banks of the clean, beautiful Middle Loup River, not far from the quaint Danish village of Dannebrog, on a tree farm, no neighbor nearer than a quarter mile, twenty-five miles from a town of any size, on a highway that goes nowhere but here, in a county without a stoplight or a single industry, among the cornfields and pastures of native grass is "My, how wonderfully quiet that must be!"

Well, no. That would be wrong. Actually, it's very noisy in a context like this, or for that matter any rural context. It may be peaceful, but it's rarely quiet. There are still the sounds of humanity: a railroad ten miles south of us can be clearly heard most days and especially most nights, not only the whistle as it crosses side roads but the rumble of its wheels on the rails. In the summer we hear kids swimming — which is to say, yelling — down at the bridge. When someone is banging on a reluctant hitch or bolt up at the co-op in town we can hear that. We hear the fire siren from town when the wind is from the north. A neighbor a half mile away has an external ringer on his telephone and once or twice a day we might hear that.

While those sounds are not really disturbing, they are certainly not on a level of urban idiots who have converted their cars into loudspeakers with the specific intention of annoying others, or drunks yelling in the streets, or as was once the case with my son's home in St Paul, Minnesota, the casual and constant report of street guns fired in anger or amusement.

Nor are those the loudest or most persistent sounds we hear in our rural home. Here it's the sounds of nature that fill our ears. Now, I understand that this may not be a universal reaction, but I have yet to hear one sound of nature so distressing or annoying that it doesn't give me pleasure. I guess I am a bit uneasy when a ferocious storm gathers and the weather warning radio tells us we are in for some rough times: wind, hail, hard rain, and maybe even a tornado. But even that doesn't bother me as much as the deliberately inconsiderate noisemaking of my fellow human beings. Even when packs of wild dogs—my beloved coyotes—come howling through here, not a hundred feet from the house, singing their insane baroque choruses, I may sit up startled in bed with the hair on the back of my neck standing at attention, but then I smile and lie back down, grinning like an idiot. Because I love the notion of there being wild dogs still running free in this country, and that they survive despite the evil and stupid warfare conducted against them. They give hope to me for my kind, and I love their wild song. God bless those free creatures and may they outlast the half-wits who would destroy them!

In fact, I absolutely glowed for a couple years with the knowledge that we had a mountain lion living in a transient sort of way in our river bottoms. We saw signs of her—a dismantled deer not ten steps behind Linda's art studio—and some of our neighbors spotted her now and then (although we sadly never did before a grinning ass with a badge in a nearby town shot her because "she got belligerent when he had her cornered"). But there was one night. . . . We were in bed reading when our big cat neighbor screamed her magic howl. I still get goose bumps thinking of it. But part of the impression was Linda, whose idea of a ferocious explosion of violent language is when, after one of the dogs once jumped up unexpectedly and split her lip, she sputtered, "You . . . you . . . you *idiot head!*" Never having heard her use language like that, we all hid under the porch for two days until she lured us out with a pork roast. Anyway, the night the lion howled, she sat straight up in bed and sputtered, "*What the &@#$ was that?*" Absolutely no other or lesser language would have been appropriate for the occasion. A ninety-year-old nun would have said the same thing. But one could never call even the sound of a lion's roar from the woods on one's own land annoying. It was, if anything at all, a thrill of a lifetime. Far worse are the sounds of guns as the various hunting seasons open: pheasants, ducks, geese, deer, possums, coons; I understand populations controls are necessary (but then why not for human beings, one must wonder?) and I am a meat eater, but in all honesty, most hunting is a matter of killing for fun, and that perversion is not exactly man's noblest side.

FOR THE BIRDS

Probably the most common sounds here are birds. As I write this the geese are headed north and in our yard you can hardly hear yourself think sometimes for the gigantic Vs of geese gaining altitude from the feeding grounds on the Platte River twenty-five miles south of here, and catching the thermals and high altitude winds for a ride north to the breeding grounds. Shortly after the geese finish their departure, about the middle or end of March, we will begin to hear the brrrrrring of millions of sandhill cranes headed north.

And before long the other birds will come back. To some of you this will really seem dumb but on the other hand I remember astonishing some young people in a university class by calling their attention to the fact that not only does the sun come up in the east every morning it also moves slowly from one extreme to another, never taking the same path each day. They'd never noticed, so maybe you haven't noticed something I missed in all my years in the city. My pal, Dan, came by one day while I was doing something on some machinery, as I recall. "Listen," he said. I listened. "I don't hear anything," I said. He nodded knowingly. "The birds are gone."

Well, I'll be damned. All at once the birds *were* gone. I knew that the mourning doves, robins, all the others do migrate, but I guess I figured they all just kind of trickled off one or two at a time. Nope, Dan informed me, they all just pack up and one day leave, just like that. From that point on I've tried to keep track, and to my astonishment, that's just the way it works. Right now the birds are gone. There are some cardinals, downy woodpeckers, flickers, sparrows, chickadees, blue jays, crows, but there is nothing like the cacophony that will shortly arrive all on one morning when the birds come back. And then suddenly it will all be the way it was last fall before they left, impossible to sleep in the morning, impossible to hear yourself think when they are in full tweet. (Where did robins get their reputation for gentle song, anyway? Is there another winged squawker half as annoying as the robin?) How could I have missed this obvious transition for so long in my life? Same way some people never notice that the sun comes up in the east, I guess.

It's gotten to the point where I miss my brown thrasher when he leaves in the fall and I am genuinely amused when he comes back. It took me a long time and some fancy binocular work to figure out who the heck that was who made such wonderfully peculiar, even comical calls first thing in the morning, repeating everything twice, but never saying any doublet more than once: "Cincinnati Cincinnati!" "Pistol pistol!" "Freebies freebies!" "Birds! Birds!" I wish I could sleep an extra half hour maybe instead of putting up with this nutty chatterbox waking me at dawn with his prattle, but like the song of the coyotes, the brown thrasher's manic recital is just so damned amusing, I can't react except with a smile.

Nor are all our avian guests as cute and cuddly as the wren who nests at the door of my shop every blasted year and scolds me every time I have to go in there for a tool. Birds can get pretty big in the country. Huge wild turkeys strut and parade at the end of our backyard fence and cow our dogs into retreating to their kennels. Eagles circle overhead eyeing our cats. Hawks scan the bottom ground for mice and voles; kestrels, small but ferocious, pick off sparrows who think they're safe in the lilac bush; turkey vultures circle over something down there in the river bottoms and I'm not sure I want to know what it is.

BIGGER GAME

To some degree this is a matter of there being more nature in
the country, or less human imposition on it. But nature is
also more obvious, more intrusive, less avoidable out here.
It's not simply that nature may come to you but that you
have by coming into the country also come into nature. I have
always been something of a nature enthusiast—that's one of
the reasons I came out here, after all—but there have
nonetheless been plenty of surprises. I can imagine that,
depending on your own inclinations, they might be delights
or horrors. Moreover, I imagine we might be subject to even
more of a variety and density of critters here along the river
than might happen elsewhere. We have deer passing within
feet of our back door every evening, and that is a wonderfully beautiful sight. A few weeks ago Daughter Antonia was
visiting from school and needed to run out to the yard to
grab something from her car . . . and ran smack into a huge
skunk. Skunks are gentle creatures; they really don't want
any trouble. Moreover, I think they are very handsome. But
they do have this problem, you know, and even worse, they
are notorious for being rabid in this area, so there are at least
two reasons you don't want your dogs to mix it up with a
skunk. (We have found that when a skunk takes up residence
somewhere close to you, the conflict can be solved with
mothballs. For a while we had a skunk living under the floor
of our outhouse; he would peek out whenever I visited what
he had come to think of as his house and while we never had
any disagreements, I was not comfortable with the double
occupancy arrangements. We threw some mothballs down
the large hole in the privy and in no time at all, the skunk
moved on. Now think about the wonder of that: he lived

under our outhouse but he moved because he couldn't deal with the smell!)

Coons and possums are a constant problem for us in this particular location, a possible function of being so close to the river and the woods. There is always a problem with raccoons being rabid and therefore a threat to pets and we have had at least one rabid raccoon come inside the yard fence and confront our dogs. Fortunately we were here and could handle the problem quickly without any harm being done. (Which reminds me, somewhere below I should tell you about the necessity of firearms in the rural home.)

We set up a live trap whenever we get hints that we are having visits from unwanted company: disturbed pets, torn garbage bags, destruction to pet food containers, tracks in the snow or mud, even visual sightings. When we find an animal in our trap, we move it to a nearby wildlife habitat area and wish it well when we release it. So far I have not had the bad fortune of live-trapping a skunk. I don't even have a plan for that contingency.

Our worst experience happened one time when I was out of town and called home about seven in the morning just to check in. Linda said she was fine, now that she was back from the hospital emergency ward. "What? Hospital emergency ward? What's going on there?" Linda said that in the middle of the night she had heard a ruckus out in the garage and finally it got wild and loud enough to get the dogs barking, so she finally went out to check. Sure enough, there was a big raccoon in the live trap in the garage. So far that was still okay; I'd be home in a few hours and could take the animal to the refuge area and turn it loose then. But in its struggle to escape, it had grabbed some fishing line and pulled it into the trap. In order to avoid an even worse mess, Linda took a small stick and reached into the trap to pull the line out. The raccoon had been quiet and frightened but as Linda's hand approached, the animal hissed loudly and slammed itself against the front of the trap at Linda's hand. Linda yanked back, noticing a stinging pain in one finger as she recoiled. She looked down, and couldn't believe what she saw; a shiny new hook complete with a plastic worm lure driven all the way through her finger.

Oh man. She managed to get into the house—thank goodness she had taken the time to get out of her pajamas and into some work clothes before venturing out in the night to the garage—and called our friends the Halseys up in town. Even though it was the middle of the night, they came running, as small town neighbors will do, and while Mel took care of the raccoon, Sue got Linda ready to go to the emergency ward. There the barb was cut off the hook, the hook was removed, and the wound was disinfected. And all that was before breakfast. . . . To this day Linda cannot even stand the idea of raccoons much less the sight of them, no matter how cute the rest of us might think the little bandits are.

CREEPY CRAWLERS

We have a lot of toads and frogs here—again, we are near a river, so that's to be expected—and we just ignore them, knowing they are important for insect control not to mention that we have come to love the songs of the frogs in the ponds and sloughs just over the bank at the end of our yard.

Linda and I have a deeper disagreement about snakes. I appreciate snakes because I know they are valuable in controlling other, worse pests around here like moles, mice, and voles. Besides, while we have the occasional large (but totally harmless) bull snake, most of the reptiles here are quite small—grass snakes, garter snakes, cute little rascals, with no greater intention than to put as much distance as possible between themselves and you. I even appreciate the bluster of the big bull snake, hissing, coiling, threatening, but all bluff.

My favorite snakes here at our place are hog-nose puff adders, again totally harmless little snakes, but to my mind hilariously amusing. They eat toads and are as secretive as all other snakes but when cornered the hog nose puts on a particularly handsome display, and one I never tire of. First it shows how tough it is, hissing, faking a strike, puffing out its neck for all the world like the dreaded cobra. If you stand your ground, the hognose thinks over its options and tries another approach; it declares (despite what you already should have noted) that it is dead. It rolls over on its back and acts for all the world as if it has gone to snake heaven. If you roll it back on its tummy, it quickly rolls back over, as if saying, "No, no, really, I *am* dead." Finally, if you insist on picking up this little creature that has done its best to convince you it is 1) dangerous and 2) dead, it uses its last weapon—it pees on you. Which then gives me the chance to use one of my favorite gag lines: "A little piss of asp never hurt anyone." I know, I know, Linda doesn't think it's funny either.

The worst single animal invader we have in our rural home is the mouse. Especially the field mouse, which is just as dirty, undesirable, and destructive as its city cousin but which is infinitely cuter, being brown and cuddly like a hamster. We live-trapped mice for many years but it quickly became obvious that that was an endless task with questionable results. As fall approaches and cold weather suggests to mice that it might be a good time to move into warmer quarters, the task of thwarting the annual mouse invasion becomes a full-time job. I would not suggest poisoning mice in the house because when they die in the walls of a house, the memory lingers on, if you catch my drift. We have had to resort to old-fashioned wood-base spring traps and simply check them every day and throw out the sad corpses. It isn't easy but one of the things you most definitely will find when you live in the country is that being closer to nature means you are going to be closer to death.

And there are bugs. More bugs than in the city? I think so. Right now as spring approaches and the house warms up, we start finding ladybugs everywhere, and box elder bugs. I don't know where they've been all winter—tucked into some cold corner, I'd guess. At least they are harmless. In the fall there are flies, desperate to get into the warm house as they sense the cold of winter approaching. We deal with them with flypaper and swatters. In the autumn we also get crickets, and I know they too can be destructive, but I so enjoy their song that we grant them clemency in our household and let them share the house until they outlive their expectancy and are gone until the next year. I have no idea how they get in but we have a continuing problem with cupboard moths, which we control with sticky papers with hormone lures. Again, while the problem is persistent, the solution seems to make the situation short term and tolerable. I told you how to solve your grasshopper problems: a biddy hen with a clutch of chicks.

OVERDOING IT

There can also be way too much of a good thing: deer are beautiful creatures and a joy to see scampering around the backyard, the song of the coyote is glorious on a night when a full moon is on a new snow, a kit fox is a beautiful thing to see, a soaring eagle is a downright honor, and then there are those cute little raccoons. Until you try to keep some chickens and see that same fox or coyote carry off your favorite hen, or the raccoons move in and clean you out the day before you were going to pick that sweet corn in the garden, or you plant a hundred new trees and the next morning the deer have clipped them all off at the ground. Sure, that kind of disappointment hurts, but I still feel there are ways around it. I am hoping that that biddy hen, a dozen ears of corn, or the trees are not the only thing between you and starvation or losing the farm. You can find ways to deal with the problems. Ask around, find some alternative solutions, hang some bars of motel soap on the trees; that'll keep the deer away. Put a fence around the chickens and make sure they are all in the coop and the door is closed when you close down for the night.

I was once told by an old-timer that he'd heard that as sweet corn ripens if you put newspapers on the ground in your garden and keep a radio turned on loud you can keep the raccoons away and enjoy the stuff yourself. But then he shook his head sadly and said that when he tried it, he came out the next morning to find three raccoons reading the newspapers, listening to Paul Harvey on the radio, and eating sweet corn.

My own feeling is that a certain amount of loss is part of the game. Hearing the coyotes is worth losing an occasional chicken. If the raccoons get too bad, I can always get sweet corn dirt cheap over at the St. Libory produce stands. And next year I'll just plant a couple extra trees. When ranchers around here complain that they need to start a war against coyotes because of calf losses, when they see a coyote eating at a still-born calf or cleaning up an afterbirth, the first thing they do is reach for a rifle. I wonder if they are in the right line of work if the difference between them making it or going broke is the possible (but not probable) loss of one calf, when the outlay for the gun and ammunition and the loss of work time to go hunting for that coyote constitutes their real bottom line loss. What is going on when a rancher lays out huge amounts of poison to kill off a prairie dog town on the grounds that aren't covered with enough grass for his cows anyway? Millions of bison and millions of prairie dogs coexisted on this same ground two hundred years ago, so why is there now not enough grass for fifty cows and fifty prairie dogs on the same acres? Research still shows that where prairie dogs prosper, grazers prosper, and ranchers who kill off their prairie dogs are at the same time killing off their own profits. Sometimes conquering nature isn't quite as profitable or pleasant as living comfortably with nature.

A problem for both our pets and us has been the disgusting spring hazard of ticks, once only an annoyance but now with Lyme disease a life-threatening emergency. Again, our proximity to the river and woods makes the tick a worse problem for us than for others, perhaps, but by keeping our dogs well medicated with tick-resisting medicines, checking ourselves carefully, avoiding entering the woods when ticks are particularly bad (especially during a wet April, precisely the time when we should be down along the river every day looking for morel mushrooms), and wearing light-colored clothes, caps, and tight cuffs we can at least reduce our exposure.

I GOT RHYTHMS

Have you noticed a hidden theme here as I've skipped over
the joys and miseries of living so close to nature? There is a
constant theme of the rhythms of life throughout the year.
Even when it's a matter of dealing with the less pleasant
aspects of rural life—ticks, snakes, grasshoppers—there is a
certain pleasure in working with the cycles and patterns of
nature's year. That is in fact a constant and comforting part
of rural life, and one I take great pleasure in. It's not just animals in nature, but the sky, the weather, and the plants, wild
as well as domestic. If you are like me, you will be amazed to
find that the nasty dandelion you so hated in your suburban
lawn is really quite a rare and handsome flower in the rural
countryside, and very welcome to my eye. It is a delight to
find that bright yellow blossom defying the approach of winter by blooming late into December, long after all other
colors have faded, and then springing back up as early as
late February, ready to go for yet another year. You will come
to appreciate and welcome the wild lilies of the valley down
by the river, and the true signs of summer in wild plum,
chokecherry, and elderberry blossoms. You'll note where the
frilly bright yellow fronds of wild asparagus are in the
autumn so you can check in on them again the next April.
You will learn to watch the cycles of plants like you never
have before because they are another kind of calendar, one
reflecting the stages of this particular year in this particular
place rather than an abstract passage of sunrises as pat-
terned millenniums ago by a Roman emperor.

In fact, it's an even more dramatic set of observations
than that. And again I would urge you to keep a journal for
your farm to keep track of the enormity of the movements

and cycles sweeping around and over you. Talk with a naturist and you will be amazed: in this area, armadillos are moving north, mountain lions are moving south and east, wolves are coming south, howling mice (my favorite! Onychomys luecogaster) are on the move. I sense that the tiny lizards that scampered across the sands in my barren uplands have disappeared or are, at any rate, far less common. Last year we had crowds of eagles—this year not a single one. One year we saw red foxes at almost every turn.

The same is true of plant life. One year the lovely blue of spiderwort inundates us, and this past year the bottom ground was infested with woolly mullein. You will be amazed and hopefully amused by the variety and dynamic nature of nature now that you are closer to it. You will find changes that can be detected from hour to hour during the day—some wildflowers are seen only in the morning hours, some only in the evening. Coyotes never howl during the day—until this past week when for some reason a pack not far from us took to singing at the sun instead of just the moon. Some days you can smell the wet ground of the woods at the river, or a feedlot somewhere well out of sight. A skunk apparently confronts a dog or coyote perhaps as much as a couple miles away, the odorous results wafting past your nose as you sleep much later that night. You will find new excitement in the signs of the seasons, because now you see them, note them, and perhaps even understand them. (Curiously, on the very day I am writing this, I awoke to find that the birds have returned for the year. I'm going to take some time this afternoon to sit in the March sun on our patio and just listen to the cacophony of conversation all the new arrivals are having discussing the best places to build nests for the summer. What an incredible joy!)

In all honesty, I'll have to admit that this proximity—
make that intimacy—with nature has its share of downsides
too. We are in the middle of a ten-year drought and every
year we watch the sky with an intensity we never felt in the
city where every foot of our small house lot was within easy
reach of a garden hose. And when it does rain, because we
are on the central Plains where there is no such thing as
meteorological moderation we watch the sky for signs of tornados, hail, and straight-line winds that easily rival Florida
hurricanes. One June day here it rained nine inches in two
hours. Oak Creek saved time by skipping the big loop around
town and ran right straight down Main Street. Our bottomlands were flooded but we had no real damage. I can tell you
this for darn sure, however—the river we thought we knew so
well sure did change. To our amazement, side channels where
water had always stood or run for a decade were suddenly
dry. It's not that the river was any more shallow but that it
was lower, that is, the bottom of the river had been scoured
and it had dropped—the entire river—a good foot, maybe
two. I had no idea such things happened, but there it was,
right in front of me. And then it didn't rain again until
September. Our state newspaper declared that our area had
had a wet summer—nine inches. Rained once . . . wet summer.
. . . Of course that newspaper is in what passes for a city in
Nebraska so what the hell do they know about weather? That
was the judgment of everyone around here anyway. On the
other hand I remember once after a very long dry spell when
it finally rained and since I was new to rural living but was
catching on to the importance of weather, I went up town to
the tavern to see how everyone was receiving the bounty of
this desperately needed rain. The tavern was full, partially

because it was full of farmers who couldn't get into the fields because of the rain but also because the tavern owner was serving up free beer. He was celebrating too, after all.

WEATHER OR NOT

It was probably in my first year or two here that I walked into the Chew 'n' Chat Café one morning after a rain and was asked the standard question, "How much rain did you get at your place?" I apparently still had a few things to learn because 1) I answered with an amount but I have since figured out that you always answer that question with your own question, "How much did you get over at *your* place?" because the first liar is always at a disadvantage; and 2) I made a total fool of myself by saying "About a third of an inch." And everyone in the café exploded in disbelieving laughter. Eric was the first to regain control of himself and between laughs said, "You idiot city puke! Rain doesn't come in *thirds*! It comes in *hundredths*! You didn't have a third of an inch. You had thirty hundredths!" Rain is too important in agricultural life, whether plenty or spare, to measure in such broad terms as thirds. Out here rain comes in hundredths.

Part of the preoccupation with weather in the rural countryside may well be that you can see it coming from farther away than you can in the city. From our house we can see weather in Kansas and South Dakota and a good hundred miles to the east. On the other hand, there is a big hill to our west, and we have to keep our eye in that direction because that's the direction from which a lot of our weather comes and it can come in mighty fast over that hill. We were once standing in our kitchen with our coats on getting ready to bid farewell to our overnight guests John and Annie, looking out our windows on a bright, sunny winter day, and with absolutely no warning, we couldn't see ten feet. We had been instantly engulfed in a dense snow squall that had crept up from over the hill and behind the house. It was obvious that no one was going anywhere on this day. We took off our coats, threw another log onto the fire, and settled down for what promised to be a long and maybe even dangerous day. And then suddenly a half hour later the squall swept past and we could see it disappearing at incredible speed toward the southeast. And it was clear again. John and Annie put on their coats and left before the Plains dealt us another hand—maybe a dust storm.

And dust storms there are. And dust devils. Hail storms, sleet and ice, wind, lightning. . . . Weather takes on a whole new intensity when there is not a neighbor's house feet away to take some of the force of it, or when you know that without power lines you have no heat or light, refrigeration or television. You quickly learn that a cell phone may not be just a convenience but a necessity when your telephone wire lines are at the mercy of wind and lightning.

If you live in a region where there are seasons (I think of my friend Walt who lives in the seasonless horrors of Hawaii), you will come to appreciate as deeply the rhythms of the year as you do the changes in days and hours. Sometimes even these larger events that you would think would move more slowly are stunning in their drama. I came here one weekend before I moved here permanently and was surprised to find that the river was bank-to-bank water. Hmmmm. I had been out here just four days earlier and the river was solid ice. Was it really possible that all that ice had gone out and down the river that quickly, and without leaving a single block of ice on a sandbar or bank? Something didn't seem right about this.

Up in town I saw Big Don walking along the main street of town toward his machine shop so I stopped and talked with him a bit, remarking, "It sure is amazing how fast all that ice went out, huh?" His face became very serious as he said, "Rog, the ice didn't go out. The river is running on top of the ice and when it does go out, it's not going to be pretty." Rain and snow melt had coincided so rapidly that the ice was still thick and solid where it had been all winter, but now two to three feet of water were indeed running on top of the ice, meaning that once things started breaking loose, there would be a ferocious rush of gigantic blocks of heavy ice downstream, smashing everything in its path. That's exactly what happened. I spent the day slack-jawed and glassy-eyed watching the brutal force and violence of this gentle river I thought I knew. The huge blocks of ice slammed against the highway bridge, making it shudder so sickeningly that people who had been standing on it to watch the drama eased their way back to the safe and solid approach, a bit green at the gills. I sat on the bank watching blocks jam into sandbars and then with the force of a roaring river behind them rise up twenty feet in the air and slam back down onto the running water. It was simultaneously terrifying and fascinating. Huge cottonwood trees were sheared off as if by a gigantic ax when the blocks came onto shore with the floodwaters and ran full force into the river woods. The spring thaw hasn't put running water on top of the ice again in the intervening twenty years but I never take my eye off the river when the thaw begins because when it happens again, I want to be there to remember again that Mother Nature can be sweet and gentle, but on the other hand. . . .

Chapter 8

THE SOCIAL LIFE:

Fitting In, Staying Out, Understanding, and Surviving

NOTHING HAPPENING

One of the most persistent—and erroneous—stereotypes of rural life is that there is nothing going
on, certainly nothing on the level of the social life
of the city. Well, think again. You will be absolutely astonished at the constant flurry of social activity roiling the
rural waters. Where you have one or two things a week
happening in the city, you have five or ten in farm country.
There's no way to keep up with the social whirl in a small
town. Okay, it's not exactly dinner at Spago with Wolfgang
or a dozen parties after the Oscars, but it is graduation
parties, a fish fry at the American Legion Club, Booster
Club meeting at the town hall, farm auction over where
the Jacobsens used to live before the Allerheiligens came
to town, a performance of *Arsenic and Old Lace* at the
school, a pitch tourney at the tavern, the town-wide yard
sale, and the junior wrestling meet down in Grand Island.
All in one evening. All you can do is pick and choose and
hope you can avoid hurting anyone's (or everyone's) feelings. And God help you if you are a parent: you will be

expected to have your kid(s) at six different places simultaneously, sometimes thirty miles apart.

I've already said it but here again part of the complication is that there is not a lot of exclusivity in small-town life as a result of a caste system. No, not everyone is going to be invited to the Baptist Church's policy meetings, nor will everyone be invited to the fanciest parties at the home of those who aspire to what social status there is, nor for that matter are those who aspire to social status likely to get an engraved invitation to the weekly poker game in Myron's basement, but whatever gatherings you do wind up at, you are sure to find a broader mix of economic, political, and social ranges than you might find in the city.

In *It's Not the End of the Earth But You Can See It from Here* (University of Nebraska Press, Lincoln) I wrote true stories (although it is labeled fiction to protect the guilty) about life in my little town of Dannebrog, which I also tried to protect by giving it the pseudonym "Centralia." It was no time at all before I was getting letters from all over America, from coast to coast, saying "Hey, I figured out what town you are writing about in that book because that's the town where I grew up, in [fill in appropriate state: Pennsylvania, Florida, Texas, Minnesota, Idaho, California, Kansas, etc.]." The point is, the events that I have witnessed in my little town are typical of what happens in not only many little towns but probably in almost every little town. What's more, the cast of characters I have grown to know and love here is the same cast that everyone who has his own little town is likely to have encountered, to wit, viz.:

GOOD GUYS

On the *positive influences* side of the social ledger are:

The Sparkplug: I start off with this character because he or she is the most important element of any town that is a going concern. The Sparkplug is a tireless worker, but importantly is not at all aware of what a pain in the rear he or she is, constantly on the make to shanghai everyone else in town to work, be on a committee, or donate to a worthy cause. Without this person a town is in trouble; with him or her you have a chance. I understand your frustration and efforts to hide when you see this one coming down the sidewalk—actually, marching down the sidewalk—but be darn happy you have him or her.

Mechanic/Handyman: The richest people in town may think they're important but everyone knows that the mechanic or handyman—usually not at all rich because he does most of his work for nothing—is worth ten riches. The Handyman is not simply a carpenter or plumber or electrician or town records keeper, but all of those things. It is also important that this actor in small town drama is always self-taught, so the knowledge he has is all the more esoteric because you don't find it in books. He just knows all this stuff. When you have a mechanical problem, you just go to this guy. It doesn't matter that it seems unlikely that he would know anything about a vacuum sweeper or deep-sea fishing reel—he'll fix it. He's not a vacuum sweeper repairman or fishing reel expert—he's a fixer.

The Good Guy: When you have a raffle or auction sale, when you need someone trustworthy to take tickets at the town rodeo, this is the person everyone knows will be tagged for the job. Like The Mechanic, he is not likely to be rich, being honest after all, nor religious, being decent after all. He may not even be considered reputable by the elitists and proper folks in town, but even they can't deny it—he can be trusted and is always ready to help where he is needed, not only where there is no profit to be made but even where he is likely to wind up covering his own expenses.

Bartender: The Bartender may be doing double duty as the town's good guy or ne'er-do-well, or even both. It's possible. But a good bartender is the closest thing most small towns have to a therapist and provides an alternative to those who don't trust, often with good reason, the small-town preacher. The Bartender may be philosophically or even religiously oriented but what's important is that he is also likely to be practical and tolerant of human failings and flaws.

Historian: Trained historians seem to have a rule that they aren't really serious scholars unless they are also boring, which is strange because history is without question one of the most fascinating studies there is. You really have to work at it to make history dull, so I suppose you have to respect and salute those who manage to make that leap. But the town historian puts the stress on the "-story" part of the word "history." While eyes may glaze over when the Bible-like genealogical recitations begin, nothing is more fascinating than sitting down over a cup of coffee or glass of beer with the town historian and hearing stories about the fight between Big Hans and Slow Lars that started in front of the tavern, ranged south all the way to the cemetery, worked its way back up Main Street again to the tavern, and ended up when both exhausted warriors decided to take a break for a beer and along the way forgot why they were mad at each other in the first place; or what dances used to be like over at Pleasure Isle; or the time someone spiked the watermelons at the Baptist Church's spring picnic.

Cook: In my little town we are fortunate in that our town cook—the competition is fierce, as you can imagine, and pride runs high—is a public commodity. Ten years ago or so she bought a small house right on the main square (our town is so small there are only three sides to the town square) and converted it into a restaurant. The main entry room seats sixteen at three tables—you just sit with whoever is already there—and the back room, another ten for overflow. You get your own coffee. There are no bills; you just step back into the kitchen to pay. If you get there too early, you may even have to reach in and flick up the chain so you can get in and get the coffee started. And the food is sublime. And plentiful. The only problem with Harriett's food is that six days later you're hungry again.

Wit/Idler/Clown: Don't confuse this character with your usual U.S. Bureau of Standards Ne'er-Do-Well, another category altogether. Some of the righteous insist the town clown is indeed a ne'er-do-well because he makes people laugh, and that can't be a productive use of energy, but like King Lear's fool, the clown is wiser than the ne'er-do-well. He or she will often have the very best take on the town and its other characters and will not only have a wonderful repertoire of clever and subtle tales that will amaze you because they seem totally *de novo*—new and unique—but he or she also has a sense of timing, diction, and wit that many of the most facile New York comics would envy. In fact, Dick Cavett, as I mentioned earlier, comes out here on occasion and has been dazzled by the comic material that swirls around me constantly as a matter of daily life. This is a resource you will want to seek out and make friends with. I married one.

Drunk: You will probably be surprised to find this notorious cast member in my list of positive community elements. But that has been my experience. Not a universal experience: there are drunks in this town we go out of our way to avoid because their most obvious trait—maybe their *only* trait—is that they are annoying. Nonetheless I have found that the drinkers in a small town are considerably more helpful, kind, honest, generous, and solid than the notoriously religious. It is indeed sad to see someone like my old friend Rod drink himself to death way too young, but I'm not sure that's any worse than being a miserable but sober wretch and living long. I truly am uneasy about seeming to praise what most people see as a moral failing but in a couple cases, I have seen for myself a perfectly good drunk go sour and mean when sobriety struck. I don't know what to say about that. And if I did, I am guessing it would be to my benefit not to say it.

Slow but Sure: I spent some time wrestling with the label to use for this character because most are so insulting we would start off on the wrong foot in talking about him. I think you'll know what I mean. This is a person of considerably

diminished mental capacity. I don't mean dumb—I am probably seen by a lot of people in this town as dumb—I mean
truly handicapped by a mental problem. But do note that I
include this person in my positives list. I don't do that out of
any sense of pity, either—this person is truly worth knowing.
He is reliable, hard working, and honest, something that
can't always be said about the smart, shrewd, cagey, and
crooked in a small town. You're not going to be comparing
notes with this guy about existentialism or chaos theory but
he may be able to tell you something about how to catch fish
or will cut you a fair load of firewood for an honest price.

COULD GO EITHER WAY

It's hard to tell what influence the following exert in a small
town's dynamics. It's not so much that they are neutral as it
is that they might fall either way. Depending on the individual, or the time of day, some would consider them assets,
some just asses:

Preacher: Obviously, a spiritual leader should be a major
asset to any community, and they sometimes are. The problem is, when they are not, the damage they cause is liable to
be far worse than that inflicted by any other role in the
drama. We have had both in my town. To some degree, church
leaders are like politicians, not simply servants, but slaves to
their constituents. Of course they should be serving higher
principles, but, well, you know . . . you're an American. You've
seen what's happening to this country. One town minister
faced some tough questions about his decision to marry
Linda and me down here by the river. One member of his
prominent and famously "Christian" flock asked, "What

would God be doing down by the river when we built Him a perfectly good house up here?" I wish I had been there to answer his question. In another case, it was a town minister who urged his youth group to steal street signs because he disapproved of the person for whom the street was named, a kind of Fagin-for-Jesus operation. He later apologized but I can't imagine such behavior happening in the first place. A current sky pilot in residence uses funerals not to celebrate the life or mourn the passing of the person who should after all be the honoree at his own funeral but to hustle mourners who might not already be adherents of his particularly narrow mindset to shift allegiances and sweeten the pot for his support or they can face an eternity in hell. Makes you proud, doesn't it?

Ne'er-Do-Well: The true Ne'er-Do-Well really doesn't e'er do well. There's not a lot funny about this one but it's possible he has a heart of gold. These days all too often Ne'er-Do-Wells are also the local drug dealers and there's nothing funny about that whatsoever. Of all the bad things about country living the very worst is the enormous expansion of methamphetamine manufacture in the rural setting. What this crap does to people is just about the saddest thing I know.

Nature Boy: This character comes in a wide variety of forms, from the organic gardening hippie to the Ted Nugent nutcase. If he or she is found at the benign, hippie end of the scale and simply takes joy in the gifts of nature, gathering mushrooms and wild asparagus, protecting birds and bunnies, living in a tipi year round, the eccentricity remains charming if sometimes odiferous, but at the other end, the

Great Hunter/Trapper, black powder muzzleloader (and we're not just talking guns here), the problem can become substantial. It's one thing for someone to want to walk through your river bottoms looking for bittersweet or morel mushrooms, quite another for a cannon-bearer to insist that as a mountain man he has every right to kill anything that moves or to leave animals struggling in agony in traps for days at a time, all on your land. You'll want to put the kibosh on this one, pronto.

Newcomer/Tourist: In a town of 350 souls, any new resident gets plenty of attention. It's always good to have a new tax-payer on the county rolls but the curiosity is instantly there—Republican or Democrat, Baptist or Hellbound Sinner, marriageable or marriage wrecker, buying groceries and gas in town or commuting to the city? Best of all, a new-comer has never heard all the old town jokes and can be counted on to buy a couple extra rounds at the tavern just to hear the end of the one about the time it was up to the Catholic boys of the Loup City Volunteer Fire Department to put out the fire at the Lutheran Church in Boelus. This citizen is either a new settler, a momentary visitor staying over at the Bed and Breakfast, or . . .

The Peripatetic Citizen: I wouldn't have known about this kind of person but then I became one. And it turns out, I'm not alone. There are a good dozen people who consider our little town a second home and return here for all sorts of events from weddings, festivals, and graduation parties to Christmas, funerals, or just a couple of weeks of vacation. Since I've been here, I understand the attraction. No matter how anonymous you are in the city, a couple of days in a town like mine and everyone knows you, you have established a presence, and you know where everything is. That is, you feel at home very quickly. That's a good feeling, and so you come back, and damned if everyone doesn't still remember you, and almost nothing has changed since you were here last. Everyone is eager to hear what news you bring and since you now know everyone in town, you are eager to hear the news of your adopted community. Pretty soon, you're here just about as much as you are at what you used to call home, and then you find you're not going anywhere else when you have time, and then, eventually, Dee asks you when you are going to be home again.

Loose Lady: Again, you might be surprised not to find this character in the questionable category. Well, it may just be my own style in things but I tend to migrate to the lower end of the social scale and find the most interesting, useful, and loyal people there. So, along with the Town Drunk and Ne'er-Do-Well, I consider the Loose Lady of the town first of all to be an interesting, kind, and helpful person but even more than that, rarely to be anything but virtuous albeit in a generously interpreted sort of way. By now you recognize the idea as a motif, but it's true—those in a small town who may be seen by the elite and maybe even the mainstream as lacking in the noble virtues are more often than not far more principled than those who take the greatest pride and make the most noise about their piety. I think Jesus found pretty much the same thing to be true in his travels and work.

BAD NEWS IN TOWN

Thief: I was once sitting at the "Big Table," the standard small-town seminar site in either the tavern or the café—this time in the Chew 'n' Chat Café—when the conversation turned to a local of dubious reputation. Out of nowhere, Bumps stopped the bad-mouthing by saying, "I don't want to hear anything more about Maynard's stealing. During the Depression, he almost single-handedly saved this town." Everyone at the table's jaw dropped and we all turned to Bumps in amazement. No one had ever said anything good about Maynard, and here it was, Bumps, the town wit complimenting him. He continued before we could ask him the natural question, "No one here had a dime to spare, and not even enough to buy feed for our chickens. Good ol' Maynard saved us the trouble of buying feed. He stole all our chickens." If you can't think of anything nice to say. . . .

Druggie: Increasingly this is the main problem in every little town just as he is in every city. At least everyone knows who it is in the small town. In this town, fathers of kids at vulnerable ages visited our local drug dealer and they had a chat. It was made clear that if his name ever came up in any conversations with children in this area, his home would be burned to the ground and he would exit the vicinity with a free ride on a metal fence post and a full three-piece suit made of roofing tar and chicken feathers. And no one was joking or exaggerating. Drug users, like drug dealers, are a growing danger in rural America because the drugs these days are not the relatively benign soothers like marijuana but are the vicious scourges of crack cocaine and, worst of all, methamphetamine. I can't imagine where this garbage is going to lead eventually but right now it puts killers on the highways and streets; at least as often as not, the victims are the users themselves, who, rendered stupid by their recreation of choice, do themselves in. While locals have a pretty good idea who the local crazies are, increasingly these stupid asses wander and drift around and then, who knows?

Pervert: A certain amount of deviance being generally and generously allowed for in small towns, the town Pervert is not so much condemned as giggled at. The demonstrations of his obsessions run to laundry stealing, window peeking, and maybe widow stalking and are therefore considered harmless if annoying. One thing you can almost certainly count on: The town Pervert is a faithful churchgoer. I have no idea how that works but it seems to be a consistency.

Grouch: I could have a soft spot in my heart for this role because I have been told I sometimes have less than the sunniest of dispositions. The problem is, the town grouch in our case was also a major problem, making life in our town uncomfortable and angry. In a rare example of true justice, however, he died before he was 110 years old, apparently the usual terminal age grouches reach before blessing us with their departure, and the job has remained unfilled since. Our late and unlamented grouch donated his body to science—for the acid and vinegar, I would guess—and the rumor was that he did it because he knew that if he were buried in the cemetery here, his grave would be the most popular spot in the county for late-night pee-ers. I was astonished when I suggested this theory to another friend and he said, "Not me. You wouldn't catch me pissing on his grave." While I was still puzzling at what appeared to be an atypical loathing of this now-dead jerk, he continued, "When I was in the Marine Corps I swore that once I got out, I'd never stand in another line again."

Prig/Missionary: I used to think this was a character restricted to rural living but now he seems to be distributed on a national scale, and not at all rare. This problem uses religion to manipulate and run other people's lives while at the same time using it to excuse his own failings. As so often happens with "religious" people, principle is for him a device used to obtain power over others but only rarely for self-control. In our town this person has actually been known to show up at town ballgames, where he would otherwise never be seen, to move around the stands sniffing for beer, which is not permitted in the town park. He then notifies the sheriff's office and some poor officer has to drag down to the field and check on violations. I make a point of taking a big coffee mug of non-alcohol beer to games in the hopes of luring this idiot into reporting me. He never does, however, because he pretty much knows that I have to be up to no good and it's always better to pick on the visitors' side of the bleachers where they don't know what he's up to. This is also the guy who killed our town Danish festival by squelching the beer garden, which he said detracted from the "Danish" nature of the day. Obviously, he's never been to Denmark.

Snoop/Gossip: This person can be a real problem in any small town. Or a wonderful resource for what's going on. He or she is something like a newspaper, but unfortunately it's a tabloid.

Cheapskate: A mooch is never any fun to be around but once you figure it out, the problem is also easily avoided. Our classic tightwad died many years ago but lives on in legend. He was a joy because you never ceased being amazed at new manifestations of his tight-fistedness. I once came into the tavern and he was sitting at one end, eating some of the free popcorn the proprietor sometimes set out late in the afternoon. "I'll take a beer," I said, "And give one to Emil too." "Well, tank you," he said [he was one of the Old Danes who was truly an original in this very Danish town]. "But you know, Roger, I'm not going to buy you one."

"Oh, I know, Emil," I said, once again staggered by the dimensions of his most notable fault, and yet somehow admiring of his frankness.

Mensa Wannabe: Again, our town pseudo-genius died a few years ago and the job remains unfilled but there are several candidates working their way up. This guy was amazing to me. Since the general standard of education in this small town is still a high school diploma, this guy—still with only a high school diploma but a great flair for performance— could simply make "facts" up and they would be accepted by everyone else, who wonderfully presumed a universal honesty. Someone would say something like "I wonder how far Mars is from Earth," and he would say "Fifty-three thousand point six-seven miles, give or take ten miles," and there it was. Since he said it with the certainly of declaring his own age, no one ever doubted him. What's more, they gave him credit for astonishing knowledge. "What's the deepest place in the ocean?" "The Mindanao Trench—27,555 feet deep." Wow. How did he know that? And he never failed to come up with an answer. He once declared that Ronald Reagan was the greatest president ever because he at least balanced the budget each and every year in contrast to those spendthrift liberals. I knew better and said so. He declared me wrong and cited numbers, right off the top of his head. It's hard to argue with information like that. So I wrote to our very right-wing congressional representative and got the figures from her. Of course Reagan never did balance the budget. He borrowed a million dollars and declared himself a millionaire, a nuttiness even the first George Bush could see through. I took the congresswoman's letter to the café the first chance I got and began to read it to the Pseudo-Genius. The moment he sensed what was happening—he was being exposed as a fraud—he put his fingers in his ears and started singing the Star Spangled Banner! He was declaring ignorance to be a matter of patriotism. Thus, another small-town character astonished me with the rigidity of his role. But that didn't end his reign of ignorance, of course. Despite this and several more such exposures, the locals continued to be dazzled by his grasp of facts . . . and the myth of his vast knowledge continues to this day.

THE DYNAMICS

The individual elements of the cast of characters in small-town life are of course part of larger processes, the dynamics of rural life. Just as you have to decide the degree to which you intend to interact with the town's citizens, you'll have to give some thought to how deeply you want to become involved in the mechanisms and machinations within, among, and around those elements. And as I think you probably sense by now, there are extremes to every feature of rural life and more often than not the overlap is substantial enough that what is a virtue can also be a vice; what is an asset is sometimes a problem.

Nothing is more pervasive in rural life than the fact that everyone knows everyone else's business, which is absolutely true. On the other hand, the single most comforting factor in rural living is that everyone looks out for everyone else. To some degree those two extremes are part of the same thing. "I've noticed that you haven't been coming to town to get your mail like you used to do every day" could be seen as prying. But then when you respond, "Well, I've been diagnosed with prostate cancer and so we have to go into the city every day for radiation treatments and just don't get a chance to come in for the mail like we used to" and suddenly the whole town is concerned with you and your family and springs into action to make sure that anything you need is taken care of during your difficulties, well, that can be reassuring.

Security works the same way. Later in the book I'll discuss law enforcement, but the fact is that we are a good half hour from law, sometimes more if the sheriff happens to be on business at the other side of the county. We therefore rely on everyone keeping an eye on everything and everyone else, not simply out of idle interest and a search for conversational materials but to protect the community. That attitude still exists in rural America, even as it diminishes in the cities and across the nation. The new politics is: "Take care of yourself and to hell with everyone else. Why should I pay for health care or education for someone else's kid? I have mine so I don't care about you." While a ferocious insistence on independence and self-reliance persists in the rural countryside too, there is nonetheless the understanding that some things require the fabric of *community*. It's not simply a matter of "scratch my back and I'll scratch yours" either. There is also a philosophical affection for the idea of us all being together in this mess and a feeling of camaraderie within it.

At no time is this sense of community more evident than on the occasion of disaster. Whether the disaster takes the form of a fire or accident attended to by the volunteer fire department or emergency medical team or a personal disaster suffered by a family or something grander like a tornado ravaging the entire town, the horror of the problem is mitigated by the truly inspiring response of the community as a community. The town's jerks may remain the town's jerks— it's not as if there are miraculous transformations of the spirit in the crucible of disaster—but so many otherwise neutral characters rise to new heights, you can't help but come out of the experience glowing with new confidence in your fellow man.

One of the most memorable such events in my experience was the time it rained something like nine inches in a matter of hours here and suddenly the creek that circles around town was running right down Main Street and through businesses and homes. That was, to be sure, nothing new. There are lots of photographs of previous floods. An area that floods once, after all, is likely to flood again the next time the water comes up. In fact, in my town they stopped having their annual ethnic festival for a couple decades because it seemed like every time they had it, it rained torrents and the town flooded; then we had a severe drought and someone had the bright idea of re-instituting the festival with the hopes of maybe bringing back the rains. The flood I'm about to tell you about happened immediately following the first revival of the festival. Don't tell me God doesn't have a sense of humor.

GOOD OLD-FASHIONED DISASTER

Anyway, the rains came and we had a flood. Our mayor was a sweet old guy, mostly put in office as a kind of honor—I mean jeez, what kind of job can being mayor of a town of 350 be?—and so he was completely out of his element in this moment of emergency. Therefore he was gently and respectfully set aside and the people of the town took over—especially my old friend Dee, who pretty much became our ad hoc, pro tem mayor for the occasion, securing supplies like sandbags, help from neighboring towns and the county, organizing as if by magic. The people of Dannebrog generally amazed this outsider with their teamwork, generosity, and good spirit in the face of overwhelming hardship. It almost makes a soul hope for another occasional disaster to remind us all how much we do need each other.

SCHOOL AND SPORT

The most persistent unifying component of the social fabric in our area, and I suspect in most others, is school athletics. In a way that's sad because the last way in the world for a small-town kid to prepare for life is playing ball; despite the inevitable graduation speech comparing life to a football game, it isn't. I despair when I see a grand educational institution like our own State University reduced to a football mill whose main purpose is not educating our youth but providing Saturday entertainments for boobs who couldn't care less about the academic underpinnings of the institution.

Things are not quite the same in the case of rural sports. While our University teams are essentially hired semi-professionals who have nothing to do with the school or the state, and even though sports are painfully overemphasized in rural schools, one cannot deny that the kids playing the games are indeed our own progeny. I'm sure you can sense my disapproval of the reduction of education to an excuse for games, and yet there was something about seeing my own daughter Antonia playing softball or volleyball. . . . Beyond that, even seeing our town team, or a neighboring town team playing takes sport to a new level. Now we truly are a part of the game when it is our friends and neighbors who are playing and not just disembodied names who have no connection to us other than the color of the costumes they wear on the field.

Even if you have no interest in sports, when you move to the rural countryside or a small town be prepared to sit—or stand—in the bleachers and cheer for the locals, especially when they play those big lugs from the county seat or worse yet the nearby city. Now it's truly not us in the abstract against them in the abstract but us in the concrete—really us! Dave and Marv and Gene, or Deb and Krystal and Carrie against them—Bob, Gary, and Justin, Susan, Heather, and Melanie.

After sports but still up there somewhere on the list of what holds rural communities together are the schools. While consolidation of small schools and the busing of students to buildings that may not be near any town at all have detracted to some degree from the pride of how small-town or farm people see their schools, the activities that go on in those buildings are still major factors in the lives of rural communities, even for those school districts that no longer have children or those members of the communities whose children have moved on. The school remains the cultural as well as the entertainment center of an area. The faculty is relied on to be the intellectual element, pride is taken in students who excel, and their achievements are reported as news in the local papers, not as prominently as athletic accomplishments to be sure, but nonetheless with pride.

FAITH AND FAKERY

One of the advantages of education as a unifying factor is that it is only in minor ways controversial. Some zealots may want to have prayer in school, there may be momentary discontent with one teacher or a program, there is the usual grousing about how expensive education is by those who insist that ignorance would be cheap in comparison, but generally speaking it is understood that we need schools, kids need to go to school, we need teachers, and we need to pay them something for their trouble. Not so with religion. Religion is by its very nature divisive, I suppose, separating those of us who have the truth from those stupid clods over there in the other church who are not simply wrong but are going to go to hell for their error. The current whiff of ugly intolerance and political muscle injected into the religious scene certainly hasn't helped, but even at its best, religion does not do much to contribute to the pleasure of rural or small-town life. Of course those who feel strongly about their church and their religion will argue with this but the fact is, they almost always feel that way about *their* religion and *their* church, not religion and churches in general. Like the politicians now in power, they insist that everything would be fine and we could all be unified if only we all accepted their vision of the truth and rejected our own errant ways. That is not a path to understanding and peace.

Please, don't presume by all this that I am somehow against religion. In fact, I consider myself to be very religious. That is in fact the problem. I object not to there being too much religion in American life but too little. And it almost follows automatically that the more vocally religious that people, community, and churches are, the less they have anything to do with honest religion. While screaming and yelling about starting the meetings of the village board with a fundamentalist Christian prayer, or campaigning for religion in the schools, or sending their children to intensely fundamentalist schools, there is little sign of principle in their own lives, no honest prayer in the home, and a total absence of charity and love for others different from themselves. Painfully, that condition is at least as sad and sorry in the rural countryside as in the cities.

COURTSHIP

If there is one rural social institution I wonder about and rejoice that I am not a part of, it's courtship. In fact, I cannot imagine trying to find a date much less a mate in this rural setting. I just cannot imagine it. I would dismiss that as my own problem—I have never been what could be described as a social butterfly—but I see way too many examples of others—attractive, interesting, solid, decent, truly fine people—who deserve and want mates and go for years and years without making contacts, reaching a point of near desperation. That's where I would be. I wouldn't know where to start. There simply aren't many institutions or processes where one can meet a range of eligible potential partners, it seems to me.

Again, I don't think that's just me because I see the same
brick wall confronting others who are looking, sometimes
intently, for a companion. What can we make of a full page of
personal ads of people actually advertising—advertising!—
for contacts in the back of the electric company's magazine
that we get every month? Right there among the warnings
about wiring our own buildings and ads trying to sell us
portable sawmills or patterns for lawn ornaments are ads
from single white males who like line dancing but are regular churchgoers flailing out to find a woman of similar
interests who might be interested in living on a ranch and
wouldn't mind helping with branding in the spring or laying
irrigation pipe while knee-deep in muck. I find myself to be
uncharitably skeptical about the ads from women who are
"young at heart, generously built but light on their feet,
active in church activities and grandchildren's lives, seeking
a comfortably situated male who enjoys watching home
improvement shows on television." If I ever found myself
back in the market for a mate—a horror I don't anticipate by
the way—I think I'd move back to the city for a while.
Nothing would make me do something as desperate as relying on personals in a rural electric magazine.

FEASTS AND FESTS

I don't want to make it sound as if it's just disasters that
bring and hold a community together. There are good things
too, events that require community effort and get it. Some
are large, formal, highly organized and some are small, spon-
taneous, and genuinely organic to the community. Whatever
the case, the situation seems to be the same as in disasters;
grudges are generally suspended (at least until closing hour

at the tavern) and folks pull together—or get out of town if they want nothing to do with the festivities.

Every town these days has some sort of annual festival, like Dannebrog's Danish Independence Day Festival generally known by its name in the romantical Danish language as Gruntlovfest, which is not nearly as much fun as the Danish phrase seems to suggest but a delightful weekend of community celebration nonetheless. It doesn't help that the Danish is also frequently bastardized to "Grunge Love Fest" or even "Grudge Love Fest" by those who take little of it seriously.

At our Gruntlovfest there are parades, melodramas, specialty meals, a bicycle rodeo for the kids, cake walks, exhibits, activities, few of which really have anything whatsoever to do with Denmark or Danish culture or even the history of the town, but that's not the point. There is the exoteric element of showing off to the outside world—and attracting that easy tourist dollar of course—but there is also the internal importance of getting everyone together and doing something as a community. I can imagine that all the small-town stuff might strike the suave and debonair (pronounced around here "swave and duBONEr") as pretty boring, even a little silly, but I find it perfectly charming that our Gruntlovfest parade goes down Main Street—all one block of it—and then comes back the other way so people on both sides of Main Street can see both sides of the items in the parade. Which may be little more than a local farmer's new tractor or an antique car that is in the parade every year and so isn't much of a novelty to anyone. It's nice to know everyone in the parade and be able to yell back and forth in friendly banter without being arrested for disruptive behavior.

So, what if you're not Danish? Like me, for example. Well, the rule in Dannebrog is that during Gruntlovfest, everyone within the village limits is Danish. So pull up your chair and have a bit of kale soup washed down with a shot of ice-cold aquavit and enjoy the parade. Look! Here comes that Welsch fellow with one of those goofy orange tractors of his!

I've always liked fairs, big or little. They are a celebration of harvest after all and what could resonate more with rural America than that? As I have become familiar with our local county fair, I have grown less and less enchanted with the big ones. It is really great to wander from exhibit to exhibit, recognizing the names of people you know or the items in the competition (prizes range from somewhere around fifty cents to two dollars), including your own wife's name on some embroidery work. There aren't as many animals as in the livestock exhibits at the State Fair of course, but the grins and beams of hope on the faces of the kids are the same. There's free watermelon from the produce stands over at St. Libory, and one of the local churches always has homemade pies and ice cream for sale. And the price for parking and admission is certainly right—you just park the car and walk in.

Of all the holidays celebrated on a community level, the Fourth of July is the largest in our community. There is a parade, a day of ball games, patriotic ceremonies, and maybe a beer garden both downtown and at the ballpark depending on what sort of majority the Baptists hold in the village board. Even if you never go to a ball game, even if you don't know anyone on any of the teams, even if it is impossibly hot and the last thing you want to do is sit in the sun at the dusty, windy ball diamond, on the Fourth of July you have to. You owe it to your country.

These days we don't even have a community fireworks show; the cost of pyrotechnics and uneasiness about liability have pretty much killed that fun, but there was a time and hopefully will be again when the Fourth was a major and old-time extravaganza pursued without fear. The old Fourth of Julys in the nearby town of Boelus are now a lot tamer than they used to be but memories of the good old days there are some of my fondest. There were amateur horse races with substantial purses, free beer, a huge picnic with food for little more than cost, a hometown rodeo, sometimes even demolition derbies. Even then I wondered how long I was going to see horse races over a steeplechase kind of course, down the riverbank, across the sandbars, through the river channel, back onto the sandbars, and up the bank again on the way to the wire. Horses fell in the water; riders ranged from little girls riding ponies cheered on by grandparents to grizzled cowboys riding hard for as much as five-hundred-dollar purses. Man, spectacle doesn't seem to be a word adequate to describe the event. People were hurt and hauled off to the hospital by the EMTs, and as often as not, it was the little girl on the pony who won, but alas, that was another day. Maybe the day will come again when we can stop worrying about things like broken arms or terrorist attacks and rejoice again in things like wild abandon and life.

When we first moved out here into the country I was surprised at the role graduation plays in the annual course of things. If you think about it, it makes sense; graduation from high school is either the final and grand terminal in a youngster's education or it marks the time they are going to go off to school somewhere else. There's nothing more here for them. The parties have mellowed some here during the last few years, as has all celebration. The raucous days of hard drinking and driving have mercifully faded into the past as the painful consequences of such actions have become ever more vivid thanks to television coverage. Such activity has become ever more risky because of increased law enforcement and penalties. Nonetheless following the ceremonies in the school gym, attended by enormous numbers of parents, relatives, and friends, there are still dozens of parties scattered throughout the often large school community, meaning that you may be attending three, four, even six or seven parties in one evening, driving many miles in between. When we first came out here, open bars were the rule at high school graduation parties but now it's mostly soft drinks, punch, and coffee, with the graduating seniors putting in a token appearance and then disappearing for the night, I don't want to know to where or for what. Increasingly, there are also planned, structured, and supervised events for them but seniors who have just received some official acknowledgment of maturity are not likely to submit to a lot of authority on this night of all nights!

I suppose it's only logical that on the rural landscape, where the occupation (the noblest of all, I might add) is growing food, that food itself would be the center of so many social activities. There are only three places to grab a meal in our small town: the bakery for modest breakfasts and an occasional lunch (pizza on Thursday nights, some of the best in the nation we're told), Harriett's Danish for breakfast and big noon meals, and the tavern for superb burgers and draft root beer; you have to go a long way if you want anything more elegant . . . unless you watch the local papers or look at posters stuck up in the Co-op or in the grocery store window.

There you will find notices of fish fries or sausage extravaganzas at the American Legion club Monday, a Danish smorgasbord over at the Lutheran Church on Tuesday, a benefit feed by the Baptists Wednesday, a Danish Sisterhood bake sale on Thursday, a wild game feed by the local hunting club Friday, and on and on and on. The food is always good on such occasions, the price is always right, and the servings are always generous.

I think fondly back on once going to a parish duck-and-dumpling dinner in a nearby Czech community and anticipating not just the great meal, but the promise too of homemade pie. And I do love pie! I came out the back end of the serving line with a plate mounded with wonderful food . . . but no pie. Hmmmm. Had I been stiffed on my pie? I got to a table and sat down with Linda and her parents, just a trifle miffed about the pie promised but not served up. Then right behind us came a no-nonsense lady with a print apron who plopped down a whole pie in the middle of our table, cutting it brusquely into four equal pieces: whole quarter pies. And that, by God, is the way pie should be served. No one goes hungry in this land of plenty!

There is always food with any community event, including weddings and funerals. Wait a minute—weddings and funerals? Aren't those pretty much private family affairs? Not when they close down Main Street, put the band up on a flatbed truck and dance right on the very pavement of Main Street. In fact, sometimes a wedding invitation is not just sent out to family and friends but posted in the window or on the bulletin board of one or several local businesses, inviting everyone and anyone to join the festivities, including the feed, the dance, and the party, free drinks and all. A good wedding is and should be after all a community celebration.

"Celebration" probably isn't the best word in most cases for funerals, but then again for the very best of us, even a funeral is a celebration of a life, which is why we always balance our mourning with food. In a community with a solid ethnic foundation even funeral food is something special. Any small-town or rural event where people bring food is bound to be something special.

By way of a side note on cuisine, while small towns are famous for solid, generous, mainstream, typical American meals with loads of mashed potatoes, gravy, fried chicken, enormous steaks, and Jell-o salads, don't for a moment sell small towns short on good ethnic food, too. Churches often retain an ethnic flavor, and so do the meals they serve. Around our town there are many European-based communities, and butcher shops still make wonderful ethnic sausages—Polish and Danish, primarily—and always at a very good price. This kind of food makes a wonderful gift because it is unique to your area and may be available at no other site anywhere, including in the original native land! A custom meats shop in our county seat is Polish and produces absolutely exquisite sausages; but recently it has been increasingly hard to find Polish workers now that we are down to the third and fourth American-born generations, so the business has been hiring instead the labor that is newly available: Hispanics. While they do still produce their long-standing line of Polish sausages, they are now wisely taking advantage of their new resource and are making and marketing Mexican breakfast sausages! We don't go hungry in America's agricultural heartland, no sirree!

Historical observances like centennials (or our own celebration of Danish Independence Day), calendral observations like Memorial or Labor Day, church festivals like Christmas or saints' days, volunteer fire department fund-raiser, even unlikely events like a customer appreciation dinner by a local farm equipment dealer is an occasion for community re-affirmation, renewing acquaintances, looking over babies, comparing rain totals or crop yields, doing business, and exchanging news. Even a newcomer should take advantage of the opportunity to see and meet, be seen and be met.

KNOWING YOUR PLACE

One word of caution, however: Do remember that you are moving into a community where you are a newcomer. You are not simply changing addresses; you are moving into a new anthropological context. You need to serve your apprenticeship and then a journeymanship and then you need to take all kinds of tests, exams, and trials before you have any idea of what's going on or how things work or even more complicated, get close to being a certified participant in what's going on. You may want to be helpful and you may indeed know some things this new community could use and they may even say that they want input from you and whatever you say or do may be with nothing but the very best of intentions, but slooooowly, slooooowly, slooooowly. You don't have to take many steps in any direction to tread on toes, so sometimes it's best to stay right where you are and listen for a while before speaking up.

Some newcomers to Dannebrog not long ago made the mistake of moving too quickly in their enthusiasm to be active, contributing parts of the community and they were, as the phrase came to be expressed, "'broged"—that is, snubbed, rejected, uninvited, dismissed, and excluded. And then, worse than starting over, they had to pick up from a new starting line ten steps back from where they had been in the first place. Don't risk being 'broged, or whatever you might call this social gaffe in your own new context. Be a good anthropologist and just sit and listen for a while before speaking up and trying to "improve" things. We all have a right to our opinion but sometimes it's like insisting that we have the right-of-way when we are about to enter an intersection within sight of a speeding and brakeless semi headed toward the same spot.

So, for example, when you first see the historical or ethnic festival in Ennui, Iowa, your newly adopted hometown, you may be somewhat—or a good deal—taken aback. Let's just say for the purpose of discussion here that Ennui is proud of its Romanian roots. And hey, that's great because while you were in the Peace Corps, you spent a lot of time in Romania. Well, you watch the proceedings of the Ennui festival with curiosity—then dismay—and then horror as you see the customs of the Romanian homeland distorted, perverted, mutilated, and misinterpreted. Okay, this may be the heritage of all these folks in your new town but how can they possibly get so many things wrong? The signs that are allegedly in Romanian are at best a hideous distortion of the language. The costumes are Czech, not Romanian, and even at that they are nothing but artificial outfits drummed up in Prague tourism offices to cater to people who don't know any better. And what is this food being served up as Romanian? It isn't even close to the wonderful fare you enjoyed while you were actually in that country. And what are these people doing drinking sodas and lemonade when any self-respecting Romanian would be enjoying good slivovitz or excellent beers?

Surely the people of Ennui will be delighted to profit from your expertise, right? Wrong-o. For one thing, you can't tell these people that what they believe about their own her- itage—and the key word there is "believe," because the historical truth fades into utter insignificance when it comes to what people cherish and hold precious as their traditions. The folklore, you see, is not what they are trying to depict but what they believe to be tradition. All you can do is comfort yourself by remembering that the forefathers of these cele- brants came over a long time ago, when traditions were different. And those traditions were re-formed and adapted to the new homeland in ways you don't know and don't understand. Finally, as an outsider, it isn't up to you to cor- rect anything, not now at least, and more than likely, not ever.

Same with historical celebrations. I have some experi- ence here myself. I have a pretty decent education, have a long interest in regional and local history, have done a lot of reading, interviewing, and researching; and I have written a good deal about a lot of things. So, let's say your new com- munity reconstructs, as in my case, a sod house in the manner of the homesteaders. But, well, uh, it isn't at all like the ones that homesteaders actually built. They knew what they were doing, and they had the tools, expertise, and materials to build a sod house right, so that it was comfortable and lasted a long time. What you see before you is a miserable mud hovel, already caving in before even the first rain falls on it. You see people looking at the wretched travesty, peer into the darkness, and express their horror at the sufferings of the pioneers, not knowing that what they are seeing is nowhere close to the truth. Nor are their eyes the eyes of their fore- bears who found the cool, dark, quiet safety of the small,

solid soddie a wonderful fortress against the ferocity of the
new, unaccustomed geography that assaulted them.

Sometimes it's hard to keep one's silence. I know that.
Annually I watch a local museum gather a bunch of re-enac-
tors in what purports to be Civil War uniforms and stage a
Civil War battle on ground that was nowhere near any Civil
War hostilities in a state where no battles took place. They
march, make a lot of noise, yell, fall dramatically in feigned
death and injury, and then arise laughing to enjoy the
applause of onlookers and then gather for a tailgate lunch-
eon. Local newspapers revel in the praise of participants and
observers who solemnly proclaim how much they have
learned and, not incidentally, how much fun the whole exercise was on this nice Saturday afternoon. Children often
comment that they have had a really great time, wondering
especially at the roar of the cannon. As one was quoted as
saying, "It must have really been fun to be alive during the
years of the Civil War!"

Okay, let's be honest here. How much has actually been
learned in such a goofy parody? And does anything that
might have been learned about, for example, the kind of
weapons or uniforms used on Civil War battlefields, come
anywhere close to balancing the hideous distortion of the
incalculable horror of an actual Civil War battle? The Civil
War was the very worst moment in this nation's history; do
we dare so much as suggest that it was a sacred thing, or an
admirable thing to kill our fellow citizens, brothers, and
children? Where are the screams of dying horses and men, the
stink of guts and fouled britches, the blood and fear? "Fun?"
If anyone comes away from any such demonstration with
anything but nausea and trauma, then the lessons conveyed

have been erroneous, flat-out, ridiculously wrong. The Civil War should be viewed with sobbing sadness, regret, and stomach-wrenching disgust.

Okay, so your newly adopted town decides to do a Civil War re-enactment even though it wasn't even founded until well after the war itself and none of the immigrant families had even entered the nation by the time the First World War was imminent. What do you say to set these people right? Not a thing. It's not up to you. At least not yet, and maybe not ever. If you are a true citizen of this new home, if you respect these new neighbors and friends, if you are truly someone who wants to learn, then look at the events before you as a demonstration of how folklore and tradition works, how people come to view themselves and their past, how formal history can become so impossibly distorted. And then enjoy the pageantry, have a lemonade, and cheer on the gallant soldiers.

INSTITUTIONAL GLUE

In addition to processes and people, there are also institutions that form the fabric of small-town life and serve as the glue to keep everything else stuck together. When people ask me how I get so much done, I have two answers: I never use the telephone and I never go to meetings . . . unless there is food there because then at least one thing worthwhile gets done. That's not true in small towns and rural settings. Meetings in social settings where there is so much remoteness serve far more than getting business done. In our community there is a Legion Club; although membership is limited and orientation runs to reactionary, the Legion does a lot of good work here and does provide a social context. There are extension clubs focusing on sewing, cooking, and reading, 4-H clubs open to children and young adults, and even the occasional service club. I became a member of our local Lions Club even though I am not a joiner just because a lot of my town friends were members and it seemed like a good opportunity to participate in town activities. I did worry when I read the brochure because first, it said attendance is absolutely required with no excuses for absence accepted short of death, and second, there was the thing about an initiation ceremony, and I'm not much of one for goofy formalities.

But I decided that membership was important enough that I would swallow my doubts and join since I'd been invited. At the time I didn't live here yet so I had to drive over two hours to get back for my first meeting—after all, there was that thing about mandatory attendance. I stopped first at my buddy Eric's place because I knew he was a member too and so would certainly be getting ready to go to the meeting hall. But no, he was under his car in his driveway. "Uuuh, Eric, aren't you going to the Lions Club meeting?" I yelled at him as he hammered at something around the transmission. "Oh I may drop by later," he said, "but then again I may not get this done." So much for mandatory attendance.

I got to the meeting in time for happy hour, which it turned out constituted pretty much most of the business for the evening anyway, and at the door I was met by Bumps, my friend who had invited me to become a member. "There you go," he said, handing me a yellow and blue cloth cap. "You're supposed to wear that to all meetings. I forgot mine tonight, but. . . ." And that was the extent of my "initiation." Sadly, the town Lions Club faded and died; it's hard to keep such organizations alive and lively with so few people in town and young people less and less inclined to join them or contribute to social benevolence, but when they are available and the newcomer receives an invitation, they are terrific places to begin to fit into a new community.

Also in our community is a standing Booster Club, a small-town version of a Chamber of Commerce, and various ad hoc committees and groups for special events like our ethnic festival, historic preservation of one building on our main street, for activities connected with the ballpark, two para-security groups like Neighborhood Watch, that kind of thing. Since these groups have real business to conduct and keeping in mind my caveat about newcomers getting themselves into a situation inviting 'broging, they may not be the best entry level to small-town social life, but attendance at their public meetings demonstrates admirable support for their activities.

Okay, if you are a delicate flower and don't like to deal with naughty thoughts, you may want to skip the next couple paragraphs but since I am telling you about small-town life, I don't think it would make sense to self-censor myself out of telling you about important elements that are, well, at the edge. Not far from here a community rehabilitated an old store front near the business district, set it up with some furniture and equipment for things like playing dominoes and pool, and made it into a club for older gentlemen in town who wanted a social setting, an activity center, and a place for some fun but didn't want to hang around the town tavern. It is very popular and seems to have become a permanent element and asset for the town and the seniors' community. So, what's so bad about that? Well, the thing is, the gents themselves named it. They call it the "Dead Pecker Club."

Also, I should perhaps note that while there is prudery too, nonetheless an element of solid earthiness persists in rural America.

Speaking of which, some friends of mine recently found themselves in a small Nebraska town on a Saturday evening and wondered what sort of entertainment might be available. Here in Dannebrog there are often special events at our tavern on weekend evenings. For a while karaoke was the craze, or "scary okie" as they called it, and scary it was. I suppose in a city of fifty thousand there are enough talented performers to give some level of entertainment to do-it-yourself shows but in a town of 350, well, I can't think of a more suitable term than "scary okie." But back to my friends—in another town, I hasten to add. Their query about entertainment brought a sideways glance from their resource person and then a whispered response, "Well, there's the old guys who get together over at the Co-op warehouse on Saturday nights. . . ."

And, uh, do what? my friends asked with trepidation.

I never did find out if my friends took advantage of this singular cultural opportunity; I know I would have just for the anecdotal value but I imagine that then I would have been as reluctant as they seemed to be to admit much else. It turned out, as their townsman friend told them, that on Saturday nights an itinerant stripper comes quietly into town and to the Co-op warehouse, where geezers gather with flashlights to watch exotic dancing amongst the feed sacks and livestock salt blocks in the dark bowels of the storage area, presumably illuminating with their flashlight beams whatever anatomical elements of the dancing lady might be of particular interest to them. As my friend notes, "Who would have guessed there was going to be Las Vegas–style entertainment in a little Nebraska town in the middle of nowhere?" I didn't ask but I have always wondered if the music of choice for the lady's performances at the Co-op isn't the polka.

Chapter 9

LAWN ORDURE —

Your Garment in Action, Your Tax Dollars at Work: What Can You Expect from Your New Government?

HE DON'T NEED NO STINKING BADGE

I had the good fortune early in my tenancy here on the rural Plains to be in the Boelus tavern one weekend before their huge Fourth of July celebration. It was a spectacular event — cheap beer served ice cold from a horse tank, wild horse races, ball games, huge fireworks, water fights — with rural fire departments wielding fire hoses, kids' games and races, incredibly good food: ribs, burgers, hotdogs. But that was the weekend before the annual celebration, remember. The county sheriff dropped by the town tavern to talk over the weekend's plans with Dick, proprietor of the Gold(en) Nugget steakhouse and tavern and pretty much de facto Czar of his little town and environs.

At any rate, my friend, Dick, as proprietor of the tavern was the most prominent citizen in town, and a central influence in how the Fourth of July celebration came together, so it wasn't surprising that the local law authorities might want some advance information on and advice about what exactly was going to be happening. The exchange between Dick and the sheriff was informative for this city boy at the edge of going rural.

The sheriff said, "I'm wondering what you have in mind by way of security and enforcement for Saturday, Dick. Would you like to have us on the grounds? Or standing by somewhere around town? Would you prefer we stay out of the way and stay in radio contact in case of emergencies? Or do you plan on handling things on your own?"

I forget which of the last two options Dick chose; it doesn't matter—probably a combination of the sheriff's office staying on the alert but pretty much leaving the details up to the folks right there in town. The main point I took away was that here the law is unquestionably at the service of the citizens, not the other way around. It only makes sense, I suppose, because after all, the sheriff is elected and regularly stands for re-election. If he does not reflect the will and inclination of the citizens who pay his salary, he won't be in that office for long—this particular sheriff, I might note, held his tenure at the courthouse for over twenty years. He knew how to do things right, and that's the way he did them, and I can say that with all honesty because over the years I was on both sides of his attention, if you catch my drift.

Compare that with the status of civil service police in the cities. My experience with law enforcement in general has been very positive and while I am a civil libertarian, a proud card-carrying member of the ACLU, I also appreciate the tough job a truly professional officer has. And yet there is something to be said about law enforcement officers who are directly beholden and answerable to their constituents.

In a later interview for network news with that same sheriff, I asked him how he felt about having to arrest the very people who would be voting for him—or against him—in the next election. He said that it was the toughest and yet most satisfying part of his job. Just days earlier he had gone to check on a car that had run into the ditch and he found a local farmer, drunk and disabled but unhurt, in his car buried in the muck and water. The sheriff said that his duty was probably to arrest the man and send him directly to jail, but he also knew that the man had lost his wife the week before and was in terrible personal pain, so his condition of despair was understandable if not excusable. So, instead of adding to the man's problems, he loaded him up in the patrol car and took him home, called his son to come over and take care of the old guy and keep him out of any further trouble. The sheriff got some friends of the farmer to come pull his car out of the ditch and get it back to his home.

That's the kind of latitude and understanding I want in my law enforcement, and that's the kind you can get on a rural and small-town level. Some of my friends would complain that that can also mean that the local law knows way too much about you and that guys like them and their kids therefore can't get away with very much of anything. That's the kind of latitude and understanding I want in my law enforcement!

Yes, it is harder to bear down hard on people who are friends and neighbors, but sometimes situations can be handled even more effectively outside of the standard legal system. For example, there was the man in my town who was sick and tired of his brother-in-law's drug use, thieving, child abuse, and general antisocial behavior. When the idiot

in-law showed up on Main Street strung out on meth, generally being insulting, my buddy, a good citizen who'd simply
had enough of this idiot embarrassment, busted him in the
chops with a fist, breaking his nose and lip. I don't know
about you, but I think that was a good plan.

On the other hand, again it was my friend, Dick, who
came out of his tavern about two o'clock one morning to find
some dumb, drunk kid squealing tires and swerving around
making tire-burn doughnuts on the pavement, throwing
gravel everywhere, smoking up the air, and disturbing the
sleep of anyone who was still trying to sleep. Dick finally got
the kid stopped, slapped him around a little, and told him
that the sheriff would be there in about five minutes and
Dick would have him put in jail for a month. Or he could
drive straight north a half mile over the hill by Marv's place
and put his car down in the ditch stuck beyond retraction,
and go to sleep. If he did that, Dick would be up to pull him
out the next morning about nine when he was sober enough
to drive. It didn't take the kid long to consider what a favor
Dick was doing him. He drove north over the hill and planted
his car firmly into the mud of the ditch. Dick pulled him out
the next morning and bought him breakfast to boot. No
damage done. Law enforced. No tax money spent on jail
time. No one hurt. That's my idea of justice.

A good rural magistrate understands this sort of situa-
tional justice. The law serves as an excellent guideline but
there are always way too many considerations to be dealt
with in terms of conditions set in cement and without true
judicial temperament. Law is not just there to punish but
also to preserve the peace and sometimes that requires more
grace and moderation than an iron fist. Treatment of miscre-

ants shouldn't be either consistently rough or genteel, but it does have to make sense. I suspect that that condition persists with wonderful consistency in rural America.

I can't imagine why people run for office on our village board, or county commission, or even our school board. They always joke about being in it for the power or money—of which there is neither—but the answer is that they really want to do the job. That approach is not always appreciated of course. There are always elements that don't want reason or justice; they want their position to prevail. They see a friend or neighbor in a governing body as an opportunity for power. The prevailing rural and small-town mood of civility and common decency, even in a larger American context where that is increasingly less often the case, seems to continue to prevail. Folks elected to public offices, even when they have their own agendas and feel a strong impulse to exercise their own will, continue to feel an obligation to those who may not agree with them and to act accordingly. God bless them. They are doing a tough job that I don't want to do.

Probably the most common violations are trespassing and crimes against property. Country people believe—and want to believe—that most such crimes are done by city people—hunters or four-wheelers who feel that all the land they see is theirs, or illegal garbage dumpers and litterers who seem to think that no one really cares about rural beauty where "there ain't nothin' but nothin' anyways." Chatter on my scanner suggests that rural folks are increasingly less tolerant of this kind of behavior, unfortunately resulting in less and less access for the considerate sportsmen and an ever deepening gap between urban and rural cousins.

CRIME AND PUNISHMENT

One of the most curious forms of rural justice is perhaps also the hardest for outsiders and newcomers to understand: the brutal punishment of not being insulted. A typical exchange at the Big Table in the Dannebrog Tavern might go this way:

MEL: Hey, Rog, come on over and sit down here. I want to talk with you about that time you tried to blow air into the hydraulic system on that 300 of yours and you were combing oil out of your hair for six weeks afterward. Sue, bring us a round over here.

ROG: I'd rather talk about the time you tried to fish your checkbook out of that State park privy with a wad of burning toilet paper on the end of a stick and the privy blew up and went into orbit like a Cape Canaveral rocket launch gone bad. Hey, Sue! I wanted to buy this one. Here, take this twenty and make sure you take the next round out of that.

DAN: Jeez, Rog, I just noticed your fly is wide open. You advertising or something?

DENNIS: I think he's just airing it out. Sue, I got the round after Rog's.

ROG: Well, it is air-cooled equipment and . . .

MEL: I heard he missed a chance once ten years ago and he just doesn't want it to happen again.

DAN: Aw jeez, here comes that cheap no-good stinking Clarence. What an asshole.

CLARENCE: Hi everyone. Who's buying?

DENNIS: It's Dutch night. Everyone's on his own.

DAN: Sure could use some rain.

CLARENCE: Dryer'n a popcorn fart. Does that beer over there belong to anyone?

DAN: Yeah, it's mine and I already took a slug out of it. . . .
MEL: Anyone wanna play some cards?

Did you spot what's going on there? No one insults the
guy they don't like. If there is a fault in my scenario it's that
when the pariah enters the scene, conversation dies and the
table goes silent. I understand that jails are a fairly recent
invention and most societies isolate undesirable miscreants
by exiling them to the worst company anyone can think of:
themselves. And that's the way it is in rural life. You insult
your friends because you trust them to understand how it is
meant. You don't insult the outcast because he wouldn't
understand how it is meant either. He'd think you liked him.

BACK TO SCHOOL

Because rural schools are involved in so many aspects of life
and constitute so much more than basic education, because
teachers and administrators (including school board members and supervisors) are our neighbors and friends, I think
citizen involvement and concern about schools is more
immediate than it might be in urban or suburban settings. I
always knew Antonia's teachers, saw them in the grocery
store, lumberyard, or tavern, felt free to talk with them
socially or professionally, did my share of complaining and
questioning. And of course made my share of mistakes. I
remember with chagrin the time I contacted Mr. Wilson,
Antonia's elementary principal and complained that she had
come home with a report of him having talked with her second grade class about evangelism. I take my religion
seriously and feel that educating my children in religion is
my business, and my business alone. I did not appreciate him

bringing his feelings about religion into the classroom. Blah blah blah blah. . . .

Mr. Wilson listened patiently and then expressed his utter bewilderment. He hadn't done any such thing. Furthermore, he wouldn't do such a thing and couldn't imagine what I was talking about. Hmmm. I turned to Antonia and asked for a bit more information. Mr. Wilson had, she said, scolded them about evangelism in the bathrooms. Evangelism in the bathrooms . . . Evangelism in the bathrooms? Then it struck him. He had indeed gone to her class earlier that day and talked with them. About the bathrooms. About *vandalism* in the bathrooms.

What was it the Gilda Radner's character Emily Latella used to say on Saturday Night Live? "Oh? Never mind. . . . "

RELAY RACE

It's probably more a human characteristic than a rural one but you will indeed find that even in small towns people can be disgustingly intolerant of others with even slight differences from themselves, but on the other hand demonstrate a wonderful acceptance of individuals of exactly the same nature. So, for example, as the Hispanic population in this area grows dramatically, there is the predictable reaction of ugly intolerance. The kindest, sweetest souls I know belch out the worst slurs and demand immediate compliance with all things "American" of new citizens. And yet when any one of the Hispanics who are our friends and neighbors are in attendance, they are heartily welcomed and treated without either deference or insult. Men who hate Mexicans for "taking white man's jobs away" will ferociously defend their own Mexican employees or colleagues as the hardest workers and the most honest guys they've ever dealt with. What is rejected out of hand in the abstract is, curiously, almost universally accepted in the reality.

I honestly think that sometimes what seems to be intolerance is unintentional stupidity. I have long known and wondered at the ability of some people to hold completely contradictory opinions in their minds at the same time without the competing truths ever encountering each other, even in what would seem to be a fairly restricted space. For example, once within a single hour I heard a friend of mine—an otherwise pretty decent guy—rail in the tavern about how sad it is that one hardly ever hears the Danish language any more, not even to the extent it persisted only thirty years ago. Only minutes later this same friend was howling just as loudly about the insult of Mexicans speaking Spanish and not abandoning their native language for the true language of the nation: American! I did call the contradiction to his attention. He said, "They're not the same thing!" Hard to argue with that. . . .

GUNNING FOR TROUBLE

By way of segueing into a brief discussion of the role firearms play in rural life, I'll offend some readers further with what is nonetheless a true story. A few years ago a man was shot and killed on the main street of our town. It was a tragic event and truly disturbing for our town but I'll never forget one element of the next day's conversation, which included the puzzled question, "How could they charge Baxter with first degree murder? He killed a *Mexican*!" You don't have to embrace the worst of social elements of rural America but you sure should be prepared for them.

I was once chided for an image in one of my CBS News stories, an anomalous shot of a pickup truck with long guns—rifles or shotguns—clearly shown hanging on a rack in the rear window of the cab. The New York City producer said we couldn't show something on national television that is clearly illegal, not to mention unlikely. Once I figured out what she was telling me, I explained that, no, those things in the pickup trucks' back windows are called gun racks, and people around here often carry guns as a part of the normal rigging of the rural pickup truck. No, she explained, growing impatient, it is illegal to carry guns like that.

Well, no it isn't. For better or worse, guns are a part of life in rural America. Part of it is a matter of hunting, part of it is "varmint control" (clearly a phony dodge but almost universally accepted), there are vague and silly intimations of self-defense, but largely it is a matter of style, the macho image, the idea of the West. A former sheriff told me that the scariest threat during his years in office were not berserk druggies, or transient desperados, or even the notorious scene of domestic violence, but the armed half-baked gun-nuts who try to seem acceptable by labeling themselves "militias," and therefore are protected by the Constitution, conveniently ignoring the part in that document about "well-regulated." I suspect that if you took all the guns out of rural America, the tilt of the earth would be seriously affected.

I am not immune. I manage to disassociate myself from both extremes by 1) really admiring guns as remarkable mechanisms and acquiring a ridiculous number of them while 2) believing firmly in the Constitutional requirement for careful and thorough regulation. I don't make a lot of noise about either side of the issue since common sense and logic don't bear much on either extreme, or for that matter my own position in the range of notions. The main thing for outsiders to understand is that guns, and therefore shooting, are part of American rural life. We built our home on a riverside hill where there had previously been nothing. For a while, nimrods continued to shoot across the river and into our backyard until we got the sheriff's office and state roads people (the shooting was from their property on the other side of the river) to bring a stop to the whizzing bullets. Still, even a good friend of mine expressed his unhappiness, saying, "I've shot across that river from the bridge all my life and I'm not about to stop." I noted that a hundred years ago hunters were shooting .50-caliber Henry rifles at buffalo right through where his house now stands and I wondered how he would feel about me hauling my own .50-caliber firearm down there and mimicking the same trajectory. You guessed it right—he said those are two different things. (He did eventually lay off the dangerous shooting in our direction and I appreciate that, Dan.)

POLITICS

I was taught that one doesn't talk about religion or politics in polite company and I find that is even more the case in impolite company. We live in Nebraska's Third Congressional District, one of the densest (and I use that term advisedly) right-wing populations in the nation. No cause-and-effect reaction is recognized here. If a politician opposes abortion, gun control, and separation of church and state, he is elected. Never mind that his or her policies are tragically destructive for agriculture in this totally agricultural area, or counter to the spirit of Christianity in this ferociously religious population, or destroys education here where the only hope for our young is education. Our current Congressional representative was a successful football coach. He admitted he knew nothing about agriculture when he ran for office. That's okay: he had a national football championship! He has no connections, no influence, no experience, no knowledge. That's okay: he could have done a little more with the passing game when he was coaching, but he can learn that when he learns about agriculture. Besides, he is against abortion, supports a generous weaponry program, and prayed before every game. What more could you ask?

No connection is drawn by folks out here between a total national disregard for agriculture and their own votes. The fact that the poor are dismissed, and that they are generally poor (the poorest county in the nation is in Nebraska), and that their painful tax payments are doled out as gifts to the already stinking rich, doesn't sink in. That they may have to drive four or five hours to the nearest medical facility and then bankrupt themselves paying for lifesaving treatment never suggests to them that they should support a national health program as a part of the national promise of "life, liberty, and the pursuit of happiness." The arguments for such things as national health or a national transportation system are swept aside with the single word "socialism." Demagogic politicians know this lesson well and coast to lives of ease and influence on clichés. I wouldn't always see self-interest as a virtue but man, sometimes you have to think of your own survival. Not in rural America, at least not when it comes to politics.

Part of the political complex is a general contempt for any sort of government—I can sure understand how that feeling can come into place—and a pervasive nonsense that we are somehow overtaxed. It could be the successful self-delusion of Reagan's voodoo economics, as so described by George Bush as we may recall, in which you borrow a million dollars and declare yourself a millionaire. Folks in rural America have nothing but contempt for tax-and-spend liberals, nothing but admiration for borrow-and-spend right-wingers. (I respect the English language too much to call these radicals "conservatives.") The understanding is, all taxes are bad and all taxes are too high. Part of that comes from the naiveté and honest goodwill of public workers who year after year after year—teachers come to mind—do their best with less and less financial resources. Sooner or later the reality of gutted programs will have to be brought to the surface so chiselers and cheapskates can see clearly the trouble they are creating: bad roads, bad air and water, bad utilities, bad law enforcement, bad schools, distinctly poorer lives. Right now no connections are made between 1) taxes on fuel and 2) quality of roads, so the very same person senses no contradiction in wanting to 1) pay less taxes and 2) have better roads. Somehow that association has to be re-established, but until it is, we'll pretty much have to sit at the tavern's Big Table and listen to complaints about 1) high taxes and 2) bad roads.

TAXED TO THE MAX

Some taxes are, admittedly, goofy—even in the country. My little town is this very day mulling over the notion of a sales tax. Uuuuuh. I wonder if anyone on the village board has noticed at all that there are only five businesses in town selling things. And at least three of them are on the edge of economic survival. So, putting together limited sales, meager profits, and few outlets, how much money is likely to be raised for municipal improvements compared to the inconvenience and damage imposed on our few struggling businesses? I imagine that a sales tax seems like a quick, easy, convenient way to extract money, especially from those pesky serfs and peasants, so let's nail *them*. Here too, sadly, no association will ever be made between diminishing business, profits, and revenue and the imposition of a tax burden on a very limited number of village citizens, and even then on the least able to pay. The obvious answer is to make the rich pay their way for once. But that won't happen. Not in today's America, where we elect our favorite football coach to Congress.

On the other hand, some civic monies are accumulated and spent with such care and success that it almost makes up for boneheaded notions like a village sales tax. I am thinking specifically of our local Emergency Medical Teams and Volunteer Fire Department. You would think that moving from a city with huge, major medical centers and full-time professional fire-fighting teams to the Middle of Nowhere would mean a major loss of safety and services. I don't sense that at all. For one thing, you will be amazed at the intensity and high level of training rural EMTs and Fire Fighters go through, all on a volunteer basis, to achieve and maintain skills, and the lengths they go to get resources to bring their equipment up to professional levels. I thought, okay, Dan's a plumber, and Brenda's a motel manager, and Jerry's an implement dealer, and Carl's a farmer, and, well, how much time and energy are they going to be able to devote to being firemen or medical technicians too? Well, the answer is one hell of a lot. I don't know how they do it, and frankly I'm not at all sure why, but from personal experience I can tell you that our emergency aid teams here are fast, efficient, skilled, and caring.

I imagine one could think that a handful of amateurs, no matter how thorough their training, constitute a fairly pitiful force against a major automobile accident or raging fire, but again, that would be a misunderstanding of how things work. Our Dannebrog teams are not alone. Within moments of assessing a situation that requires additional attention, a call goes out from the dispatcher in our county seat to teams in neighboring towns and villages until the forces are brought to a level where there is plenty of manpower, equipment, and supplies to deal with the problem.

Whatever disadvantage there is in having voluntary emergency services is offset by the unlikely benefit of increased rapid response. You'd think that if you live six miles outside of town, you would therefore be almost out of reach, but six country miles are not six city miles. Once our village services get the call, they are out of here, hustling along the roads and highways from wherever they are, summoned by personal pagers, toward the emergency, facing absolutely no urban traffic. Out here six miles is maybe seven minutes. You know what six miles can mean in the city: That famous "New York minute" there is so much talk about is also a "New York 20 yards."

I suppose some might be troubled by the notion of having medical emergency personnel you know personally tending to possibly intimate physical problems. I know from experience that it can be disconcerting to have a neighbor who is a nurse from just over the hill conversing with you about our daughters and their shared school activities while she gently pushes your nether parts from one side to the other and she shaves your groinal region for an impending hernia operation. Or encountering in the supermarket and exchanging cheery holiday greetings with the lovely young radiation technologist who only weeks before inserted a prostate stabilizing balloon into the orifice providing the most convenient access to your troubled gland but generally reserved for exits only. But professionalism seems to overcome such potential embarrassment and only in truly non-threatening situations are you likely to experience what one friend of mine did when he wrenched his back, wound up lying in agony on the kitchen floor, called in the EMTs all of whom know him well, was attended to, examined, and transported to the nearby city's emergency ward only to be informed much later by some of the giggling ER staff at the city hospital where the EMTs had delivered him about the smiley face drawn in magic marker over his lower back when he arrived. Drawn on his *very* lower back, if you catch my drift.

THE WIDOW'S HARVEST

One of my favorite *CBS News Sunday Morning* Postcards from Nebraska essays was a difficult one to corner because while it is a phenomenon that happens in rural American very often—way too often, in fact—you almost never hear about it until it is over. This time I was lucky, although the farmer in the story was not. He was out doing some work on his tractor when the tractor rolled on a hill—they often do— and he was killed. He left behind a young wife and some nice kids, and a farm with fields full of crops to be harvested that autumn. At the time of the accident one of the newspapers we read did a report on the accident, interviewing one of the EMTs who happened to be on the scene, finding the farmer dead. During the course of the interview, she mentioned that there would probably be a community effort to bring in the crops for the widow.

The thing is, this happens all the time but no one needs to give notice. Everyone in the community knows what has happened, and what needs to be done: the crops need to be brought in. And then there is a report in the paper about the harvest having gone well . . . and I missed another chance to cover this grand example of the good in humanity.

Not this time. This time I talked with that EMT and got the details of when and where the harvest of the widow's crops would start, and my crew and I were there at sunrise. But no one else was. Uuuuh, where was everyone? And all the machinery? And the organizers? Who was running this operation? Shouldn't there be food and water for the workers? Man, had we been stiffed? Could it be that this thing had fallen through? My three friends—Izzy Bleckman with his camera, Danny Gianneschi with the microphone, Bud Lamoureaux with his notebook, me with my script—waited in the cold and silence. Bud said, tentatively, "Uh, Rog, what happened? Where are the. . . ."

About that time there was a faint rumble off in the distance and over the crest of a distant hill on the gravel road came a combine. Whew! Okay, so only one harvester showed up, nonetheless we could . . . Oops, here comes another one from over there. And there's a grain truck right behind him. And two more combines coming from the other direction. And three pickup trucks. And they have food and coffee! And before long, we had so many people swinging into the widow's fields, we couldn't focus the camera or recite lines fast enough.

It was even more difficult to capture on tape because no one stopped to talk. Of course! They don't need organization for a HARVEST! They all know what to do, so they are just going about doing it. They don't need directions! It was like an assault by a well-oiled army. People picked corn, people loaded trucks, people put out food and handed it up to men and women in pickers and trucks, people waved at us to get the hell out of the way.

And then, just a couple hours later, it was over and done. And just as they had appeared and swung into the fields to bring in those sheaves, they went back out onto the gravel and headed to their own fields to the harvest on this perfect day for the task. These good neighbors and friends not only didn't need directions, they didn't need thanks. When someone did stop to talk to the widow to hand her tens of thousands of dollars of receipts from the grain elevators where they had hauled the crop, they mostly stood around looking uncomfortable as she expressed her thanks. There were some runny noses and I thought I even spotted a tear or two, but mostly they didn't figure thanks were necessary because they were only doing what needed to be done. Nothing so special about that, after all.

You'll find the same thing happens after any death in the rural countryside. Or any storm, or flood, or fire, or car accident. The "isolation" of the boondocks, especially where the population is at its thinnest, is pure baloney. You will find that you are never so surrounded by friends as you are where there's no one around for miles.

MUSEUMS

It's a long way from such necessary services as fire and medical teams and not nearly as obvious as institutions like religion or education or as universal as the town drunk, but you will be surprised to find how many towns manage to put together and take pride in their museum. Small-town museums tend to be along the lines of what were called "cabinets of curiosities," random collections of two-headed frogs, fossilized mastodon bones, fragments of a meteorite, a turnip that looks like an alligator, and a hard roll with a burned spot on it that looks like George Washington if you squint just a little and the light is just right. These collections were meant to surprise, amaze, maybe inspire, but rarely to make even a passing gesture toward any sort of education.

We had a privately owned and operated "museum" in our town for a number of years, displaying some antiques to some degree connected with the community, or the community's Danish origins, but it had few visitors and when the building came to constitute more of a danger to the artifacts than a shelter, the museum was discontinued and the collection dismantled. Now we have a sort of parody museum, the National Liars Hall of Fame, in the back room of the gift shop, featuring tall-tale and joke items expressing American folk humor and the tall-tale tradition that has always flourished on the Great Plains. Remarkably, the "Hall of Fame" has drawn an unlikely volume of attention and visitors and is at this point probably the primary tourist attraction we have. You never know. . . .

Chapter 10

BE PREPARED:

Considering the Inevitable Emergencies

POOP HAPPENS

One of the reasons you have moved to the rural countryside is for privacy. Privacy equals isolation. Being away from the prying eyes, noise, problems, annoyance of nearby neighbors also means that you no longer have the security and convenience of nearby neighbors. I hope I have convinced you that this remoteness is more than compensated for by a stronger sense of community on the rural landscape, but nonetheless you need to consider taking care of as many problems and emergencies as you can on your own. As much as anything, it's not so much what you do as it is being prepared for what you need to do.

Some things you simply have to prepare to accept. A major problem around here (and I sense around the country) is city people moving into the country for all the charms of rural living and then recoiling when they find out what that entails, insisting that agriculture and nature somehow change to suit their own tastes they brought from the city. That's no way to make friends. Or, for that matter, to get things changed. Farmers themselves are occasionally guilty of this attitude and I chide them too when I get the chance. They too have moved into an environment of which they are a new and unfamiliar part: the Great Plains and raw nature. And they should be making allowances, learning, and adjusting. They can't simply run over the top of whatever they don't happen to like, that doesn't fit in with their plans, that isn't what they expected, that they don't want to include in the mix. That is, sometimes you have to take some losses—some short term, some long term, some permanent—as a part of the larger picture. Killing off every coyote, bear, mountain lion, porcupine, raccoon, possum, field mouse, and prairie dog from the Mexican to the Canadian border would not only not pay for the bullets it would take to accomplish the slaughter, even the most superficial research shows that it would be counterproductive since even elements that may seem pernicious on the surface are in the final analysis a part of what makes the Plains what they are. They are, that is, indeed some of the essential parts in making man's survival here possible, comfortable, and even profitable.

Severe weather can happen just about anywhere but may not be as threatening to one's livelihood in the city as in the country. For example, while severe drought may cause some annoyance with restricting car washing or limiting lawn watering, it scarcely endangers your very survival as it very well might in the country with dying windbreaks, raging brush and grass fires, or loss of surface cover. A blizzard may pose a clear threat to life but even then the moisture it provides may very well be celebrated by some in an agricultural community. The heat and humidity that discomfits the gentleman farmer working in a vegetable garden means increased income for the corn or cotton farmer. Even if you don't locate next to a livestock feed lot or downwind from a cornfield that spews clouds of black dust during planting season and blizzards of cornhusks and dust at harvest, if you are going to live in the country, you need to expect that kind of thing because on a humid night odors may drift your way from miles away and during a dry season dust and wind may be region-wide and not just a local annoyance. You're on a farm now so you expect some dirt is going to be tracked into the house in the spring and some snow in the winter; if you insist on putting down white carpet, well, you're an idiot and you're only getting what you deserve. You have to understand such things and deal with them; be sure you have a mud porch where boots can be taken off and left before entry to the house, put out mud scrapers at the stairs leading to that mud porch, teach everyone in the family to think about what's on their boots and shoes before they come in.

Do what you can to yourself to prevent blasphemies like water, air, noise, and light pollution in your area . . . and elsewhere, because when you come right down to it, what happens in any one part of the rural countryside affects you and yours too. While you can't complain about the natural consequences of agricultural processes and rural life, you can and should watch for abuse and do what you can to enforce regulation against such abuses. You can't count on federal inspectors out here, or even county regulators. That is part of self-reliance too. The main thing is that you do what you can to reduce your own impact on the environment and others around you but if you see major violations, you are doing the world a favor by calling official attention to the violators.

Here, too, there are tools and equipment you can have to deal with emergencies.

CLOTHING

Perhaps the most immediate and important preventative tool, and yet one that is often ignored (I am thinking of my friend's idiot cousins who wore Birkenstocks while trying to raise cattle in Texas) is appropriate clothing. If you are headed toward country that is notorious for murderous winters, it only stands to reason that you are going to need clothing suitable for cold survival in a rural setting—not for a ski resort or arctic exploration or ice fishing, but for working outdoors on a tractor in the rural countryside. Go to a local farm supply store and see what they are selling; go to the tavern or café on a cold day and see what everyone is wearing. You can pretty much bet that folks familiar with the environment will know what they are doing. You may need not only warm headgear in the winter but also protective cover when you spend long days in the sun, something you may not have had to do in the city. Mud boots in the spring and fall, snowshoes in the winter or cowboy boots in cattle country may not strike you as very fashionable but we are talking about function, comfort, and maybe even survival now. Who knows? You may wind up actually feeling completely at home in overalls or coveralls eventually . . . just like someone else I know.

COMMUNICATIONS

A cellular telephone may be a fashion statement in the city, or perhaps even a convenience, but in the country it can be important when you are fifteen miles from home and nowhere near a wired phone, and a downright lifesaver if you are stranded in your home when a blizzard or tornado knocks down your power and telephone lines and you need help *now*. I know it sounds nutty, but I once had to rely on the cell phone in our car when I was stranded in my office in a building maybe twenty steps from the house. I ventured in the morning with my cup of coffee and was three or four steps out onto the inch-thick ice before I realized the hazard I faced. The path was literally and absolutely impassable. With great effort and jeopardy I managed to make it to the door of my office. I worked a while until I realized a freezing rain was still falling and an impossible situation was only getting worse. I needed to get back to the house for lunch but I also wanted to warn Linda not to venture out herself, even to head toward her studio. The icing conditions were that bad. I honestly worried that she might hurt herself simply covering the thirty or forty feet between the house and her studio. But I couldn't call her on my office telephone because it's the same line as our house phone. Fortunately I thought of the cell phone in the car in the same building as my office and so I called Linda in the house from the cell phone and warned her of the hazard.

CB radios have faded out of fashion except with truckers on the highways but there is still some CB traffic from tractor to house and even farmer to farmer. Communications by CB are considerably more public of course and you can't call your stockbroker in the State Capital like you can with a cell phone. It's your call, as long as you have some way of getting word out without relying on the vulnerability of telephone lines.

Even if you have no need for a powerful transistor radio bringing in your favorite music while you lounge on the beach, you will want one tucked away with fresh batteries in whatever you use by way of a storm shelter, even if it's only the little triangular room under the stairs like ours. I recommend a radio that picks up not only radio, a medium that is less and less useful as it become increasingly formatted, but also television audio. That substantially increases your ability to find out what is happening outside with all that banging and roaring while you cower in the dark of your storm shelter. Even more importantly, I recommend— no, I insist—that you have at least one, preferably two or three weather radios. We have one in the shelter, one in the front room, and one upstairs in the bedroom, all operable either from household electrical current or, if that fails, internal batteries. I don't know how these things work but there is a network of weather broadcast operating on a full-time 24/7 basis, constantly broadcasting weather information for your specific area. I simply cannot over-estate the importance of this kind of information in the country. These radios can be left on, in which case they will sound an alarm if there is dangerous weather approaching you, but when we have accidentally left our weather radios in this mode, it only scared the bejeezus out of us when the alarm fired off, usually when we least expected it. You'll know when the weather looks threatening, or you'll get some notice from other media, and then you can turn on your radio to get a constant feed of detailed information. You have to have at least one of these. I have mentioned elsewhere that I also have a scanner feeding information into my office about emergency calls, law enforcement communications, and that kind of thing, and while this is useful and interesting, it isn't usually a real matter of life and death like your weather radio.

LET THERE BE LIGHT

I called up the image of you cowering in your storm cellar in the dark. Hopefully you're smarter than that. We have candles and oil lanterns in our emergency equipment but we are uneasy and cautious about using them. If the threat is a tornado or windstorm, an open flame may not be the best thing to have sitting around, just waiting to ignite the place when it blows down. In the winter they can be helpful when snow or ice takes down our power lines, however, especially if our other sources of light and portable power fade in a long-time situation.

And those other sources would be . . . ? First, a supply of handy flashlights with fresh batteries . . . and a supply of additional batteries in a convenient, established, and well-stocked place. We have only a few times had our power out any longer than our flashlights lasted. But then we also don't just sit there with our flashlights on like those guys in the Co-op watching the stripper—wouldn't want the lights to go out in a critical situation like that! Our next fall-back line for emergency power is one of the best things we have found for situations like this: booster packs originally meant for jump-starting cars with dead batteries but now increasingly adapted specifically for household emergency use, or for campers who want power for lights, radios, even television sets while they are far from power lines. I am an enthusiastic believer in these things. Most have a light on them that will give you light for hours if not days on the energy stored when they are recharged. They often have a plug like the old automobile cigarette lighter so you can plug in radios and even small portable TVs designed for 12-volt operation. And the really good ones also have a plug just like the one in your house system so you can plug in anything requiring 110- to 120-volt service. Of course you start loading up these handy little packages with a radio, a television, maybe some emergency lighting, and of course the daiquiri blender, they won't last long, but during storms we have managed to keep a small portable television on and informing us about the progress of the storm for many hours during a power outage. We now have three of these power packs in our home: one in my office and two in the house. At the slightest threat of bad weather I haul them out and charge them up but I try to keep them powered up even during fair weather because you never know when some drunk is going to knock down a pole somewhere and put you out of lights and power for a few hours.

Knowing how such things go and being something of a worrywart, I also have a gas-engine generator that we could use to power the house during a really long-term power outage. Our house is built around a huge, beautiful fireplace that I made darn sure has a Heatilator insert so that it can be used to produce heat as well as charm and comfort. Every autumn I make sure I've laid in a good supply of firewood within easy reach of the back door. When there is the threat of heavy snow or freezing rain, I build a cautionary fire in the fireplace just in case I need to rely on it to keep the house from freezing up. But even with all that in place, each fall I make sure my gas-powered generator is in running condition and that I have 5 gallons of fresh fuel in case we need it. We never have. But it makes us more comfortable knowing it is there. (Ours is started with a rope pull; if I ever have to replace it, knowing that Linda might have to start it if I am not here and that as I get older I may not be in condition to find the strength necessary to pull the rope, I would invest in a portable generator with an electric starter.) You don't want to run a loud, stinky, and dangerous generator indoors because of the carbon monoxide of the exhaust; you will want to be sure you have enough heavy-duty extension cords suitable for outdoor use in rain and snow to bring the generator's power into the house. A friend of mine has just the ticket: a large, electric-start generator, and he has it and his household rigged so that he could if necessary use the generator to power the essential parts of his household appliances — the furnace, the refrigerator, maybe the freezer, the lights, and of course his computer!

I can't imagine a situation where we would need more emergency food than we already have in our cupboards and refrigerator but we do have a small supply of military MREs — Meals Ready to Eat — just in case. Far more important than food, or even power, is water. A real problem for us is that our water supply is our well, and that depends on our electrical system. So, if we lose power, we lose water. A couple gallons of distilled water in gallon jugs in our larder will keep us in coffee for a few days and if worse comes to worst, we can live on the beer I keep stashed in the cellar in case of just such an emergency(!). But we've never had an emergency even close to requiring that kind of provisioning. Far more important and not likely to be something you'd think of is water to flush the toilets. I am perfectly happy with our outhouse but the ladies of the family are less sanguine about that exigency. When we know rough weather is headed our way, we fill our bathtub with water — hot water in the winter to add to the heat reserves in the house — and know that if we have to we can simply dip water out of the tub with a small bucket and pour it into the toilet to flush it. Again, we have only had to retreat to this last resort once in almost twenty years.

FIREARMS AGAIN

As crime gets steadily worse, even in the rural countryside, incidents of assault, robbery, household attacks, and just plain drugged-out nut cases showing up on doorsteps completely out of control have reached the stage where they are a real and serious consideration for the country home. Some friends of ours have had a couple real scares in the last few weeks and so we are all thinking seriously about the problem.

It's not easy. I'd say just get a gun but it's also not that simple. My friend's wife, Deb, is occasionally home alone. She is very petite and not at all familiar with firearms. They picked up a 12-gauge shotgun, far and away the best weapon for home security (and the weapon favored whenever possible by Old West gunfighters, I might add, the Hollywood six-gun being the last thing you want to have to fall back on) but after firing it once it became clear that she would probably never be convinced to shoot it again. It is simply too big and powerful for her. I bought Linda, a slightly larger person, a .410 shotgun for the same purposes but again, it's more of a firearm than she is likely to take up in defense, no matter what the situation. Another friend and I have been trying to help our mutual friend weigh the advantages and disadvantages of various handguns but again, it's not as simple as one might think. Both of us who know a bit about guns would choose for ourselves as large-caliber a weapon as we can handle because if it comes down to us actually having to fire a gun in self-defense, we want the most power we can muster. If you shoot at someone, you want to stop them, not just make them mad. For our own home the smallest caliber I have is a 9mm; I prefer a .38-caliber, .357, or even a .45. There is no way in hell Deb would be capable of lifting and aiming a gun that size much less shoot it effectively. A .22 magnum or .25-caliber semi-automatic isn't much of a gun, I'll admit. It's almost more of a toy. But the thing is, a gun of that size is likely to be something Deb might actually use. The caliber isn't going to make much difference if she won't or can't shoot it, after all. Yes, a firearm's effectiveness is to some degree its ability to intimidate an intruder but still, you don't want to aim a gun at someone unless you have every intention and ability to fire it. You can't imagine how sad it makes me to recommend that you have firearms in your home for self-protection but in today's America, that does indeed seem prudent, if not necessary.

We have considered alternatives—pepper spray, Mace, even an electric Taser gun—but all have their drawbacks and dangers, not to mention their expense. Ultimately I would still recommend a firearm. Don't like to, but pretty much have to.

SIGNAGE

We have had only a couple cases in which suspicious or dangerous intruders have entered our property or threatened to enter it. (There was once a one-mile police cordon for a murderer and we fell within that area.) Our cabin was burglarized once before we lived here. We have had some trouble with minor vandalism (the usual Saturday night drunks demonstrating their manhood by bashing mailboxes, may they die of terminal hangovers). It may seem trivial, but a big problem for us, in part a result of my minor celebrity from television appearances and my long writing career, has been folks dropping in to visit us. Now, they are all lovely people and all they want is a half hour or hour to chat, look at my shop, ask about how they can get their own books published, share some stories. But the problem is, as Linda puts it, there is only one of me and hundreds—or thousands—of them.

It was one nice Sunday summer afternoon when I was trying to work or get some family time in and twelve separate carloads of unannounced and uninvited visitors drifted into our yard that we decided we had to do something to stop the problem or we were going to have to give up making a living and simply open a reception center for tourists. There are several steps one can take short of shooting at amiable intruders. First, I highly recommend a yard fence. That will stop most people at least from approaching your house and door. You increase the effectiveness of the fence by hanging a sign on the gate. I understand that if you have a sign warning trespassers of a dangerous dog and your otherwise thoroughly benign house pet decides to bite the lady delivering flowers to your wife on Valentine's Day (ask me about this one sometime!), then you only increase your jeopardy because you have indicated that you knew the dog is dangerous . . . even if he isn't. We solved that problem by getting a sign from Gempler's farm supply catalog saying: "Danger—these monkeys bite and cause serious injuries! Do not approach." That did the job. You'd be amazed: people who don't seem to be the least bit intimidated by big, barking security dogs won't risk mixing it up with dangerous monkeys. I know I wouldn't. That's still the scariest part of *The Wizard of Oz.*

If you want to back the threat of your signs with something more substantial than bluff but less dangerous than a shotgun, I would like to suggest the unlikely options of . . . birds. Yep, birds. Guinea hens are incredibly goofy looking, are quite good to eat, and are living, walking alarm systems.

Only peacocks (another option by way of avian warning sirens, by the way) make louder, more terrifying noises than guinea hens. If you have a half dozen of these birds, you will instantly know when someone enters your farmyard. You won't need to fence them in, or more precisely, there's no sense in fencing them in, because they pretty much go wherever they want to. If there's a problem to guineas, it's that they tend to roam. Keep them well fed and sheltered however and they'll stick around.

Now, if you want to ratchet that threat mechanism up a couple more notches but still not loose the pit bulls or resort to warning shots over an insurance salesman's bow, get a couple geese. Geese are grand birds. I love them. They do tend to be a bit messy, not being particularly fussy about where they deposit their, well, their deposits, but they loudly announce the arrival of visitors and what's more, attack unwanted guests with a terrifying ferocity, but without doing any particular damage. (Hint: There is a reason a goose is called a "goose." Protect your flanks if you have geese.) We had some geese for a while; we worried at first about our big black labs being a hazard to them, but it turned out to be the other way around. Even big dogs learn that the best policy is to stay the hell away from a big gander. Drawback: Geese are not partial to those who pay the bills, so you may also find that your house, home, and property are being protected by your geese . . . from you.

A big dog—even a big friendly dog—inside that fence does indeed discourage most people from risking going through the gate. And it should, because even the friendliest of family pets is territorial, senses danger, and will spring to the defense of family members disregarding any danger to itself. I strongly feel that an excellent security system is 1) a yard fence, 2) signs clearly indicating you do not want intruders or trespassers, and 3) a big dog or two. And maybe a monkey.

A MAN, A PLAN

Finally, we have also developed and written out a clear plan for what to do in the event of most emergencies we might anticipate for our house and farm, for ourselves, and also for anyone who might be caring for the house, farm, and animals for us. We outline precisely what to do in the case of a power failure in the winter: the closing down of most of the house, the importance of keeping bathrooms heated to keep pipes from freezing up, the operation of the fireplace, generator, and power units, the location of the storm cellar, flashlights, radios, and supplies. We have listed the names and numbers of people and offices that can be called for each emergency. We have clearly established escape plans and routes, put ropes in place for exiting windows, and placed fire extinguishers in visible and carefully thought-out locations (near doors from which we could retreat and escape in the case of fire but near where fires are most likely to be a problem: the fireplace and the kitchen). In short, we have tried not only to anticipate emergencies but to put in place the tools we might need to deal with them well in advance of the problem.

AFTERWARD:

Last Words

Well, there you have it. I would not for a moment mislead you by suggesting this is a complete guide to country living, anticipating every single problem you are going to encounter in your big move, or for that matter every single rural joy you are going to experience. My intent in these pages has been to give you some idea of the kinds of things you may discover, just as I did when I made the move from city to country. There is not a doubt in my mind but that you are going to find conditions unique to the environment from which you are coming and to that where you are going, to your individual experiences and needs, to the very region and acres you are adopting as home, to the communities you are entering, right down to the very model and year of tractor you wind up driving.

Wife Linda has a habit of saying things like "Looks like the first thing I'll have to do this afternoon is mop the kitchen floor." Reading between the lines, that means the next time you come in, Welsch, why don't you take your boots off? Not everything can be anticipated or said. We all need to do some reading between the lines, or even a lot of reading between the lines. What I have offered you in the above words and pages is only the lines; you're going to have to fill in the spaces between my lines. Okay, so you're moving to the Colorado mountains or the East Texas Thickets, not the Plains where I live. Okay, you are a single parent with six kids and not with a mate and one child, like me. Okay, so you're a skilled mechanic rather than a hopeless doofus. Well, I can't piece together the puzzle for all such things in all you human beings looking at country living. You're going to have to do the calculus yourself. But hopefully I have pointed you in directions to help you smooth the path.

Most of all, I hope that with all my warnings, caveats, and cautions I haven't discouraged you from making the move. Just yesterday my pal Mick was out here, lusting to live in the country himself. He looked around at our very modest home and "farm" and said, "Welsch, you are one lucky man." And I guess I am since a lot of what has worked out for me is just plain dumb luck. All I could respond to Mick was that yeah, I am a lucky man, because if I hadn't thrown away what seemed to so many to be the cushiest job in the world, and a nice house in a nice neighborhood, and come out here to the Great American Desert, in the middle of nowhere, to a piece of wretched ground with no suitable living quarters on it, and made my new home in a village where I am to this day inevitably an outsider, I'd be dead by now, killed by everything I didn't like about city living and my grinding lust to live out here, where last night a coyote choir sang me to sleep.

In my opinion the worst feeling a human can have is regret because it is a pain that can scarcely be healed. We get one life (unless you believe in reincarnation, I suppose) and I feel we should live it to the hilt, with good and virtue, and in a way that makes the living worthwhile. I found that sense of satisfaction living in America's rural farmlands, among farmers and villagers, where the style is overalls and mud boots rather than suits and ties, where the "rush hour" is, as my friend Eric once put it, "when the Lutheran Church lets out on Sunday morning."

If that kind of thing speaks to you then my very best advice is: "*Do it!*" But then my first amendment to that shout would be: "And insofar as you can, do it right!"